WOVEN IN KIDL Е. ІІNSTER

An Illustrated History of the Carpet Industry in the
Kidderminster Area including Stourport, Bridgnorth
and Bewdley.

1735 - 2000

Written and compiled
by
Melvyn Thompson

Old Weavers Toast - 1886
' May the trade of Kidderminster be trodden under foot by all nations '

The "Bull" signals the end of the working day, Brintons in the 1940s

Cover Picture

Thomas Lea's Slingfield Mill in 1923.
Taken from an oil painting by local carpet designer Roger Sullivan.
The photograph is part of the impressive Carpet Trades collection which is owned by the Charter Trustees of Kidderminster.

Inside Cover

The office buildings, past and present, photographed at the Millennium.

Tomkinson & Adam, Church Street   Brockway Carpets, Hoobrook
Tomkinsons, Duke Street   Victoria, Green Street
Union Offices, Callows Lane   W. & R.R. Adam, Birmingham Road
Chlidema, Green Street   Brintons, Exchange Street

About the Author

Hand loom weaving "Kidderminster" Carpet in Kidderminster Library
as part of the "Peoples & Patterns" exhibition, January 1999.

Melvyn Thompson is now retired after a lifetime working in textiles. He started an engineering apprenticeship with Carpet Trades Ltd. in the early fifties. After a period with British Nylon Spinners (Bri-Nylon) in Pontypool he returned to Carpet Trades in the mid-sixties and stayed through all the mergers and changes until 1990 when he moved to Brintons.

His involvement with the Carpet Museum Trust and Brinton's extensive archives stimulated his enthusiasm for writing the history of the carpet industry.

ISBN 0 9529937 3 2   FIRST PUBLISHED MARCH 2002

Published by
David Voice Associates, 9 Redwing Court, Kidderminster, Worcs. DY10 4TR
Email: davidvoice@waitrose.com

Printed by
Stargold Ltd., Digital House, Stourport Road, Kidderminster

HAND LOOM

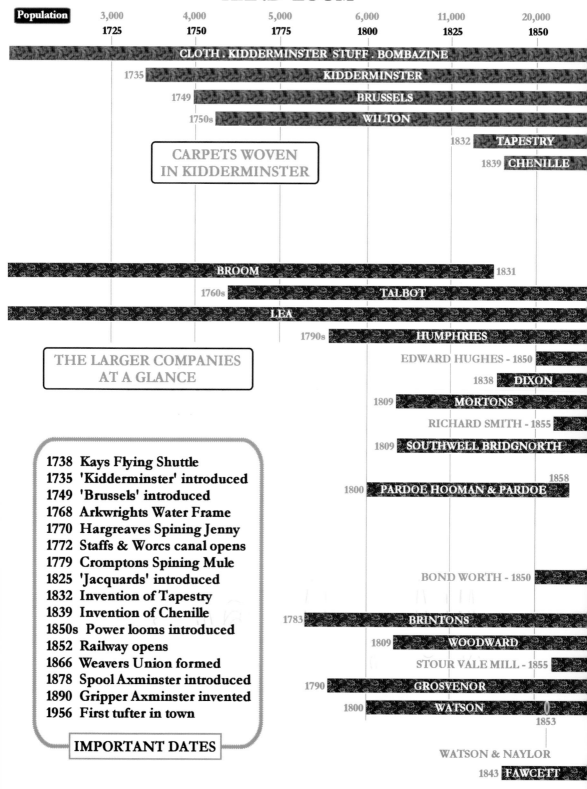

Population | 3,000 | 4,000 | 5,000 | 6,000 | 11,000 | 20,000
| 1725 | 1750 | 1775 | 1800 | 1825 | 1850

CLOTH . KIDDERMINSTER STUFF . BOMBAZINE

1735 KIDDERMINSTER

1749 BRUSSELS

1750s WILTON

1832 TAPESTRY

1839 CHENILLE

CARPETS WOVEN
IN KIDDERMINSTER

BROOM — 1831

1760s TALBOT

LEA

1790s HUMPHRIES

EDWARD HUGHES - 1850

THE LARGER COMPANIES
AT A GLANCE

1838 DIXON

1809 MORTONS

RICHARD SMITH - 1855

1809 SOUTHWELL BRIDGNORTH

1800 PARDOE HOOMAN & PARDOE 1858

BOND WORTH - 1850

1783 BRINTONS

1809 WOODWARD

STOUR VALE MILL - 1855

1790 GROSVENOR

1800 WATSON 1853

WATSON & NAYLOR

1843 FAWCETT

IMPORTANT DATES

1738 Kays Flying Shuttle
1735 'Kidderminster' introduced
1749 'Brussels' introduced
1768 Arkwrights Water Frame
1770 Hargreaves Spining Jenny
1772 Staffs & Worcs canal opens
1779 Cromptons Spining Mule
1825 'Jacquards' introduced
1832 Invention of Tapestry
1839 Invention of Chenille
1850s Power looms introduced
1852 Railway opens
1866 Weavers Union formed
1878 Spool Axminster introduced
1890 Gripper Axminster invented
1956 First tufter in town

POWER LOOM

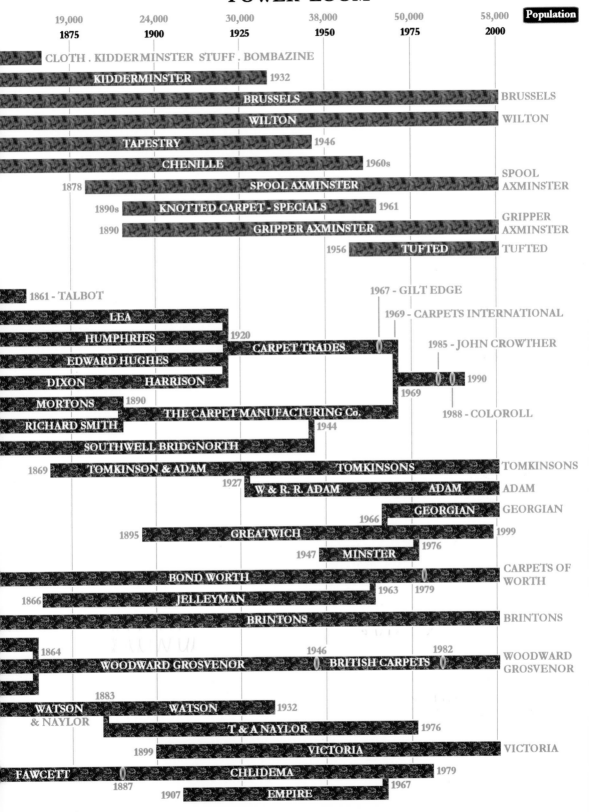

Population					
19,000	24,000	30,000	38,000	50,000	58,000
1875	**1900**	**1925**	**1950**	**1975**	**2000**

CLOTH . KIDDERMINSTER STUFF . BOMBAZINE

KIDDERMINSTER — 1932

BRUSSELS — BRUSSELS

WILTON — WILTON

TAPESTRY — 1946

CHENILLE — 1960s

1878 — SPOOL AXMINSTER — SPOOL AXMINSTER

1890s — KNOTTED CARPET - SPECIALS — 1961

1890 — GRIPPER AXMINSTER — GRIPPER AXMINSTER

1956 — TUFTED — TUFTED

1861 - TALBOT

1967 - GILT EDGE

LEA

1969 - CARPETS INTERNATIONAL

HUMPHRIES — 1920

CARPET TRADES

1985 - JOHN CROWTHER

EDWARD HUGHES

DIXON   HARRISON

1990

MORTONS — 1890

1969

THE CARPET MANUFACTURING Co.

1988 - COLOROLL

RICHARD SMITH — 1944

SOUTHWELL BRIDGNORTH

1869 — TOMKINSON & ADAM   TOMKINSONS — TOMKINSONS

1927 — W & R. R. ADAM   ADAM — ADAM

GEORGIAN — GEORGIAN

1966

1895 — GREATWICH — 1999

1947 — MINSTER — 1976

BOND WORTH — CARPETS OF WORTH

1963 | 1979

1866 — JELLEYMAN

BRINTONS — BRINTONS

1864

WOODWARD GROSVENOR   BRITISH CARPETS — WOODWARD GROSVENOR

1946   1982

1883

WATSON & NAYLOR   WATSON — 1932

T & A NAYLOR — 1976

1899 — VICTORIA — VICTORIA

FAWCETT   CHLIDEMA — 1979

1887

1907 — EMPIRE — 1967

Foreword

In the 18th century Kidderminster was a small market town with a thriving cloth weaving industry. The hand loom weavers were industrious and already noted for a crude floor covering. Therefore, it was not surprising when, in 1735, John Pearsall and John Broom became the first carpet weavers at their loom-shop on Mount Skipet overlooking Park Butts and the town.

A period of change followed as cloth production diminished and the demand for carpet grew to the point where it became the predominant product.

The carpet industry went through turmoil during the mid to late 19th century when the "Industrial Revolution" hit the town bringing the power looms and the factories. The skyline changed as the mills and their chimneys were constructed and the surrounding fields and open spaces became roads and factories.

The population grew rapidly creating a need for more housing and public services. The town centre also developed with new shops and a Town Hall.

In the 20th Century the industry continued to grow. The war years were difficult but the postwar boom of the 1950s injected new life and prosperity into the town. A second revolution became a reality as new, more productive, processes were introduced.

From the 1970s onward the industry was restructured: many companies merged or were taken over. Some failed to meet the challenge and the number of people employed in the carpet industry was significantly reduced.

The history of these companies, their owners and the employees, makes interesting reading and becomes a major section of the book. Over two hundred and fifty companies are reviewed.

In the following chapters you will find out how, and why, carpet weaving came to Kidderminster and who the weavers were. The town's history, photographs and many anecdotes combine to tell the story of Kidderminster's carpet heritage.

The book is dedicated to my father, Cyril Thompson, who was a carpet loom tuner of the town. He was a character who worked for many of the companies and knew the industry well. When I was young he shared with me his wealth of knowledge. Consequently it was perhaps inevitable that I should eventually work in the carpet industry myself: a career I never regretted.

Melvyn Thompson CEng MIMechE
January 2000

Contents

Before you start ...

This book is intended to be an easy and informative read. It is inevitable that the technical "jargon" of the carpet industry will creep into the text. The Glossary, starting on page 192, should help to sort out most of the queries.

The story starts in the East with the early developments of spinning,
dyeing and weaving.
The craft of weaving spreads into Europe and the Huguenots become skilled artisans.
Kidderminster becomes a centre for the cloth trade but it is also renowned for its "Stuff".

The Weavers of the Orient and "Turkey Work"

Many thousands of years ago the nomadic tribes of Asia and the Orient wove natural grasses and palm leaves to make simple floor coverings. The Turks and the Persians were particularly adept and they invented ways of spinning useable threads from grasses, animal hairs and fibrous roots. They also developed techniques for dyeing the threads with plant juices and the extracts from flowers and insects. And so, with the coloured threads and the knowledge of weaving they were soon producing simple patterned fabrics.

The craft spread rapidly. The Egyptians wove fine woollen and linen cloths, the Indians spun cotton; the Chinese learned how to extract the silk threads from the silkworm's cocoon for even finer and more luxurious fabrics.

So it was that the weaving of patterned cloth became an established craft.

This old sketch map shows the towns and districts of Asia and the Orient where simple fabric weaving later developed into the production of carpets with a pile.

CARPET Producing Districts OF ASIA & THE ORIENT

Europe gets weaving

By the early 8th century patterned fabric weaving was well established and the craft had worked its way westward into Europe with the Saracens settling in Belgium, Spain, Italy and France.

The tales and songs of the monks of old Flanders refer to the markets of Ghent, Courtrai and Bruges. Brussels became renowned for its lace, tapestries and simple flat weave floorcoverings.

By the 15th century the Crusaders and the French and Dutch merchants were offering these expensive fabrics to the wealthy nobility of England.

"Turkey Work" on a vertical frame

The first carpets with a pile were developed by the Turkish and Persian weavers. They introduced a very laborious method of hand knotting pre-cut tufts of coloured yarn around the warps on a vertical frame. Frames for weaving are generally referred to as looms.

A number of "knotters" sat side by side on a bench across the width and,

working from a pattern above their heads, gradually produced beautiful deep pile carpets in traditional designs.

The carpets took some months to produce and it is interesting to note that they both used a different style of knot.

The Turks called theirs the Ghiordes and the Persian the Sehna knot.

This type of carpet with a pile was commonly known as " Turkey Work ".

GHIORDES
OR
TURKISH
KNOTS

SEHNA
OR
PERSIAN
KNOTS

Aubusson, Savonnerie and the Huguenots

By the 16th century the demand for floor coverings was spreading rapidly throughout Europe and in France two names had already become well known.

In the town of Aubusson weavers produced a flat tapestry carpet known by the name of the town. Aubusson carpet was a popular floor covering for the mansions and palaces of Europe. However, even more famous were the hand knotted Turkey Work pile carpets called Savonnerie.

In 1608 the French King Henry IV set up a weaver, Pierre Dupont, in a factory in Paris at the Royal Palace of the Louvre. There, he made textile fabrics and the hand knotted Turkey Work carpets. His business flourished and more factories were established. These included the famous factory on the outskirts of Paris known as *La Savonnerie*. The actual buildings were originally a soap-works. (In France a *savonnerie* is a soap-works.)

Over the years Savonnerie carpets became renowned and were much in demand. But, others were producing in volume. And so, in 1825, this factory had to close with production transferred to a smaller factory at Gobelin in Beauvais, north of Paris. The Dupont factories employed the orphans of Paris as hard working cheap labour. However, the real skill was in the hands of a group of French Protestants who were known as Huguenots. The Huguneots were also employed in the factories of Aubusson. They were accomplished spinners, dyers and weavers.

Duhamel du Monceau's "Art de Faire les Tapis Facon de Turquie" drawn in 1766 shows the knotter or weaver at work in Dupont's Factory

Note the pile yarns in the boxes by the weaver and the carpet design just above his eye level. The lady on the left is winding pile yarn on to bobbins.

Section of AUBUSSON CARPET

Section of SAVONNERIE CARPET

3

The Huguenots come to England

By 1685 the Catholic King Louis XIV was in power and he allowed the persecution of the Protestant Huguenots under the Revocation of the Edict of Nantes. Many of them fled the country; some settled in Holland and Germany but a few came across the channel to England.

In this country the skilled Huguenots were welcomed. They were integrated into a developing cloth weaving industry which had many locations including the towns of Wilton in the South and Kidderminster in the Midlands.

Kidderminster in the 1700s and the cloth looms

The Domesday Book of 1086 refers to Chideminstre.

Around 1700, before the canal was built, Kidderminster was a small rural industrial market town with a population around 3,000. There was an established cloth weaving cottage industry with many hand looms in the houses around the town. The river valley location gave a good climate for the industry and there was a potential for wool from the sheep on the surrounding hills.

All Saints Church looked down over the river and the activities on its banks.

The River Stour flowed in from the north. The weirs, pools and tributary splits in the meadows around the town provided good facilities for dyeing and washing the hanks of yarn. The water was said to contain inclusions from the industrial Black Country and that these enhanced the dyeing.

High Street was the shopping centre; "Behind Shops", later Swan Street, ran parallel. The old Guildhall stood at the bottom near the junction with Vicars Street. In those days, Vicars Street was the road out of town into Vicars Meadows. At the end of the street, opposite Tythe Barn, was the Vicarage which was destined in future years to become the site of a new Town Hall.

The river diverted at a point behind the vicarage to form a branch known as Vicars Brook. This travelled through the meadows beyond to rejoin the Stour near the Worcester Road. This branch later became more popularly known as Back Brook. The area around the bottom of High Street and the Bull Ring was the real town centre. Small factories were located on the river in Mill Street, Church Street and Vicars Street (popularly Vicar Street).

Extract from the Survey of John Doharty in 1753

John Doharty surveyed the town in 1753. From his detailed plan, we can see the clusters of housing and the factories beside the River Stour. It is interesting to note that in those days Blackwell Street was called Black Star Street; Dudley Street was Barn Street and both led to the Horse Fair.

Cobblers Corner, at the end of Church Street led into the Bull Ring then across the bridge into Mill Street. Caldwall Tower stood on its own in open meadows and Park Lane ran through open parkland.

Two "Carpet Halls" are identified, one at Mount Skipet and one near Pytts Lane.

John Doharty's Plan Of Kidderminster 1753

Kidderminster Cloths and Bombazine

From early times several of the towns in Worcestershire, including Worcester itself, had a connection with the cloth industry. In the north of the county Bewdley was a small producer. Kidderminster had a thriving and organised spinning and cloth weaving industry.

By the 1600s the master cloth weavers had become very protective of their trade. The Society or Fraternity of Weavers regulated production and the quality of the cloth sold in the area, issuing a seal of approval for each piece. They also kept a strict eye on the weavers. They controlled the training given to apprentices and journeymen, who had to weave for seven years before they were allowed to own a loom. In 1677 records show that there were over 150 master cloth weavers controlling more than 400 looms.

Kidderminster became known for a variety of cloths with strange names such as Linsey Woolseys, Cheneys, Damasks, Prunellas, Friezes, Tammies, Ratteens, Silks, Woollen Camlets, Glossanetts, Poplins and several types of Crape.

However, Kidderminster was particularly noted for an expensive quality cloth called Bombazine. Bombazine was a lightweight twilled or corded dress material made of silk and worsted yarns generally woven in black for mourning. It was also produced in other clerical colours and extensively sold to the priests of the Catholic Church in Spain and Portugal.

Bombazine hand looms were small and ideally suited to the upper floors of the town's houses. Queen Street and Paradise Row were centres for Bombazine.

At the Millennium three derelict cottages in the Horsefair are thought to have been occupied by Bombazine weavers and their families.

Author's Recommendation: A detailed account of the early years of cloth production in Kidderminster is contained in "Collections for the History of Worcestershire" (1782-82) by T.R.Nash, there are two volumes.

"Old George" Talbot makes a Killing

In the early 19th century the Talbot family were well established Bombazine cloth manufacturers and they kept a good stock. The story is told about George Talbot Senior, known as "Old George", who was a very shrewd business man.

In 1817 Princess Charlotte died in London. With an urgent need for black Bombazine cloth for the mourning clothes of the royalty and nobility, two clothing companies immediately sent their representatives on horseback to George Talbot's factory in Mill Street. The object was to buy the complete stock at a good price before the news had reached Kidderminster.

The first arrived in the dead of night and hammered on the door but Old George would not get out of bed. The second arrived just after. Again he remained in bed but he sensed something was up. In the morning the men had to explain the circumstances before they were allowed in.

They left with their packhorses laden and Old George's bank balance considerably more healthy.

"Simple" Hand Looms are Horizontal Looms

It is important at this stage to establish the difference between the Turkey Work looms and the cloth looms. Turkey Work looms were vertical whereas the cloth looms were traditionally horizontal with the weaver sitting at the front and the cloth travelling towards him.

Coloured warp threads were fed from a beam or beams at the rear. The coloured weft was inserted with the weaver selecting from a number of shuttles, one for each colour. The weaver had to work to the pattern and this was very involved. The warp threads were raised and lowered with a complicated device called a Mounture which sat on top of the wooden frame of the loom. The working of the Mounture for the carpet loom is fully described on page 11.

Hand looms with a Mounture were called "Simple" looms. The photograph, below, shows a typical hand loom used for cloth production. However, looms of this size and construction would have been necessary for a heavier cloth known as Kidderminster "Stuff".

The "Ell" is 27 inches

Cloth widths were varied to suit the requirement, but they were always within the capability of the weaver to pass the shuttle through the warp ends by hand.

Even in those days a popular width was 27 inches. The dimension probably derived from the influence of the Huguenot weavers who used a measurement called the Ell. The Flemish Ell is approximately 27 inches.

Strangely, there was also a Scottish Ell at 37 inches and a French Ell at 47 inches. It should be noted that in the carpet industry today 27 inches or 3/4 yard is still regarded as the standard "body" width of the narrow carpet loom.

Kidderminster "Stuff"

Over the years the town's weavers gained a national reputation for a woven product known as Kidderminster Stuff. This was a coarse wool-based patterned heavy cloth woven on the Simple looms of the town.

It was a multi-purpose product and it was used as a covering for beds and furniture. It was also hung on the wall, used as a curtain, or it could be made into outer garments because of its warmth and durability.

Kidderminster Stuff was sometimes used as the theatre back-drop instead of scenery. In a play called "The Generous Enemies" performed at The Kings Theatre in 1672, part of the prologue went as follows:

> "Our aged fathers came to plays for wit,
> And sat knee deep in nut-shells in the pit,
> Coarse hangings then instead of scenes were worn,
> And Kidderminster did the stage adorn."

In 1619 the inventory of Naworth castle in Cumbria referred to "seven items of Kitterminster Stuff"; similar records exist for Worcester cathedral, Much Wenlock church and the council chambers. Richard Baxter, in his 1664 autobiography, said "My people were not rich, but there were few beggars, because their trade of Stuff weaving would find work for them all".

But the Stuff product had another use. It looked good as a floor covering and in this form it was sometimes referred to as a "Fote Cloth".

By the early 1700s Stuff weaving was increasing rapidly particularly as a carpet.

The Stuff looms were heavier in section making them unsuitable for the upper rooms of the houses of the town. Therefore, the master weavers brought a number of looms together into a purpose-designed building called a "loom-shop". The Carpet Halls shown on John Doharty's map were in fact loom-shops.

At the Mount Skipet loom-shop John Pearsall and John Broom were typical Stuff weavers. Over the years to come they would have a significant influence on the future of Kidderminster and its role in the textile industry.

Another hand loom photograph taken at Woodward, Grosvenor in 1938, the weaver is hard at work weaving a "Finger Rug".

HAND LOOMS AND THE RIVERSIDE FACTORIES

The first carpet is woven by Pearsall and Broom. 1735 - 1851

Chapter 2

Other areas get weaving but Kidderminster is ideally situated at the centre of the country.
The Masters and the Weavers - how they lived, worked and spent their leisure time.
The rapidly expanding industry creates tensions resulting in strikes and riots.
The town developes and the industry settles down to a period of stability. The calm before the storm !

1735 - Pearsall and Broom weave "Kidderminster"

With the Huguenot weavers now integrated into the cloth weaving industry of the country new products were developed. For example, in the year 1735 the first real carpet was said to have been woven in Kidderminster. The carpet was flat, without a pile, and it was a natural progression from the Stuff product. Manufactured entirely out of coloured woollen yarn it was cleverly woven on the Simple loom as a double thickness to give it some bulk. It was an instant success and became known as "Kidderminster" carpet.

Kidderminster double or two-ply carpet could be described as two thick patterned cloths joined together in the weaving process. The pattern appeared on both surfaces in reverse colours; therefore, the carpet could be turned over.

However, the weave was not confined to Kidderminster. It was also known as "Scotch" and in 1824 a Scottish weaver from Kilmarnock succeeded in achieving a triple thickness with even greater bulk and wearing capabilities. Another name for the same product was "Ingrain", particularly used in America in later years.

Pearsall and Broom on Mount Skipet

By 1735 the population of the town had grown to 3,500 and there were over 600 cloth looms weaving in the houses and loom-shops. The credit for the first carpet with the Kidderminster weave goes to John Pearsall and John Broom who adapted their heavier Stuff looms to weave Kidderminster double carpet at the loom-shop on Mount Skipet.

A document, dated 1758, indicates that John Pearsall was the tenant of the land at Mount Skipet owned by Francis Clare. It is therefore assumed that he was the first weaver and John Broom worked with him. In later years they had a joint agreement and eventually Broom became the sole named tenant.

The 1758 document also refers to two dwellings as part of the lease.

Note. The document can be examined at Kidderminster Reference Library - Document 12012.

The Town gets weaving

Word got around the town and it was not long before other companies learned the techniques and were selling Kidderminster carpet alongside their cloth products. Pearsall and Broom's monopoly was short-lived.

9

Mount Skipet

Mount Skipet, in January 2000, could be reached by climbing the steep steps from Park Lane which ascended alongside the derelict Rock Building, formerly owned by The Carpet Manufacturing Company. At the top of the steps, the row of cottages on the right was considered to be the site of the actual "Carpet Hall" or loom-shop referred to on Doharty's 1753 plan.

The 1758 document describes the loom-shop as being twenty-five yards long with two storeys, each capable of housing sixteen looms. The agreement also states that the two dwellings were occupied by weavers John Tanner and William Foster. While the loom-shop no longer exists it could be that the current Mount Skipet Cottage, the white building to the right of the photograph, forms the actual dwellings referred to in the document.

Another building near the cottage at the end of Hill Street has the structure of a smaller loom-shop, see the lower photograph.

Incidentally, the existing steps were built in 1927 when the Rock Building was extended towards Mount Skipet. The original steps were further down Park Lane.

1749 The Introduction of "Brussels" Carpet

The production of Kidderminster carpet continued to grow with many of the manufacturers investing more of their profit in new looms and the building of loom-shops. But John Broom had been actively following developments elsewhere and in 1749 he introduced the "Brussels" carpet weave to the town.

There are two versions of the story. The popular relates John Broom's journey to Brussels and Tournai to learn the weaving techniques. On his return he brought with him a Belgian weaver to help him convert looms at his loom-shop on Mount Skipet. The second version suggests that the weavers actually came from Wilton and that they were, in fact, John Tanner and William Foster who occupied the dwellings thought to be Mount Skipet Cottage. Whichever is true, the fact remained that he had an advantage and he tried to keep it a secret. However, the word got around and other manufacturers went to great lengths to find out what was going on. It appears they even climbed ladders to look through the upper windows of the loom-shop as Broom and his weaver worked at night by candle light.

Patterned Brussels was significantly different from the Kidderminster weave since it was the first to be woven on a Simple hand loom with a raised pile surface. In the Brussels weave the raised pile remains uncut in the looped form.

Author's recommendation: Don Gilbert's "Kidderminster's Early Carpet Industry" discusses the introduction of Brussels in great detail and is worth a read. It can be found in the Reference Library under - Transactions for Worcestershire Archeological Society, Series 3, Vol.12, 1990.

The Brussels "Simple" Loom

The looms were set up to weave patterns with up to five colours in the design. The Brussels weave was more complex than the Kidderminster weave for it required a number of other materials to hold the raised pile in position. These were called the "backing materials" and were generally natural spun fibres such as linen, cotton and jute. Jute only became available in the early 1800s.

The warp backing materials were fed from a beam or a number of beams at the rear. The backing weft was inserted by a single shuttle containing a "cop" of yarn. The coloured pile yarns were fed from individual bobbins held in a tray at the rear behind the loom. This was called the "creel". Five trays made up the creel: a tray for each colour. Very often the colour bank was referred to as a "frame" of ends.

As outlined in the previous chapter, the Mounture was the device above the loom which enabled the coloured pile ends to be selected for weaving into the pattern of the carpet. It was a complicated structure with "simple" cords, known as the "harness", hanging down. Each cord controlled an individual pile warp end and there were 1,300 in the 27inch width. With five possible colours, 260 ends had to be lifted for each row of loops in accordance with the pattern.

The weaver's assistant was called a "draw-boy". It was his job to lift or "draw" the selected ends to the up position for weaving into pile surface of the carpet.

When the yarns were raised up, the draw-boy passed underneath the "sword". The sword was a long batten of wood which, when turned on its side, formed an opening called the "shedding". The "pile wire" was inserted to form the loops. The sword was then withdrawn and the shedding changed position to bind in the pile wire with the passing of the weft shuttle. A number of pile wires remained in the carpet. At the point of removal the draw-boy would "draw" out the wire to the side, leaving a row of pile yarns in loop formation. He also had to look after the creel. This entailed mending broken ends and replenishing empty bobbins.

The draw-boys were kept very busy!

Brussels takes over

Brussels was a real carpet and it was an instant success. Soon the whole town was adapting looms and reorganising the workplace to accommodate the creel and the additional materials. Many thousands of square yards was produced each year to the detriment of the Kidderminster weave. Brussels carpet rapidly became the principal product of the town

1825 The Jacquard replaces the Mounture

The Mounture had had its day. It was slow, heavy and complicated - a fact well known to Joseph Marie Jacquard in the French town of Lyon. As far back as 1801 Jacquard had perfected a device to replace the Mountures on the patterned cloth looms.

The "Jacquard" was a complex mechanism using punched cards and needles to select the coloured warp ends. But it was not until twenty years later that the Jacquard system was adapted to the carpet loom. Pioneer John Broom's grandson, also John, was the first to hear about the development and he successfully installed Jacquards on to his Brussels looms in 1825. Jacquards slowly replaced the Mountures but not without problems for the smaller loom shops where the ceiling height was not enough. The weavers and draw-boys were happy to see the end of the Mounture. Productivity increased. The boys effectively became general assistants, though it was much later that they became known as "creelers".

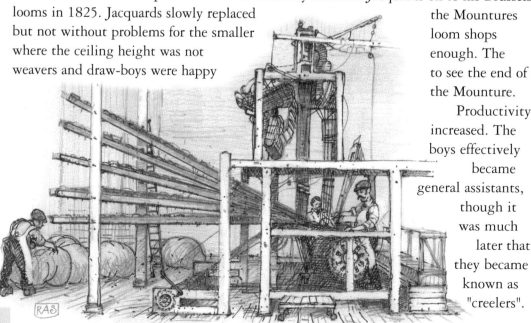

"Wiltons" from Wiltshire and "Axminsters" from Devon

Kidderminster was not the only place where things were happening. In the 1730s Henry, the 9th Earl of Pembroke, was doing the Grand Tour of Europe. As he travelled through Flanders and France, he became attracted to the beautiful hand-crafted carpets of the area. He persuaded two French weavers, Antoine Duffosee and Pierre Jemaule, to return with him to Wilton. There they joined the established cloth industry on the banks of the rivers Wylye and Nadder.

The Wilton cloth industry had also deviated into the production of carpets. Like Kidderminster, they had a number of Brussels looms. Antoine Duffosee was a Brussels weaver and he conceived the idea of cutting the Brussels loop to form the pile. Cut pile or "Velvet" carpets produced in this way became known as "**Wiltons**". The Wilton weave and the Simple loom was exactly as described for Brussels but the weaver now had the additional job of cutting the warp pile ends.

Like many pioneers Antoine Duffosee did not profit from his invention. He married a local girl, Mary Tanner, and they had a number of children. However, when he died penniless in 1785 his widow ended up in the local poor house.

In 1755 Thomas Whitty, a cloth weaver in the Devon town of Axminster, constructed a vertical loom for hand knotting imitation Oriental designs in the style of Turkey Work. With the growing demand for floorcoverings these expensive multi-coloured knotted pile carpets were very popular and christened "**Axminsters**".

The industry in Axminster continued until 1835 when the Whitty company ceased production following a devastating fire. A Wilton manufacturer called Blackmore bought the business and what was left of the equipment. He transferred everything to his factory in Wilton, including some of the weavers.

Blackmore's historic Wilton factory changed ownership over the years. In 1905 it received the Royal Warrant to become the famous Wilton Royal Carpet Factory.

The original Wilton factory was erected in 1655. After a fire it was rebuilt in 1710. Today, it is a Museum where the Turkey Work knotting looms are for demonstration only.

There were other areas

Other cloth manufacturers were experimenting with floorcoverings particularly in Frome, Fulham, Kilmarnock, Halifax and Donegal in Ireland In the early 1800s the Kidderminster weave was introduced to the cloth looms of Barnard Castle in County Durham. In the Bowes Museum of that town a hand loom is set up to weave Kidderminster double.

Growing Kidderminster

Canals and Transport give the Advantage

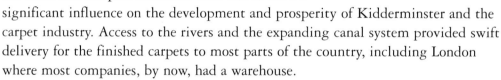

Between 1766 and 1772 James Brindley constructed the Staffordshire and Worcestershire Canal which linked together the Trent and Severn rivers. The canal passed through Kidderminster following the River Stour to the point where it joined the Severn at Lower Mitton, some 4 miles away.

The town of Stourport on Severn soon grew around the canal and the port facilities. This was to have a significant influence on the development and prosperity of Kidderminster and the carpet industry. Access to the rivers and the expanding canal system provided swift delivery for the finished carpets to most parts of the country, including London where most companies, by now, had a warehouse.

The canals also were the perfect way to bring raw materials into the town. A good support industry was created as the many wharfs and basins of the town became busy with the bales of carpet awaiting the narrow boats of the canal.

Pickfords and others provided horse drawn wagons to link the canal with the factory. So, with Kidderminster's central location coupled with river and the

expanding canal system it had a good commercial advantage over the other carpet towns.

The Old Wharf under the shadow of St.Mary's Church, one of many in the town.

Kidderminster Carpets the White House

The carpet industry was now well established and by the early 1800s Kidderminster, Brussels and the cut pile Wilton products were all available alongside a variety of cloths which still included the popular Bombazine.
One of the earliest prestigious export deals was struck by an architect called Benjamin Latrobe. In 1809, he sailed from Bristol to America to design the interior of the White House for Dolly Madison, wife of President James Madison. Henry Woodward and Company of Church Street were commissioned to weave the carpet for the Blue Room which is today called the Oval Office.

Barclays Directory 1810 reports on Kidderminster

KIDDERMINSTER - A town of Worcestershire, the principal manufacturing place in the county, and long celebrated for its different manufactures of woollens, carpets, poplins, crapes, bombazines, etc. Its former trade of Stuffs, however, is much declined, on account of the general use of cotton goods; but its carpet manufactory has greatly increased, and it is still the first market in England for pile or plush carpets, which for beauty and colour and patterns, exceed any other. These are frequently called Wilton, from having been first made in that town; but, at present, by much the greater part is made in Kidderminster. The silk and worsted trades have also been introduced here and employ about 2,000 hands. The goods go chiefly to Portugal, and their carriage has been much facilitated by the late canal communications. It is seated under a hill, on the river Stour.

Kidderminster grows with the Carpet Industry

At the turn of the century the population had grown to 6,000. There were now more than 1,000 carpet looms in town, the majority of which wove Brussels. The town authorities had difficulty keeping up with this increase in population. Sanitation became a major problem and drinking water from the wells dried up in the summer months. The *Worcester Chronicle* reported that the town had an average of one well to every twenty-five houses.

Carpet sales continued to flourish and the owners, the "Carpet Masters", became rich and powerful men. But not so the workforce who were forced to work long hours in appalling conditions to earn a meagre wage. Despite these adverse conditions people continued to come into the industry and by 1811 the town had to cope with 8,000 inhabitants.

Some progress was made in 1813 with the "Paving and Improvement Act" which widened roads, provided pavements and cleaned obstructions from the river. Five years later the Kidderminster Gas & Coke Company opened in Pitts Lane. Within the next year the company had installed gas lighting in the town centre but only for the winter months.

But it was not until 1835 that the town gained its small full time Police Force.

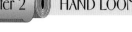

Kidderminster has Vacancies !

By 1820 there were over 2,000 carpet looms and the population had again expanded to around 11,000. The influx came mainly from the surrounding Worcestershire towns although a few came from Wilton in the hope of better wages. This rapid development of the industry led to a serious shortage of looms and skilled weavers. The manufacturers were building more loom-shops and the carpenters were busy constructing the heavier carpet looms with the tray creels. However, the burning issue was the shortage of skilled craftsmen. All who qualified quickly became a weaver leaving a critical shortage of assistants at the loom.

The industry desperately needed more draw-boys, but they would also take girls! These children were apprenticed to the weaver. He looked after them and paid them a weekly wage. In return for the training, the weaver received a bond payment, generally from their family.

In 1808 a number of weavers were so short of help that they wrote to other towns in Worcestershire seeking suitable apprentices.

The following letters are held at the County Records Office..

To the Overseers of Evesham in the County of Worcester.

Sirs,

I take the liberty to inform you, that I have been informed that you have several Boys to put out as apprentices, if so, be pleased to Let me Know of what ages and sizes they may be and on what Terms, if there may be any from the age of ten years to fourteen. I would be willing to accept of them provided we can come to terms,

My Business is Carpet Weaving & my Master John Broom Esq. will give me a Undeniable Character to be Creditable hours keeper & Sobriety also that I am a good workman, if you Should have any of the above mentioned ages & description please to let me have a answer & I will Endevour to come to Terms if possible, if you Should answer this as I hope you will please direct for Benjamin Crundall Carpet Weaver in the Church Street Kidderminster in the County of Worcester.

in Complience of the above you will Greatly Oblige.

Your Humble Servt.

Benj'n Crundall.

Be pleased to let me have a answer as soon as possible.

Kidderminster. 28th Oct'r 1808

A Mr Scott replied to Benjamin Crundall and the contact resulted in the first draw-boys coming from Evesham to work in the carpet industry.

In the Inns of the town the word soon got around and other weavers put quill pen to paper - but they didn't all want a boy!

Mr Scot Sir,

this is to Acquaint you that Benjamin Crundall Informs me that you have several young Gearls to Put out Aprentice if so Please to send your Proposal and the Age of the Gearls as me and a naibor of Mine can take one Each at this time, Please to send word as soon as Posable

Sir I Remain yours
Wm Jevans.

28th August 1809   Direct Wm Jevans Near the New Inn Kidderminster.
Worstershire.

When you write I shall come over

Author's comment: I'm sure the requests were genuine but would you trust your young daughter with a weaver who lived near a pub!

Another joint letter on the same theme.

Kidderminster 31 st Augt 1809

Sir   We have been Informed by Benjamin Crundall a man that as Lately had a Boy from your Parish that you have Several Girls from the Age of Eleven to Thirteen that you would Like to Bind out as Apprentices and We shall Esteem it a favour if you will by a Line Inform us if you have any such at this time and the Details of the Terms you put on tenure with Bombazeen Weavers and can bring suffcent Carractor from our Different Masters if you think surfice to Return an answer Please to say when will be the Most Suitable time for us to come Down that the Business may be Finished at one Journey
you will Please to Direct for William Kirby Blackwell Street near the Red Man Kidderminster Worcestershire.

in so doing you will Much Oblige your Humble Servants
William Kirby and William Frost.

Having created a demand, the letter from William Beal gets straight to the point. The weaver goes to church, he's expensive and it's first come first served !

March 28   1810
Sir
In Complyance of your Request I have sought for a Master for the Children you wish to Put out Apprentice the Person I Recomend is a Steady Industerious man & one of Mr Wesley's People But he will not take one under the sum of 6 pounds if you should think Proper to Comply an answer as soon as possible is requested or the Person is in suspence as he waits for an answer from another Place & under similar Circumstances.
Yours ....   W'm Beal

A Present for the Queen

Queen Caroline was estranged from her husband King George IV. He refused to recognise her as Queen and barred her from his Coronation at St.Paul's Cathedral in 1821. Her name was struck from the Church Litany and she was excluded from court. However, she was much loved by the people. In Kidderminster 5,000 townsfolk signed a petition of loyalty and support which was delivered to London together with a present of a carpet, some 10 yards square, paid for by 3,000 weavers who each contributed one shilling towards the weaving.

Kidderminster Carpet Manufacturers

The history so far has referred to the names of John Pearsall, John Broom and his descendants. The Woodward company has been mentioned and we know that George Talbot was a Bombazine weaver, but who else controlled the carpet industry in Kidderminster?

In 1783 William Brinton started spinning at Hill Pool and before the turn of the century his family had formed partnerships with Richard Green and John Cooper. The family names Lea, Woodward, Morton, Watson, Hooman and Pardoe were all established and in the following years would continue to be major forces in the carpet industry. But there were others who were equally important at the time.

The 1823 Ward Price Directory lists 22 registered carpet manufacturers. All the companies had their address at the riverside factories in Mill Street, Church Street and Vicar Street, but their Simple looms were located in the loom-shops around the town. It is to be remembered that there was still a diminishing trade for cloth.

To get a feel for the total production leaving the town each week consider 2,000 looms weaving an average of 25 linear yards and multiply by the 3/4 yard width. You will be amazed to know that nearly 40,000 square yards was produced - by hand! Many of the names listed below will be familiar but only the Brinton family remain in the industry today.

1823 Ward Price Directory lists the following -

Baker, Joseph & Son	Mill Street	Lea, Francis & Thos.	Mill Street
Bowyer, Joseph	Vicar Street	Lea & Newcomb	Church Street
Broom Sons & Horne	Mill Street	Lea, John & Son	Mill Street
Brinton, Henry	Mill Street	Newcomb, John & Son	Mill Street
Cole, James Junior	Church Street	Pardoe, Hooman & Pardoe	New Road
Cooper, Joshua C.	Vicar Street	Robinson, George	Church Street
Cooper, W. [and rug]	Mill Street	Shirley, Robert	Church Street
Dobson, Timothy	Church Street	Talbot, George, Henry & George	Mill Street
Gough, John, Son	Mill Street	Watson & Son	Church Street
Hooman & Co. Spinners	Vicar Street	Woodward & Morton	Vicar Street
Lea, Francis & Thos. Spinners	Mill Street	Wright, Chas. (and rug)	Vicar Street

Masters, Weavers, Draw-boys, Factories and Leisure

Author's recommendation: The "Carpet Weavers and Carpet Masters 1780 - 1850"
by Len Smith is an excellent book with an in-depth study of the hand loom period.

The following pages give a quick overview what life was like in the town and the carpet industry in those times.

The Carpet Masters

The term "Master" referred to the owner of the company who controlled the business with a rod of iron. Some of the masters originally came to Kidderminster to invest in the new industry; others worked their way up through the weaving ranks into partnerships. Many came from the existing carpet families but the clever ones married into these rich families. Dinner parties, civic functions and attending church provided the opportunity to meet each other socially and to discuss the problems of the industry. Partnerships and marriages resulted from these meetings.

The dissenting church in Kidderminster started with the congregation of Richard Baxter who had left the town in 1661. Many of the town's cloth weaving families were part of this congregation and in 1693 they provided funds to build a Meeting House in the Bull Ring. During the 1700s the families of Lea, Brinton, Fawcett, Dobson and Cooper together with the Talbots, Pearsalls, Brooms, Watsons and Penns all attended the Meeting House.

In 1781 the latter named group above, together with others, broke away to form a New Meeting House in Church Street. The original building became known as the Old Meeting House. Today it is better known as the Baxter United Reformed Church while the New Meeting Church is of the Unitarian faith.

For many years the New Meeting School existed alongside the Church. The school was originally called Nicholas Pearsall's Grammar School and many of the carpet masters' children attended.

The Church of England and other faiths also had loyal members from within the carpet industry.

The masters became involved in the running of the town's affairs. They were appointed Mayors of the Borough and in later years a few became Members of Parliament. As the town grew in size new streets were given the names of the early carpet masters - Broom Crescent, Lea Street, Talbot Street, Radford Avenue, Green Street are typical examples. There are more.

Author's note: Many people alive today, including myself, went to New Meeting Junior School. The school was housed in the historic buildings of the old Grammar School. Now demolished, the area forms the rear of The Swan Centre. This, incidentally got its name from Swan Street which was the road running parallel with High Street referred to in the Doharty map as "Behind Shops".

"Behind Shops"
or Swan Street
in the mid 1800s

The Carpet Masters' Houses

In the early days the masters lived at the factory where they could keep an eye on the business. But, as the profits rolled in, they appointed managers to run the factory and went to live in fine houses on the edge of town. The houses had extensive grounds. They had servants, gardeners and good stabling for the horses and carriages. Heathfield, Honeybrook House, Elderslie, The Shubbery, Lyndholm, The Larches, The Croft, Greatfield House, Blakebrook House, Whitville and Franche Hall are all good examples of the grand houses owned at some time by the carpet masters.

Author's Recommendation: "Ridiculous Refinement" by Nigel Gilbert is an excellent a book about the Mansions of the early Carpet Barons in Kidderminster.

"Oaklands", Chester Road North.

Built by Henry Talbot in the early 1800s, Oaklands was a fine house with extensive grounds. After a period as Tomkinson's company Sports and Social Club, the house was demolished in the 1960s and the grounds, like many others, became a housing estate.

The Factory by the River

With the hand looms scattered around the town in the loom-shops, the factory was the core of the business and always situated on the river. The factory unit was often no bigger than a large shed. It consisted of the office called the counting house, yarn store, dye house, riverside washing area, drying room, bobbin winding room, finished carpet store and a show room.

A few manufacturers had their own spinning operation at the factory where a water-wheel drove Arkwright's crude spinning machinery. After spinning, the wool based yarns were wound into hanks or skeins ready for the dye vats. The hanks were lowered into open topped wooden vats and the dye stuffs added. A wooden paddle stirred the whole concoction.

With the dyeing complete, the hanks were removed and washed in the river. This precarious operation involved the dyehouse men standing on platforms projecting into the river and manipulating the hanks on poles. It was nice work on a summer day. However, in the winter or when the river was in flood, things were a little different with many lost hanks and an occasional soaking for the dyehouse men. The River Stour regularly changed colour as the dye vats were emptied directly into the flow. With a number of dyehouses lining the banks the more up-stream the location, the cleaner the water. The hanks were suspended on poles and dried naturally in large well-ventilated drying rooms. Hot stoves were sometimes used to speed up the drying process. Finally, the yarn was wound on to bobbins and stored ready for the weaver to collect.

Author's note: Carpet Trades was downstream from Jelleymans and I can remember the river regularly changing colour, even in the early 1950s!

The Weavers' Houses

The weavers and their families lived in the streets of the town away from the river. The streets leading up the hill from Church Street towards the Horsefair were particularly well-populated. Hall Street, Barn Street, Orchard Street all contained houses laid out in "courts". This was a popular way of building communal housing since the "courtyard" at the rear contained the wash house, privy toilet and water pumped from the well. These facilities were available to all.

The houses themselves were fairly small with shared bedrooms. In some, the upper room would have housed the looms of the cloth industry. It was not unusual for the master to own the house and the loom. Yet people were happy; the ladies chatted and exchanged gossip as they did the washing; the children played together in relative safety and the men folk gathered in the yard to air their grievances about the working conditions and the luxurious lifestyle of the landlord. Doors were never locked and there was always someone to help in times of trouble.

However, the growing town and the lack of public facilities meant that the alleyways and streets were often filthy. Uncaring people threw rubbish directly into the street and stagnant puddles needed to be avoided.

Loom-shops

Loom-shops were long narrow buildings with the looms located on the outside walls near to a window for the best natural light. They varied in size from four looms to the shops with sixteen looms on each of two floors.

This grouping of the weavers and their looms meant that the master could control the quality, keep an eye on production and hopefully prevent any pilfering. The bobbins and materials were untidily stored around the looms and in the gangways. An open-topped tub of starch was available for coating the backing yarns. A coal stove provided the heat in winter. Additional light came from tallow candles precariously positioned around the loom, always a fire hazard.

Sanitation was a problem. Although there was a privy in the yard, the weavers were encouraged to use urine bins. The stale urine was collected for use in the yarn dyeing process down at the factory. The walls of the loom-shop remained unpainted and the whole area was dirty and covered in a film of yarn dust. The smell from the starch and the urine made appalling working conditions.

The draw-boys and girls were fully occupied at the loom but they were also expected to clean up. These were not ideal conditions for young people especially the developing young draw-girls who had to be very wary of the advances of the weavers, especially in the hours of darkness.

It was hard graft for the boys and girls. If any were seen to be slacking they would get a clip behind the ear or feel the weight of a thrown shuttle. These poor working conditions for young people caused the Government of the day to form a Royal Commission on Childrens Employment. Draw-boys and girls gave evidence. The full report entitled "Employment of Children in Factories" was published in 1843.

Edward Hughes' Mill Street loom-shop photographed in the 1920s

Weavers, Apprentices and Half-Weavers

Carpet hand loom weavers were male only and they were very proud and possessive about their craft. Years of training preceded weaver status at the minimum age of twenty-one years. A limited number of apprenticeships were on offer whereby a young person was assigned to a weaver on payment of a bond. It was not unusual for the apprentice to live with the weaver.

Half-weaver was the name given to a weaver in waiting. He received half pay and wove on a loom owned or rented by a qualified weaver who could profitably control a number of looms in this way.

It was a big occasion when the young weaver was given his first loom; always a cause for celebration at the local public house.

Draw-boys and Girls

Draw-boys, sometimes draw-girls, started work at a very young age, generally before they were ten years old. They were hired by the weaver and entered into an apprenticeship with him. The working relationship between them would greatly affect the yardage produced and hence the money earned. Draw-boys graduated to half-weavers. However, the draw-girls would have to work in the spinning mill or become a bobbin winder in the riverside factory. They were not allowed to weave.

The variety of jobs in the carpet industry provided potential employment for the whole family. Dad, the weaver, could have half-weaver sons and his children working as draw-boys or draw-girls. Mom and the elder daughters could be spinners or winders working at the factory.

Recollections of a Draw-boy [from the records of Sir Thomas Lea, Bart.]

James Porter, aged 12, was a draw-boy for the weaver Timothy Lloyd who worked for Timothy Dobson and Son at his loom-shop in Church Street. He told how he had been a draw-boy since he was seven. Before that he had been to school and could read and write "a little". He worked six-days-a-week; generally from 6am till 10pm, and on Sundays went to Sunday School in the morning and the evening. To finish a piece by "fall-day" the weaver and draw-boy would sometimes start at 4am or work all night. After payment for his work the weaver would always go to the public house and get drunk.

The draw-boy's pay was about 4 shillings-a-week.

James Porter recalled that he ate dry bread or toast for breakfast and "taties" with salt for dinner.

Girls were not so lucky, one girl who worked for a Bombazine weaver recalled working up to 16 hours a day, 7 days a week, with two days holiday a year on Mothering Sunday and Christmas Day.

"Fall-Day" was Pay Day

Fall-day was the name given to the day when the weaver, helped by his draw-boy, took the finished "piece" of carpet to the factory counting house and was paid for his production. Fall days were Thursdays and Saturdays and on no other day would he be paid. Therefore, the whole working week was structured around the completion of the piece by a fall-day.

After weaving, the weaver had to tidy up his piece by clipping all the loose ends and shearing the cut pile Wiltons. This was a hard job which he hated doing. At the factory the carpet was rolled out for inspection. If all was well it was measured and the weaver was paid by the yard woven. He then received the pattern and yarn for the next job.

The working day depended entirely upon the weaver. It was very often from early morning to late at night. A good weaver and draw-boy could finish a piece, 30 yards long, in a week. This was exceptional, however, and on average 25 yards was woven.

In the cloth trade the male weavers would earn about 12 shillings a week. Carpet weavers were better paid at 1 shilling for every yard finished, say, 25 shillings per week. Out of this the weaver would pay his loom rental, his coal and candles and his draw-boy. Draw-boys earned between 4 and 6 shillings a week. At best, the weaver would end up with 18 shillings in his pocket.

If a special order was being woven the master would declare "12 to 12" working with two sets of weavers and draw-boys working day and night in shifts. One of the problems of this system was security of materials. The theft of yarn and the "cutting" of a piece from the roll was not unusual. These could be sold for good profit in the local Inns. This became a big problem in later years when the relationship between the weavers and the masters was strained and all the trust had gone.

Leisure Time

With money in their pockets the weavers went off to one of the many Taverns of the town for a jar of ale and a game of skittles, dice or cards. The Inns became the meeting place for the various trades. The weavers gathered at The Freemasons Arms and the Seven Stars, while the spinners and woolcombers met at the Coach & Horses in Mill Street.

A lot of the leisure time seemed to be spent fighting in one form or other. Cock and dog fighting were popular and also bare knuckle "prize fighting". This pursuit was frowned upon by the town Magistrate who posted notices around the town. The children passed the time with hop-scotch, clay marbles, kite flying and hoops.

Sunday was a day for church, and then back to the Ale House. The drinking often continued into Monday. When this happened they called it "St.Monday" and the poor draw-boys knew they were in for some long hours before the next fall-day.

Around the town and in the villages markets and fairs were held in the summer time.
Author's comment: Today Kidderminster's Retail Market days are, would you believe it,
Thursday and Saturday - the old Fall-Days!

Masters v Weavers - Trouble and Strike

The masters controlled the industry. They set the terms and conditions. The weavers were at a disadvantage and led a very servile existence. In complete contrast the masters were becoming very wealthy men. And so, the Inns were not only a place of recreation but became the place to share grievances about poor pay, the dreadful working conditions and to observe and comment on the high living standards of the carpet masters.

The weavers discussed the need for some collective action to improve their lot. But in those days unions, as we know them, were unlawful. So the men got round the problem by organising themselves into Sick Clubs and Friendly Societies. The Friendly Society of Operative Carpet Weavers was one such group. They had an active committee who met at the Freemasons Arms.

The carpet masters were also organised, particularly when it came to fixing the piecework rates of pay. During the early 1800s the element of unrest increased and a number of confrontations took place. One of the most notable was in November 1817 when £20,000 worth of damage was done when Hooman, Pardoe & Hooman lost their complete Spinning Mill in an arson attack following a pay related dispute.

Up until this time the Combination Laws had made it illegal for the weavers or the masters to formally combine together, but in 1825 Parliament passed a law allowing collective bargaining. The weavers immediately formed a Weavers Committee.

The troubles of the industry were not confined to Kidderminster. A few weavers were on strike in Wilton while in Bradford the Woolcombers and Weavers had been engaged in a bitter twenty-three weeks battle over rates of pay. The local Weavers Committee kept a close watch on proceedings and provided significant financial support. Unrest was in the air and, therefore, perhaps it was inevitable that a major issue would cause both masters and their workforce to confront and test each other. Things came to a head in March 1828 when the masters dropped their bombshell.

The 1828 Weavers' Strike

Brussels carpet was still the town's predominant product and it was sold with a good reputation for quality, but quality wasn't the only criterion. In the north of England and Scotland the masters had successfully controlled their piece-work rates and, therefore, were able to reduce the selling price. Kidderminster began to loose valuable orders and so the masters decided to take action.

Without any consultation whatsoever on Saturday 15th March 1828 they posted notices around the town informing the weavers that the payment for one yard of Brussels was reduced from one shilling to ten old pence, a 17% reduction. The Weavers Committee immediately got together and called a town meeting on Monday 17th. The noisy gathering resulted in a march of over 2,000 angry weavers through the town centre. Unanimous in opposition they voted to strike. And so began the nationally reported Strike of the Carpet Weavers of Kidderminster.

Discussions started but the masters remained firm and unrelenting. The strike became bitter and prolonged with much anger and civil unrest. On the 17th May one worker decided to return to work at Barber & Cole's factory in Church Street. He was stoned and the weavers also turned their attention to his house and family. The following day the Military, in the form of the 14th Light Dragoons, marched into town to restore order and the riot act was read.

After three months without income starvation was setting in. So the committee sent delegations to other towns to drum up support. They received little help. The masters were losing good orders and they tried to bring in labour from out of town. The blackleg weavers were pelted with stones and horse manure. Henry Brinton received a letter threatening his life. On the 11th July one of the masters offered a compromise of eleven pence a yard for an early return to work. However, things had gone too far and the weavers resolved to remained united.

On the 15th July 28 weavers arrived by canal barge from other areas. They were taken, under the protection of constables and magistrates, to work at Joseph Bowyer's factory in Vicar Street. They were described as "a motley gang". Cracks started to appear at the end of July as a new company was started up outside the town boundary at Lower Mitton, Stourport, away from the influence of the Weavers Committee. A factory was also built on the River Severn at Bewdley. While further upstream in Bridgnorth the cloth weavers were also converting to carpet.

Kidderminster's economy plummeted as the inns and local shops lost business. Along the banks of the canal the empty narrow-boats waited patiently. In early August a few weavers had given in and about 300 hand looms were again weaving in the town.

Throughout the strike the weavers had the support of Kidderminster-born Reverend Humphrey Price, Vicar of Needwood near Lichfield. Many of the handbills and notices distributed during the strike were unsigned and it later became evident that these had been written by Humphrey Price.

By the 4th August the Magistrates had issued ten summonses to William Chalton, President of the Weavers Committee, all designed to bring matters to a head. More meetings followed and on 12th August the masters offered a payment of 30 shillings to every married weaver and 20 shillings to unmarried weavers in return for an immediate return to work - a very tempting offer! On Saturday 16th August, after twenty-one weeks, the weavers capitulated, took the money, and the strike ended.

Confidence in Kidderminster had taken a severe knock with many faithful customers placing their first orders in the north. The industry was now fragmented around the neighbouring towns and some of the disillusioned weavers had emigrated or gone to work in the north. The town's economy had also suffered greatly.

The defeated Weavers Committee disbanded and William Chalton's summonses were withdrawn. To make sure that there were no further troubles the Military remained in town until the middle of September. The carpet masters wasted no time getting back to work. They immediately introduced "12 to 12" working and the industry gradually returned to normality. Sadly, the Reverend Humphrey Price was later jailed.

WEAVERS,

REASON I fear you will not—men who abandon their own judgement to the controul of others have none—neither can you in the past read the prospect of the future, equally deaf to the voice of truth and insensible to the admonitions of experience.

THERE is no branch of Manufacture but has suffered a reduction within the last Twelve Years, both of Profit to the Master and in the price of Labor to the Workman; those Places have P succeeded which first yielded to the necessity of the times.—Owing to the want of foresight on part of your Masters in this respect—what has become of the 4-4th, or Scotch Trade? by paying more than was paying elsewhere for weaving, they were in effect giving a premium for its est ment in other places—you know that it is no longer carried on here to that extent and with t fit it was in 1818—had wages then been reduced upon that particular description of work, i not have been lost, and you in common with your townsmen would at this day have been the benefit of more extensive employment—men who of late have taken a Piece to the V only every third or fourth week, might have taken one in every ten or fourteen days, and you so dull as not to comprehend that that man is richer who is paid 33s. 4d. for a pi which he performs in a fortnight than another who receives 40s. for the same quantity, a month in producing it.

THE reduction in the value of Labor encouraged the growth of the Trade i as a natural consequence the sources of employment were lessened here in exact pro crease there—what then have the Weavers been the richer, receiving a penny pe those in other places? in the one instance less per yard has been paid with perman other case more per yard, but precarious employment—apply this principle to and those who run may read—encourage who you will to build Looms—erect th but depend upon it they will ultimately be found in the greatest numbers whe est—multiply them as fast as you can, and then drink of the cup you have f derstand that if the world only requires as many Carpets as can be made in every additional loom put on, tends to render your work less certain? will t pets to find you employment? the cruelty of your Masters is more tolerable such a case—if you doubt it, go on in the course you have, and prove it.

YOU say you CAN only get 15s. a week ; you know well that y you DID not—although there be those who have only had that much, lo not spent half their time in idleness, and with the same breath confes been better clothed—their children better fed—and themselves more b pence a Yard and their time industriously occupied.

TO THE

CARPET WEAVERS

OF KIDDERMINSTER.

BELOVED COMRADES,

The Storm is high ;—The Battle rages ;—But Success is sure. To hold on, and to hold out, is Victory. "England expects every man to do his Duty," said one of our Glories. "You and I and every man must die in his place, or gain the Victory ;" said another, and the last. The first won, and died. The last won, and lived. We, Beloved Comrades, may die, or we may live ; BUT WE MUST WIN. Our quondam Employers threaten Machinery, let it come.—They taunt Starvation, we will abide. By Starvation, they force upon us Death ; by Machinery, Pauperism.—What then ? In Death "the wicked cease from troubling, and the weary are at rest." In Pauperism we shall exchange semi-starvation with oppressive toil, under the dominion of private tyranny ; for sufficient food and raiment, with moderate labour, under the protection of public and righteous Law. Comrades, it is true, we are upon a lee shore, but there are three Ports; Death, Pauperism, and Requited Industry. Into one or other of these we shall all escape, with all our prizes and with certain Victory. The Storm is high ;—The Battle rages ;—But Success is sure. The Ships of Private Tyranny must sooner or later strike, or founder at Sea, with the indignation of man upon them.

Committee Room, Freema
May 5th, 1828.

KIDDERMINSTER
CARPET WEAVERS,
TO A
Discerning Public.

In consequence of many statements being in circulation respecting our earnings at the reduced prices, we do declare that the following would be a correct average.

If a Weaver makes one piece of Brussels Carpet Thirty Yards long, every Nine Days throughout the Year, at Tenpence per Yard, it would amount to 16s. 8d. per Week.

	s.	d.
Deduct for Weekly Expences.		
	4	2
	2	0
	0	0
Drawer's Wages.	1	6
Coals.	0	1½
Candles.	3	1
Soap for Washing.		
House Rent.	10	10½
Oil.		
Total.	5	9½
Remains for Cloathing and Living for a Family.	9	1½
If 36 Yards in Nine Days it would be		

SIGNED, THE COMMITTEE.

Committee Room, Freemason's Arms,
Kidderminster, Aug. 2, 1828.

DEIGHTON, PRINTER, CHURCH-STREET, KIDDERMINSTER.

TO THE

Carpet Weavers
OF
KIDDERMINSTER.

AS your Chief Magistrate, seeing that you are upon the brink of ruin, I cannot refrain from writing these few lines, which contain my sentiments relative to the unhappy dispute between you and your Masters. The last time I addressed you was verbally on your turn-out. I wish, for your sakes, the advice I then gave had been attended to, namely, for a few of you to wait upon your Masters, and respectfully submit to them your grievances; instead of which you have relied upon your Committee, whose avowed object has been the ruin of the Masters and of the Town. But, as these are evils which are passed, and therefore cannot be remedied, look at your present situation, and see what steps might be taken to prevent troubles which are fast coming upon you. Your late employers are applying elsewhere for hands; some have arrived; and as many as are wanted are desirous of coming. Those men must be employed; and will always, as long as their behaviour merits, be properly treated, and kept in employment. The Masters also will be induced to take Apprentices, who will soon be enabled to weave Carpets, as is now the case at Bewdley. When these things are effected, how much the value of your labour will be reduced! Your Committee will tell you the parish must maintain you; so it must,—but not without work; and should you unfortunately be compelled to apply for relief, the Parish Officers will be obliged to rent or build Shopping, and provide Looms, and you must weave therein, and perform as much work, and in as good a manner, as you can, but receive wages; for the Parish Officers will receive those, and you must receive the Poor House. Should these plans unhappily be resorted to, the Manufacturers be benefited, by having their Carpets wove probably at two pence or three pence a yard under what they now offer you; the Scotch trade brought back; and the al interests of the Town advanced.—Your late Masters, you may depend upon not let their large capitals, embarked in Buildings, Machinery, &c. lie idle; ill exert themselves to get the same brought into action. The respectable part of avers, many of whom I have long known, and whose conduct I have always and to whom I particularly address myself, let me entreat you seriously to this statement of probable results which appear to me may be prevented. My advice to you is, to return to at the proffered wages, will receive and treat you kindly, if they find that your con- s them is respectful; and those grievances which may have existed in the r injury I have no doubt will be remedied. These are, in my opinion, the at can avert the ruin which threatens you and your families.

I am,

Your sincere friend and well-wisher,

GEO. HALLEN,
High Bailiff.

July 17th, 1828.

T. PENNELL, PRINTER.

This is a small sample of the many notices posted around the town.

Author's recommendation: The 1828 strike and formation of the unions is told in great detail in Arthur Marsh's book "The Carpet Weavers of Kidderminster".

Not all Gloom !

Some of the weavers were poets with a sense of humour. One of the poems of the day reflects the masters' attempts to bring in the motley gang of "weavers" to the factory in Vicar Street.

The Funny Rigs of Good and Tender-Hearted Masters in the Happy Town of Kidderminster.

1. Come townsmen all and women too
    There is no end of fun,
    When masters will, as masters may
    The rig of fancy run.

2. Of old and steady workmen late
    Our masters sadly tired,
    Searched England through and through
    and then -
    Some new ones briskly hired.

3. Lean-fleshed and lousy, scant of clothes
    Almost as when first born,
    Cooked meat they never could have seen,
    Nor smelt John Barleycorn.

4. We wonder much; some ask how long
    Unhandcuffed they had been?
    And other some, if ever they
    The carpet loom had seen.

5. No, never in their lives, i' troth
    They one and all did say,
    Or otherwise, 'twas plain enough,
    They'd not been there today.

6. However into Looms they got
    And to work they tried their best,
    And Masters and their Foremen too,
    Thought they could do the rest.

7. But here events unthought of rose,
    To baffle such design,
    What animals were set to work
    The looms could not devine.

You can't trust anybody

Thomas Potter was the secretary of The Friendly Society of Operative Carpet Weavers during the strike. Samuel Walford was their London fund raiser who, it was reported, had not been too successful in the capital - or had he? By a strange coincidence in 1830 the pair had amassed sufficient capital to set up on their own as manufacturers.

In 1832 Potter, Walford and Company had twenty looms and were doing very nicely. Two years later, without warning, Samuel Walford absconded to America with the firm's capital and material stocks. Thomas Potter was left on his own but quickly recovered and formed another partnership soon after.

Tension remained - 1830 Dispute at Coopers

Tension remained between the masters and the weavers for many years to come. The weavers would never forgive the masters for 1828.

In the years soon after the Weavers Strike there were a number of serious confrontations where the weavers once again resorted to mob violence. Typical of this unrest was the August 1830 dispute at William Cooper's factory in the Park Butts when weavers attacked the factory buildings in another argument about piece-work payment. The mob continued to Cooper's residence where they broke his windows and destroyed his furniture and belongings. They then turned their attention to the houses of the carpet masters who caused the 1828 strike; these included Henry Brinton, Thomas Simcox Lea, George Gough and James Dobson. In the darkness, the Black Horse Hotel in Mill Street was also attacked. At this point the town's magistrates sent to Birmingham for assistance. The troops arrived and restored calm about midnight.

Schoolboys can always tell a tale   [A true account related to an observer.]

"I and the other lads, on leaving New Meeting School, ran through the Bull Ring and down Mill Street waving our caps over our heads in unison with the draw-boys and draw-girls of our acquaintance. In the Butts there was a band of weavers returning from a meeting. At the meeting the leaders of the weavers tried to curb the more turbulent spirits but the meeting broke up in disorder.

Outside the gates of Mr Cooper's factory in Mill Street a crowd had gathered. Mr Cooper was there with an iron bar threatening the mob if they tried to force an entrance. With him was Butcher, Law, Jenks, Clive, Old Trafalgar, and other of the town's watchmen. As we came up stones began to fly. Stones and cobbles were thrown at the windows of the factory and surrounding buildings. We schoolboys did our share. Then there was a rush and the defenders were hurled into the gutter as the mob broke into the factory.

The mob then moved along to Mr Brinton's house where, it was said, that a party was being held to celebrate the christening of his son. The guests sat facing Mill Street, separated only by an area from the mob. The windows were soon shattered. At the rear of the house the river was in flood so that the escape of the guests in that direction was cut off. They banded together, sallied out of a side entrance and got away.

The mob and others like it smashed other factories and shops, followed some workmen home and wrecked their houses. It was dark by this time, the oil lamps mostly broken. The old lamplighter had been severely shaken and had a broken leg when he was knocked off his ladder while lighting a lamp in Coventry Street. The Spinning Mills and Comb-shops left off work at 8 o'clock and added their quota to the mob. Employers caught in the Street were maltreated. Mr Gough ran for shelter to the Black Horse, where windows were soon shattered.

Here the upholders of order gathered. The old pillory stage was brought from the Horsefair. A Mr Charles replaced the lamp at the corner of the Chapel. Dr Custance, spectacles on nose and Riot Act in hand, fearlessly got up onto the stage and began to read the Riot Act.
Although surrounded by the remaining Magistrates and Watchmen, who were by now engaged in the general melee of fisticuffs with the weavers, the stage was eventually overturned and the Doctor sent sprawling into the gutter in front of the Black Horse".
At this point the story ends because the lad's father turned up and he was promptly marched home to bed!

Action is Needed

On the following day the High Bailiff and the town Magistrates called a public meeting in the Guildhall "for the purpose of taking such measures on the Disgraceful and Riotous Proceedings of the preceding night". George Custance, High Bailiff, chaired the meeting. After much discussion and debate William Butler Best moved a motion, seconded by Henry Brinton, that "the inhabitants of this Borough request the Magistrates to communicate with Sir Robert Peel upon the subject of the late disturbances, and to inform him that it is their decided opinion, that peace of this Borough cannot be maintained without sufficient Military Force; and further that it is likely necessary that such Military Force should be permanent".

The meeting went on to resolve a number of other issues including rewards for the detection of offenders, a request for volunteer Special Constables to patrol the streets and the collection of funds to defray the cost of the damage to property. Some rioters were ultimately arrested and lodged in Worcester gaol.
The total cost of the damage was estimated at £3,000.

But the rapidly growing town had other problems!

"Black Death" strikes Kidderminster

The strikes and disorders during these troubled times brought poverty and a general decline in standards of health. These factors coupled with the town's poor water supply and sanitation resulted in a number of outbreaks of cholera. On the 16th November 1831 the Board of Health, from their Guildhall office, distributed handbills around the town warning that "a Pestilential Disorder called CHOLERA has broken out". The notice went on to advise townsfolk to "avoid drunkenness and other profligate and irregular habits" and to open windows for fresh air and remove manure, rubbish and filth from their premises.

It was a serious problem and many people died during the epidemics. In the 1850s cholera returned to the town with so many deaths that it was said that the bodies were buried, without coffins, in a corner of St.Mary's churchyard near the canal. Houses affected by the disease were marked with a cross.

Anthrax was another malignant disease of cattle that caused deaths in the town. The disease was brought in with the raw wool, particularly the Persian wools. In the spinning mill the bale opener was most at risk.

The Growing Industry - 1830s onward

In 1830 the growing population had reached 15,000 and Kidderminster boasted 30 carpet manufacturers with 23 dyehouses lining the river. The larger companies were now concentrated around the area of Brussels Street, Mount Skipet, Mill Street, Church Street and Vicar Street. These included the factories of George and Henry Talbot; John Lea; Butcher, Worth & Holmes; James Humphries; Pardoe, Hooman & Pardoe; Bowyer & Dixon; James Morton; Richard Watson and also John Broom & Son. Henry Brinton owned the Vicar Street factory behind the Vicarage.

But Kidderminster was also helping the developing carpet industry in America. In 1831 John Humphries, who was a brother of James Humphries, was not doing too well, so he sold up and emigrated to Massachusetts taking with him a number of Brussels looms and weavers. His American company became so successful that the President presented him with two silver medals for his achievements in developing the industry in America.

Back in this country a downturn in orders made trading very difficult. In 1832 a number of companies became insolvent. The most significant was John Broom & Son who, at the time, employed over a 1,000 people with 200 looms scattered between twelve loom-shops. He also had three large spinning mills.

By 1835 the industry was stable again with six companies having more than 100 looms. But there was still unrest on the shop floor despite the efforts of some of the masters to improve relationships. For example, in the summer of 1839 Thomas Simcox Lea treated 200 employees to a dinner at the Lion Hotel. They consumed 180 gallons of ale at the company's expense!

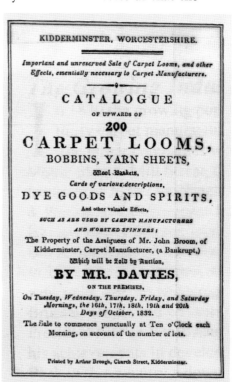

KIDDERMINSTER, WORCESTERSHIRE.

Important and unreserved Sale of Carpet Looms, and other Effects, essentially necessary to Carpet Manufacturers.

CATALOGUE

OF UPWARDS OF

200

CARPET LOOMS,

BOBBINS, YARN SHEETS,

Wool Baskets,

Cards of various descriptions,

DYE GOODS AND SPIRITS,

And other valuable Effects,

SUCH AS ARE USED BY CARPET MANUFACTURERS AND WORSTED SPINNERS;

The Property of the Assignees of Mr. John Broom, of Kidderminster, Carpet Manufacturer, (a Bankrupt,) which will be Sold by Auction,

BY MR. DAVIES,

ON THE PREMISES,

On Tuesday, Wednesday. Thursday, Friday, and Saturday Mornings, the 16th, 17th. 18th, 19th and 20th Days of October, 1832.

The Sale to commence punctually at Ten o'Clock each Morning, on account of the number of lots.

Printed by Arthur Brough, Church Street, Kidderminster.

Brussels is still the Best Seller in 1836

The advertisement on page 33 gives a good indication of the range of products coming from the hand looms of the Kidderminster factories. Brussels remains the big seller, Kidderminster is still available and there is a good variety of Venetian products on offer. Venetian was a striped carpet suitable for corridors and stairs. A study of the carpet widths is interesting. Whereas the full range covers from 2/4ths or half a yard up to the maximum 4/4ths or one yard wide the predominant width is 3/4ths yard - the 27 inches "body".

PRICES
of
CARPET & RUG WEAVING,

TO TAKE DATE FROM THE 15th of AUGUST, 1836.

BRUSSELS WEAVING, PER YARD.

	4-4ths wide.	7-8ths.	3-4ths.	5-8ths.	2-4ths.
Comber	16¼d	14d	11¼d	9¾d	8½d
Point....	13½d	11¾d	10d	8½d	7¼d

Additions per Yard, for 3-4ths wide.

OTHER WIDTHS IN PROPORTION.

1d. for Medium Pile, No. 11 or 12 wire.
2d. for High Pile, 9 or 10 ditto
¼d. for a three-thread frame, or where more than half the frame is three-thread
½d. more for all fine Yarn
1½d if ten wires to the inch
½d. for an extra Linen Chain of 260 ends, and
½d. more if a full Chain, 520 ends
4d. for a double Shuttle.

Deductions per Yard for 3-4ths wide.

OTHER WIDTHS IN PROPORTION.

½d. for two on a Lash
½d. for every Frame not worked
2d. for Common Brussels, viz: 110 Point Cords and 100 Lashes in 3-8ths work
2d. for Cottage Brussels, viz: with two fine Frames, nine wires to the inch
Knots to be woven in without charge.

RUGS, PER YARD.

	COMBER.		POINT.	
	3-4ths	5-8ths	3-4ths	5-8ths
Imperial	1s10d	1s 7d	1s 7d	1s 5d
Best Brussels............	1s 5d	1s 3d	1s 3d	1s 1d
Mock Imperial..........	1s 8d	1s 6d	1s 5d	1s 3d
Wilton	12½d	10½d	11d	9½d

These Prices for Imperial Work include a 3-thread Frame, where it is woven with a Wire instead of Wadding.

For Piece Work of these qualities 1d. per yard less.

FINGER RUG WEAVING, PER SQUARE FOOT.

	90 Pitch.	80 Pitch	Opening, Shearing, and Finishing, per Square Foot.
Figured Worsted	5½d	5d	1¼d
Ditto Woollen............	4½d	4d	1d
Stormant Worsted	2¾d	2½d	0¾d
Ditto Woollen............	2¼d	2d	

ALTERING.

For every Frame, 1s.
For Piecing Back, 1s.
If more than 4½ yards, 1s. 6d.
Comber Lashes, 6d. per score
Point ditto, 4½d. ditto
Simples, Comber 2s. Point 1s.

Winding out Thread 6d. per lb.
Day Work, 2s. 6d. to 3s. 0d. per day
Winding Linen, ½d. per lb.
Winding Worsted, common, 6d. per score

Winding Worsted, fine, 7d. per score
3d. for Warping Linen Chains, 5-8ths and 3-4ths wide
4d. ditto, 4-4ths.

KIDDERMINSTER WEAVING.

	4-4ths	7-8ths	3-4ths	5-8ths	2-4ths
Super, all Points or Comber....	5d	4½d	4d	3½d	3d
Common....................	3½d	3¼d	3d	2¾d	2½d

¾d. for every Lash put an a Barrel Engine.

VENETIAN WEAVING.

	4-4ths	7-8ths	3-4ths	5-8ths	2-4ths
Common and Plaid..................................	3d	2¾d	2½d	2¼d	2d
Super	3¼d	3d	2¾d	2½d	2¼d
Twilled	3¾d	3½d	3¼d	2¾d	2½d
Super Super Venetian, 14 Shoots to the Inch, Plain or Twilled ..	5d	4½d	4¼d	3¾d	3¼d
Ditto ditto, 16 Shoots to the Inch..................	6d	5½d	5d	4½d	4d
British or Damask, usual Pitch..........................	5d	4½d	4d	3½d	3d
Ditto, high Pitch..................................	5½d	5d	4½d	4d	3½d

Price 2d.

SAMUEL BROUGH, PRINTER, HIGH-STREET, KIDDERMINSTER.

Worths Rare Brussels Hand Woven Rug

At the Millennium a rare fringed patterned Brussels rug manufactured by Butcher, Worth & Holmes in the early 1840s is hung in the Board Room at the Carpets of Worth Headquarters in Stourport. The hand woven rug had been originally supplied to an eminent Russian Family. Miss Sarah Worth found it in a shop in St.Petersburgh.

Scottish Developments - "Tapestry" and "Chenille"

1832 The Invention of Tapestry

While the Kidderminster masters and weavers were arguing amongst themselves the weavers and engineers in Scotland were working hard to establish new ways for making carpet. In September 1832 Richard Whytock, a hand loom weaver from the village of Lasswade near Edinburgh, patented the Tapestry carpet yarn printing and weaving process.

It was a two-part process. The first involved winding undyed warp pile yarns continuously around an extremely large drum so that they lay side by side. The yarn was then printed in sections across the width in the sequence of the pattern at weaving. After steaming, washing and drying the yarns were wound on to a beam in readiness for the loom.

The second part wove the carpet on a traditional Brussels or cut-pile Wilton loom. The weaving operation was considerably easier. Since the warp yarns were already printed, the loom did not require the complicated pattern making Mounture or the Jacquard, nor did the loom need the five-tray creel of bobbins.

Cut-pile carpet was called **Tapestry Velvet** and loop-pile **Tapestry Brussels**. Tapestry was an immediate winner. It was quicker and cheaper to produce. It used fewer materials and yet it was a traditional patterned woven carpet.

Whytock's initial progress was slow. In 1846 he applied for an extension on the grounds that he had made little profit from the invention. He was given another five years but on completion he leased the patent to the Halifax company John Crossley & Sons for £10,000. They were able to further develop and market the process.

Tapestry became very popular in Kidderminster. It used the established technology of dyeing together with a simple weaving process. However, the introduction was not without its problems for the workforce on the shop floor. More details later.

Note: Although Tapestry first came into the industry towards the end of the hand loom era, it really made its mark when the equipment was mechanised.
In Chapter 3, page 65, some good photographs give a better idea of the Tapestry process.
Robert Hall & Sons made the equipment.

ROBERT HALL & SONS, BURY, LTD.,
BURY, NEAR MANCHESTER.

Carpet Yarn Printing Machine or Drum,
With Rack and Pinion for Collapsing the Drum when Doffing.

MADE IN ALL CIRCUMFERENCES AND WIDTHS.

1839 The Introduction of Chenille Axminster

James Templeton started work in Glasgow as a draper. In 1829 he went to work for a shawl weaver in Paisley who developed a good selling line using a silk "chenille" cloth. William Quiglay was a weaver at the factory and he saw the potential for the weave as a carpet. He shared his idea with James Templeton. And so Templeton and Quiglay worked together to develop the **Chenille** Axminster carpet weaving process which they called "Patent Victoria Axminster".

William Quiglay wanted the early profit from his invention. Therefore, James Templeton bought out his interest and in 1839 invested his own money in premises in Kings Street, Glasgow where he started his own carpet factory. Templetons of Glasgow became one of the carpet industry's giants.

Chenille Axminster was also a two part process using pre-dyed coloured yarns. The first part involved weaving these coloured pile yarn threads in pattern order on a Weft Loom. The pile threads were taken across the loom by the weft shuttle and held in position with strong warp threads which were spaced apart in such a way that, when cut, the pile yarn would form the "V" tuft of the carpet.

The product of the weft loom was called the chenille fabric. The fabric was steamed and cut into strips which now contained the individual coloured tufts of pile yarn. The delicate strips were known as the "fur" and they resembled a caterpillar - the French word for caterpillar is "*chenille*".

In the second part of the process the Chenille Setting Loom wove the fur into the carpet. Since the pile tufts were held in pattern order, the setting operation had to be very precise. The Chenille process gave the opportunity to introduce even more colours and at the same time to reduce the manufacturing costs. Not surprisingly, it also became very popular in the town with most companies having a large plant.

Chenille Axminster was another hand process that came into its own after mechanisation. Most companies have good photographic records of the chenille equipment, a selection of these are included in Chapter 3 on page 66.

The Foremen move on

Templeton's factory grew rapidly as the Chenille product became more popular. Like many other pioneer companies the employees grew up with the development of the product. They became specialists in their own right eventually leaving to form their own companies. John Lyle was one of these, he was the works foreman. After fourteen years he left to form his own Chenille carpet company with his brothers. His replacement was a young man who had ideas and the skills to further develop the process. In future years this young man was destined to make his mark and fortune in the factories of Kidderminster. His name was William Adam.

Kidderminster in the 1840s

Rowland Hill introduced his Penny Post in 1840. By that time Kidderminster was well established as the centre of the carpet industry in this country. Although the troubles of the previous decade had caused the population to decrease slightly, recovery was now under way and the demand for carpet was again rising.

Brussels was still the best seller but Kidderminster double and treble was produced in volume. Venetian carpet had its own market sector with 45 looms in production, while the cloth trade was hanging on with the still popular Bombazine being made on a small scale. In 1843 Queen Adelaide was staying with Lord Ward at Witley Court and she paid a visit to Lea's Mill Street factory to see the hand loom weaving.

The town centre was expanding particularly around Mill Street and Park Butts. Factories appeared between the canal and the river in the town centre. The Land Societies were building houses on Sutton Common and other parts of town. They were also busy buying land in Greenhill and the Blakebrook area.

At the top of High Street the Lion Hotel was the principal hostelry for visiting representatives. It boasted good stabling for 60 horses and was the resting point for the many stage coaches that passed through the town. L'Hirondelle and Hibernia were the fastest coaches in the country and they both used the Lion Hotel for a change of horses on their way between Cheltenham and Liverpool. In 1846 the Talbot factory still retained its own team of pack horses!

Kidderminster's manufacturers were now looking seriously at the new technologies developing in the North and Scotland, particularly the printed Tapestry process and Chenille Axminster. It should be remembered that these were still manual processes. In 1847 weavers fought at the factory gates for a job on the first Tapestry looms brought in by Pardoe, Hooman & Pardoe. It was not long before plants were installed at James Holmes' and Henry Brinton's factories. In the very early years the pile warp beams were printed at John Crossley's factory in Halifax and brought to Kidderminster for weaving into carpet.

By 1850 the town's growing population was approaching 20,000, while in 1852 yet another vital link with the outside world opened up as the Oxford, Worcester & Wolverhampton Railway came to Kidderminster with its station on the outskirts of town just at the top of Comberton Hill. Ten years later the Severn Valley line came into service.

Humphries Carpets the House of Commons by Hand !

Around this time one of James Humphries biggest ever hand loom orders was for 7,000 yards of Brussels for the House of Commons together with 3,000 yards of Velvet Wilton with "VR" in the centre of the pattern for the library of the House. No less than 40 hand looms worked day and night to complete the order on time.

High Street in the mid-1800s

Comes the Revolution

By any standards Kidderminster was a good industrial town at the heart of the Country with a Carpet Industry hungry to invest in the latest weaving technologies. Communications with the town were the best available with transport links to all parts of the country. It was a settled period and the manufacturers were contented as they prepared their luxury hand crafted carpets for the 1851 Great Exhibition in London's Hyde Park. But, what the community didn't know was that the industrial revolution was just around the corner.

In the years to come the skyline of the town would be drastically changed. There would be more trouble and strife as the old hand loom industry was replaced by the mills and the factories. It was the calm before the storm: the industrial revolution was at hand. Was the Kidderminster carpet industry prepared?

*The Industrial Revolution and an American weaver comes to Kidderminster.
The Masters reluctantly accept the Power Loom and start to build the Mills.
Power production brings serious problems and the "Associations" are formed.
Times are hard, unemployment results in emigration and the industry reorganises.
Kidderminster continues to grow and modernise. New production methods are introduced and
female labour becomes an issue. The industry welcomes new companies but the slump continues.*

Bigelow and the 1851 Great Exhibition

Queen Victoria's Great Exhibition in London's Hyde Park was a big
International event inspired by Prince Albert. In the six months it was
open it attracted over six million visitors to the 1851 feet long temporary
"Crystal Palace" running the length of Hyde Park.

The carpet section contained a disappointingly small area for the carpet industry
of Kidderminster. Nevertheless, a committee chaired by a young John Brinton set
out the stands of James Holmes; James Humphries; Joseph Kiteley; James Morton;
George Price Simcox; Henry Woodward; Pardoe, Hooman & Pardoe and Henry
Brinton.

However, the Great Exhibition was very significant to the carpet industry for a
totally different reason. It introduced a development that would change the lives
and prosperity of the people of Kidderminster for ever.

Part of the exhibition was devoted to the new technology of power transmission
and this involved steam engines, line shafting, belt drives and working machinery.
In the textile section an American engineer called Erastus Bigelow exhibited his
power driven carpet weaving loom.

The Contented Masters

The British had taken the craft of hand weaving to the Americans and they
had developed a good industry for themselves. But their engineers were
forward thinking and so, with the developing use of steam engines and
power transmission, they quickly saw the potential for power and the carpet loom.

Not so the masters of Kidderminster. Prior to the Great Exhibition they had
received reports from across the Atlantic and these had caused much heated debate
at the Meeting House. Henry Brinton pronounced "*... there is no dispute as to steam
power succeeding with Tapestry, but there will be great difficulty with five-frame Brussels work.
If it is successful at all, which is doubtful, it will still be years before success is accomplished ...*"

Generally speaking the masters of Kidderminster were content with their lot. The
hand loom business was buoyant. They were still making a good profit; so what was
all the fuss about? At the Great Exhibition they looked on and passed by. On the
other hand, the weavers were hearing stories from the cotton industry and fearing
any change, they quickly fell into line with the thinking of the masters.

Erastus Brigham Bigelow 1814 - 1879

Erastus Brigham Bigelow was born in Massachusetts in 1814. His father was a farmer and a wheelwright. Erastus trained as an engineer and went to work for the Lowell Carpet Manufacturing Company. Lowell were looking hard at mechanising the carpet loom. So, with Bigelow's expertise, they produced the first power loom weaving Kidderminster double carpet in 1840.

The loom was patented in 1842 and by 1845 the Lowell company had fifty narrow looms in production. Other American companies soon took out production licences.

The Bigelow Carpet Company and John Crossley

Following the success with the Kidderminster loom, Bigelow turned his attention to the popular Brussels weave, but the Lowell company was not very enthusiastic. Consequently, with their agreement, Erastus left in 1848 to form a company with his brother, Horatio Nelson Bigelow, in Clinton, Massachusetts. In the following years their extremely successful business eventually became the renowned Bigelow Carpet Company.

Bigelow succeeded in developing the Brussels power loom just in time for the 1851 Great Exhibition. He was disappointed at the lack of interest from the Kidderminster industry. However, being a persistent salesman, he decided to give them another chance. At the time, Hoobrook Spinning Mill had a large and powerful water-wheel. It was the only one in the area capable of driving the power loom. Bigelow hired part of the Mill and installed his Brussels loom for all to see.

Again the local masters ignored the opportunity. So the loom, together with the production rights, was bought by the ambitious northern competitor John Crossley & Sons of Halifax for £10,000. Kidderminster had again missed the boat.

Crossleys immediately commissioned their engineer, George Collier, to team up with Bigelow to further develop the powered carpet loom. Collier had already designed a powered cloth loom. With this experience under his belt it was not long before a range of looms known as the Bigelow-Collier Power Looms were offered to the carpet industry.

Crossley's policy of buying a stake in all new processes was beginning to pay off. They could now offer the industry in Kidderminster licences and the powered equipment to produce Kidderminster, Tapestry, and Brussels. John Crossley & Sons was a powerful company. They had cornered many markets. They made and sold the equipment. They issued the licences and took the royalties. Moreover, they were manufacturers of carpet in their own right.

Weavers v Masters - the Conference

So, having delayed the Industrial Revolution in Kidderminster the masters and weavers got on with their business as though nothing had happened. However, they continued to be very suspicious of each other.

The one exception was George Price Simcox who was reported to have installed a Brussels powered loom made by the Lancashire company James Bright. At the Great Exhibition he exhibited samples alongside his hand woven products.

In 1853 the weavers and the masters were still at loggerheads with issues of the hand loom industry. In April of that year the Weavers Committee organised a conference in the Guildhall at the bottom of High Street to settle a number of problems once and for all. Delegates included 24 shop floor workers from Kidderminster and one each from Stourport and Bridgnorth. There were eight agenda items ranging from the duties of the foreman to a claim for an additional one penny for the woven yard. All items related to the hand loom industry. The first four were -

1. *Weavers should not have to shear their own woven piece - (an old chestnut!)*
2. *Hours of work would be agreed and controlled.*
3. *A "Board of Arbitration" should consider all disputes, it should be made up with an equal number of masters and weavers.*
4. *All work should be paid for once a week, preferably on a Saturday.*

Henry Brinton spoke on behalf of the manufacturers, William Daniels spoke for the weavers and Lord Ward acted as an independent mediator.

Very little progress was made. The masters took their usual stubborn stance and would not concede any ground and the conference ended in stalemate. After further negotiations and a few concessions no real progress had been made and so the issue became a dispute with yet another strike, this time lasting eight weeks. The masters held out and the familiar drift back to work occurred. Once again the masters had gained the upper hand.

The Inevitable Conversion to Power

In the years immediately following the Great Exhibition competition from the North increased and it became increasingly obvious that the manufacturers would have to invest in the new power equipment or go out of business. But it was not as simple as that: the loom-shops of the town were totally unsuitable for the cast-iron framed power looms and the necessary line shafting drives coupled to the heavy steam engines. As the *Worcester Herald* observed " *The introduction of steam power into carpet weaving not only renders the old looms nearly valueless, but places the factories in the same predicament, as these buildings are not fit for receiving the steam looms*".

The riverside factories and the loom-shops were out of date. To make matters worse there was a general slump in the trade which resulted in mass unemployment.

The workforce became disillusioned and the weavers and their families sought work elsewhere. Some moved north to Yorkshire and Scotland while others emigrated to America. In a short period 4,000 people left the town.

Some of the larger companies decided to take up the challenge. The medium and small concerns were in a dilemma - but the Mayor of Kidderminster had an idea!

Lord Ward and The Stour Vale Mill Company

Wil128illiam Grosvenor was elected Mayor of Kidderminster in 1851. He inevitably became involved in the town's struggle to convert from hand to power loom weaving. His civic duties brought him in contact with Lord Ward who was the High Steward of the Borough.

Lord Ward was well aware of the industry's problems. In 1855 William Grosvenor persuaded him to put up £20,000 to finance the building of one of the first purpose-built steam powered carpet factories in the town. Lord Ward, together with William Grosvenor and local manufacturer Joseph Kiteley were the partners in a venture to be called The Stour Vale Mill Company.

They purchased Glebe land on the outskirts of the town situated on the Back Brook branch of the River Stour near Worcester Cross. There they built a large single weaving shed capable of housing the new power looms. Manufacturers could rent a section of the shed and connect to the common line shafting powered by a 35hp steam engine. There were nine sections to let.

Initially, a dyeing facility was not included since most of the small companies still had their own dyehouse and only needed the factory space and the power. The building was designed by local architect J.G.Bland. The builder was Henry Ankrett and the many cast-iron roof support columns and gutters were cast in the Clensmore foundry of Austin & Brown.

The main shed was designed to house 120 x 3/4 width Brussels power looms. It was christened "The Lord Ward Shed" after the benefactor.

At the front, on the unnamed new road, a two-storey building provided offices and warehousing.

The Stour Vale Mills.—Messrs. Woodward, Grosvenor & Co.

To the side and rear other smaller buildings housed services to the tenants including starching and beaming. Initially, the nine units were taken by James Morton; Thomas Humphries and Watson & Naylor who were worsted spinners, they had two units each; Henry Woodward; Samuel Fawcett and John Lloyd Dobson who were weavers and had one unit each.

The enterprise was a total success. However, as the years went by the number of tenants diminished until only the Woodwards and the Grosvenors were left with an interest. So, they bought out Lord Ward and formed their own company.

At the Millennium, the original owners have long since gone but the Lord Ward Shed is still occupied by a company with the name Woodward, Grosvenor. The cast iron columns and the roof have been replaced but there is still evidence of those early days of steam power and the line-shafting.

"Lord Ward Shed". A later photograph taken when the roof was being replaced. Note - the cast iron columns with line shaft fixing brackets, the oil marks on the wall, the cast iron gutters and the brick floor.

William Humble Ward, First Earl Of Dudley, 1818 - 1885

Lord Ward bought Witley Court from the Foleys. He made his wealth from the industrial Black Country where he owned more than 200 mines from which he extracted iron, coal, limestone and fireclay. These, together with iron-smelting works and other industrial concerns made him a very wealthy man. He also owned much of the land in the Kidderminster area.

His civic duties brought him into close contact with the town and the carpet industry and, on many occasions, he played an active part in the industries' affairs.

Stour Vale is a good place to start

Many of the town's developing companies started in the Lord Ward Shed where they were given the opportunity to experience the powered loom and make a good profit before building mills of their own.

James Morton, later The Carpet Manufacturing Company; Samuel Fawcett, later The Chlidema Carpet Company and many others all made a start at Stour Vale. However, perhaps the person who did the best was William Green who earned enough money to build a fine "New Road Mill" further down the road. He became Mayor and they named the new road Green Street after him.

Larger Companies make their own way

The larger companies did not need Stour Vale. They made their own plans. In 1852 James Humphries opened a new shed at his Mill Street factory. His son, John, was married to George Collier's daughter and this connection gave them a good deal for a plant of the new Bigelow-Collier Brussels powered looms. Two years later Henry Jecks Dixon built Long Meadow Mills for a similar loom installation. Brintons were also planning the future of their town site. Charles Harrison introduced Brussels power looms in Stourport.

George Price Simcox had a factory on the Worcester Road called The Beaver Works. It was there that he experimented with the early power looms. However, he also experimented with a block printing system which added the pattern to a cheaper form of the Brussels weave. The flat corded carpet was known as "stouts".

After 1855 - Kidderminster in Turmoil

The town was now well and truly in the grips of the change. Kidderminster's initial reluctance to convert to power was not shared by the whole of the British carpet industry. Scotland and Yorkshire, in particular, gained a short term advantage. It was a critical period as the companies had to make some expensive decisions about their future.

Not everyone got it right. One of these was the town's largest and most respected manufacturers, Pardoe, Hooman & Pardoe who failed, leaving 800 people without work; 50 of their workforce left the town to work in Halifax.

James Holmes, Pemberton Talbot and George Price Simcox all ceased trading.

The surviving companies were proud of their modern equipment. Through the medium of advertisements they made sure the buying public knew they now had the latest technology.

BENJAMIN WOODWARD & Co.,
MANUFACTURERS BY POWER OF
Brussels & Velvet Carpeting
AND RUGS.
Works and Offices:
Mill Street, Kidderminster.
London Warehouse:
18, Newgate Street, London, E.C.

PRIZE MEDAL, PARIS, JUNE, 1867.
WOODWARD AND RADFORD,
BRUSSELS CARPET
AND
AXMINSTER RUG MANUFACTURERS
BY STEAM POWER & HAND LOOM.
OFFICES:
13, CHURCH STREET, KIDDERMINSTER.
WAREHOUSES:
145, CHEAPSIDE, LONDON, E.C.; AND YORK STREET,
MANCHESTER.
WORKS: WATERSIDE MILLS, KIDDERMINSTER.

JOHN HEAD, BROOM & CO.,
MANUFACTURERS OF
VELVET & BRUSSELS CARPETS, RUGS, &c.
HAND LOOM AND POWER LOOM.
Worsted and Woollen Yarn Dyers,
KIDDERMINSTER.
LONDON WAREHOUSE, 18, BERNERS STREET, OXFORD STREET W.

The faster power looms were available for all weaves including Brussels, Wilton, Kidderminster and also the new techniques of Tapestry and Chenille. Compared with the speed of modern carpet looms the early power loom was not all that productive, but it was significantly better than the hand loom it replaced. For example, 700 Brussels power looms replaced 2,000 hand looms.

John Crossley & Sons were doing good business in Kidderminster. Brussels 3/4 yard wide power looms were selling for £100 each. This included a Jacquard valued at £16 and the tray creel. In the 1850s this was a lot of money. A good steam engine would set you back £300. However, the slump in sales, the failure of the companies coupled with the changes in the workplace made it a period of uncertainty and speculation.

Kidderminster Cotton Spinning Company

Linen was the popular backing material for the Wilton and Brussels weaves. However, cotton was becoming more popular and so a consortium of Kidderminster businessmen set up their own spinning operation. In 1860 the Kidderminster Cotton Spinning Company opened in The Sling, just off Pitts Lane. The company was unprofitable and lasted only ten years.

1860s and 70s - The Building of New Mills

Tall chimneys began to dominate the skyline as the boiler houses, factories and mills were built. The mills were particularly fine buildings constructed in the style of the cotton mills of Lancashire with their multi-storeys and featured ornamental coloured brickwork over the doors and windows. Much of the credit goes to the architect J.G.Bland who set the high standard with Stour Vale.

Watson & Naylor built the very impressive five storey Pike Mills in 1857. Five years later The Waterside Mill Company opened in Back Market Street, now known as Corporation Street. It ultimately became part of Brinton's town centre factory. Clensmore Mill was built in 1863 and Stourport gained its Severn Valley Mill in 1868. A year later William Green built New Road Mills. This became better known as the home of Victoria Carpets. In the 1870s Morton's Mill, Castle Mills, Worcester Cross Factory, Chlidema Mill were all completed. Barton's large mill, warehouse and office block dominated Vicar Street. The mill still remains at the Millennium, the ground floor is converted to shops and the upper floors are offices.

Over these years the whole town seemed to be involved with the building work of the carpet industry.

Brintons 1870

Pike Mills

THE PIKE MILLS, THE PROPERTY OF MESSRS. WATSON AND NAYLOR, KIDDERMINSTER.

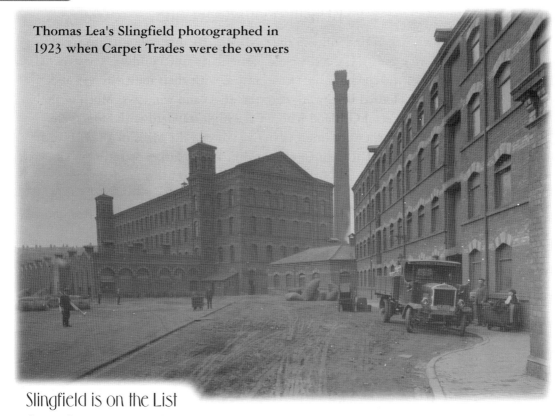

Thomas Lea's Slingfield photographed in
1923 when Carpet Trades were the owners

Slingfield is on the List

Thomas Lea was only 21 years old when he built Slingfield Spinning Mill on the canal side in 1864. On completion of the tall square boilerhouse chimney he promptly climbed to the top to survey his investment. He would have been very proud of what he saw.

The complex consisted of a main five-storey mill facing the canal with a smaller four-storey mill angled to the side. Near the canal and a purpose-built basin was the boilerhouse and the 180 feet high chimney. The boundary was formed by the canal towpath, The Sling cartway and Pitts Lane. The main entrance from Pitts Lane was guarded by a small gatehouse built in the style and character of the mill.

Two 40hp steam engines drove the extensive line shafting to all mill floors. The mill was designed by the Bradford architects Lockwood & Mawson who were well known throughout the country for fine textile mills. The red Staffordshire brickwork had blue and white string courses which formed the arches over the doors, windows and other features. Internally, the mill had traditional cast-iron columns supporting timber floors. The roof was slate.

In 1885 a factory-style extension was built on to the side of the large mill. From 1920 onwards Slingfield had other owners and it eventually became part of Brintons. The inside of the main mill was gutted. The cast iron columns and timber flooring were replaced with steel and concrete. In the mid-1990s the main mill, boilerhouse and chimney stack were given Grade II listing.

Brintons Grand Piano and Tall Chimney

B rintons came to the town centre in 1819. As part of an expansion
programme they bought the land between the river and the canal. At one
point their boundary included a narrow arm of the canal, with a basin,
which travelled towards the town centre finishing near the Bull Ring just short of
the river. This waterway was intended to service the factories near the end of Pitts
Lane and the town centre itself. By the mid-1800s the arm was no longer needed
and so it was filled in, leaving a short length off the canal for Brintons own use.
A curved path or cartway ran near the waterway. Over the years it became a right of
way and was known locally as "The Sling".

In 1867 Brintons built a five-storey warehouse on the canal side together with
sheds and a new boilerhouse and chimney. The warehouse wall followed the curved
boundary of The Sling. From above, the building looked like a grand piano, so it
got its name. The "Piano Building" was actually built over the shortened canal arm
in order that narrow-boats could be brought into the ground floor of the mill and
unloaded directly by hoist to all levels above through hatches in the timber floors.

Adjacent to the Piano Building, on the boundary of The Sling, was the chimney
stack of the boilerhouse. It stood over 180 feet from ground level and was said to
be as tall as London's Monument. It was the tallest chimney stack in Kidderminster.
It took one year to build and was completed on Saturday 14th May 1870. A Mr
Baines supervised Brinton's own workers as they laid more than a quarter of a
million bricks. It measured 26 feet diameter at the underground base and tapered to
8 feet inside at the top. The chimney was bound together by 7 tons of cast iron.
The original drawing is retained in Brinton's archives.

The Early Carpet Designers

Good carpet designers were hard to get and so it became common practice for the manufacturers to buy their carpet designs from freelance designers living in and around the town. The local studios produced some outstanding work. Many designs were based on the beautiful Turkish and Persian patterns. Others had a floral theme. All were intended to grace the noble houses of the day.

The restriction to five colours for the Brussels and Wilton did not defeat these clever designers and they devised a method called "planting". Individual coloured ends were planted to replace the original thus enabling the final design to contain many more than five colours though there remained only five in any one warp row.

The design paper had to be durable because it was used directly in the factory. The heavy weight paper was called "point paper". It was ruled into squares. Each square represented a tuft and the colours were meticulously painted in by a designer. The advent of the power loom and the central factory caused the manufacturers to consider hiring and training their own design staff. The industry needed a School of Art and Design and so discussions started with the Borough Council.

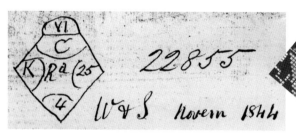

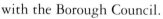

Woodward, Grosvenor's Design Archives

Every manufacturer valued his carpet designs and he kept them in a library for his customers to inspect. The older established companies today have good design archives. Brinton's designs go back to 1842 but the Woodward, Grosvenor collection beats all with a floral square design clearly dated 1798. Unfortunately, the work is unsigned.

Woodward, Grosvenor hold over 20,000 hand-painted designs of the neo-classical, rococo revival of the Regency and Mid-Victorian era, the aesthetic movement of the 1870s, arts and crafts and the Art Deco periods. Other designs are by Owen Jones, William Morris, Charles Voysey and in the 1960s by Robin Day.

One of their most prized possessions is the original design paper for Queen Victoria's sitting room at Osborne House on the Isle of Wight. The design was selected and signed by Prince Albert.

Local designer I.Arbuthnot provided over seventy designs between 1803 and 1818. They also have many more from the 1800s - John Christie (1841), Edward Perrin and Edward Poole (1850), Robert Christie (1854) and J.Bouet (1856).

Second Half of 19th Century sees a New Surge

1865 Recovery, Troubles and the Associations

A recovery began as the American Civil War ended and new markets opened up across the Atlantic. Again, there was a shortage of qualified labour. Some weavers had left the town during the recent slump. The younger men had chosen other professions and the older hand loom weavers would not get involved with the power looms or accept the factory discipline. So, with things in their favour the weavers took their opportunity to demand more money and better working conditions.

The manufacturers immediately closed ranks and formed The Brussels Power Loom Carpet Manufacturers Association with John Brinton as their Chairman. The first objective was to solve the shortage of skilled labour by training more apprentices. The weavers declared that they would not train anyone without additional payment. Stalemate again and for twelve weeks the two parties battled it out. But the weavers had the advantage and they knew it!

The manufacturers were losing good orders and so a compromise was agreed: the employers got their apprentices and the weavers got a rise. This was a big step forward for the weavers and they decided to get even more organised. Up until this time the Weavers Committee had fought the battles. However, the laws had changed and they were now allowed to form an "Association".

In 1866 The Power Loom Brussels Carpet Weavers Association came into being. Only Brussels male weavers were allowed to join. They met at The Vine Inn in the Horsefair. Ben Arnold was the first president and they had 457 members. Initially, the Association was run by the President, the Secretary, the Treasurer and a committee of delegates who met on alternate Saturdays. The officers were unpaid but they did get generous expenses. After several name changes, in 1872 it became The Power Loom Carpet Weavers Mutual Defence and Provident Association. The Association had offices at 28 Church Street from 1870 until 1887.

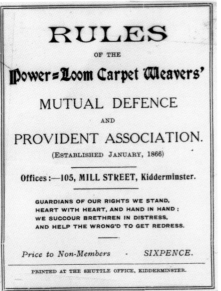

RULES

OF THE

Power=Loom Carpet Weavers'

MUTUAL DEFENCE

AND

PROVIDENT ASSOCIATION.

(ESTABLISHED JANUARY, 1866)

Offices:—105, MILL STREET, Kidderminster.

GUARDIANS OF OUR RIGHTS WE STAND,
HEART WITH HEART, AND HAND IN HAND;
WE SUCCOUR BRETHREN IN DISTRESS,
AND HELP THE WRONG'D TO GET REDRESS.

Price to Non-Members - SIXPENCE.

PRINTED AT THE SHUTTLE OFFICE, KIDDERMINSTER.

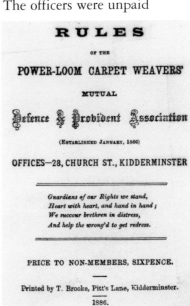

RULES

OF THE

POWER-LOOM CARPET WEAVERS'

MUTUAL

Defence & Provident Association

(ESTABLISHED JANUARY, 1866)

OFFICES—28, CHURCH ST., KIDDERMINSTER

Guardians of our Rights we stand,
Heart with heart, and hand in hand;
We succour brethren in distress,
And help the wrong'd to get redress.

PRICE TO NON-MEMBERS, SIXPENCE.

Printed by T. Brooke, Pitt's Lane, Kidderminster.

1886.

Noah Cooke the "Weavers Poet"

The inspiration and enthusiasm to set up the Weavers Association seems to have come from local-born Noah Cooke. Noah's father was a Bombazine weaver. Noah himself was a draw-boy at the age of seven. He knew the industry inside-out. His teens were spent in Yorkshire. In 1852 he returned to the town as a hand loom weaver for Wright, Crump & Crane. He later graduated to the power loom at Bartons in Vicar Street.

Noah Cook was also President of the Association in 1868.

He is best remembered for his poems reflecting his feelings for the industry. He became a regular contributor to the local newspaper's weekly feature "Poets Corner". This is one of his offerings -

Free Labour *by Noah Cooke, published in the* Kidderminster Shuttle *8th December 1877.*
The poem contains eight verses, these are the first and the last.

If I bargain with employers	*...........Tell me not to be submissive*
For the labour of my hands	*When my soul is crushed and bound*
And I do what's fair and lawful	*Ask me rather to be silent*
To obey their just commands,	*While I'm punished like a hound*
Then I've done my honest duty.	*Humble let me be but never*
More than that may none require	*Let me lose my self-respect*
'Tis the limit of my service,	*Or the glory of my being*
For my soul is not for hire!......	*Like a stranded ship lies wreck'd.*

Emigration Fund

The industry itself was growing. There were good opportunities abroad so the Association decided to support weavers and their families who wanted a "better life" in America or one of the British Empire countries.

For many years there was a special office to deal with enquiries. The Association also set up an Emigration Fund. The rule book of 1868 shows that £3 was paid for America or Canada; £5 for Australia, New Zealand and the Cape of Good Hope.

All were repayable if the weaver returned within two years. The first President, Ben Arnold, took advantage of these offers and emigrated to America where he lived to a great age.

Kidderminster Carpet Manufacturers in 1873

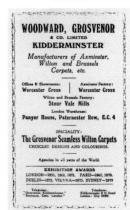

In chapter 2 the Ward Price list of companies of 1823 is a good example of the hand loom era at its peak. Fifty years on, the power loom has taken over and things have completely changed. Only the names Brinton, Woodward, Morton, Lea and Watson have survived but their companies have significantly altered.

The mills and factories have also changed the industrial architecture of the town. Mill Street and Vicar Street still have factories but the industry, apart from some offices, has deserted Church Street. Factories at Hoobrook, New Road, Mount Pleasant, Arch Hill, Clensmore and in Stourport are now listed.

1873 Littleburys Directory lists the following:

Kidderminster Carpet and Rug Manufacturers

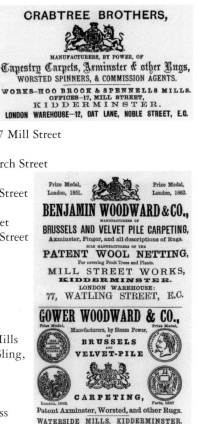

John Everard Barton	11-13 Vicar Street
John Brinton & Co.	Office and works, Vicar Street
Crabtree Brothers	Hoobrook and Spennels, Office 17 Mill Street
Henry Jecks Dixon & Sons	Long Meadow Mills
Fawcett & Spurway	Severn Valley Mills, Office 9 Church Street
William Green	New Road Mills
Isaak Hampton	Green Valley Mills and 108 Mill Street
George Holloway & Son	30 Worcester Street
Edward Hughes & Sons	Town Carpet Mills, 131 Mill Street
James Humphries & Sons	Offices and works, 119-120 Mill Street
C.E. & H.Jefferies	Clensmore Mills, Clensmore
Morton & Sons	New Road
Palmer & Co.	Park Wharf Mills, Park Butts
Perrin and Griffin	Vicar Street
Edwin Shaw & Co.	35-38 Mill Street
Richard Smith & Sons	97 and 100 Mill Street
John Stooke	Exchange Street and Stour Vale Mills
Tomkinson & Adam	Mount Pleasant, Arch Hill, The Sling, Office Church Street
Watson & Naylor	Pike Mills
Moses Whittall & Co.	Park Mills and Park Butts
H.R.Willis & Co.	Offices and works, Worcester Cross
Winnall & Fawcett	Chlidema Mills
Benjamin Woodward & Co.	Mill Street Works
Gower Woodward & Co.	Office and works, Waterside Mills
Woodward, Grosvenor & Co.	Stour Vale Mill and Waterloo Street Office, 10-12 Church Street

Registered Worsted Yarn Spinners

John Brinton & Co.	Mitton Mills, Stourport, Office Vicar Street
Crabtree Brothers	Hoobrook and Spennells Mills, Office Mill Street
Thomas Lea	Slingfield Mills
Watson & Naylor	Pike Mills - listed also as the only Woollen spinner

The Stourport Section lists the following Carpet and Rug Manufacturers

James Bough	Severn Valley Mills - Office, Severn Lane
Fawcett and Spurway	Severn Valley Mills, Office and works
Charles Harrison	Mitton, Office and works
Thomas Bond Worth	Severn Valley Mills

IRVIN & SELLERS,
TIMBER & COAL MERCHANTS,
Prize Medal, Paris, 1867.

SHUTTLE
AND
BOBBIN
MANUFACTURERS,

STEAM
SAW MILL
PROPRIETORS,

Mill Furnishers, and General Merchants
Park Wharf Mills, Kidderminster.
(MR. HENRY SCOTT, MANAGER)
And at PEEL HALL WORKS, PRESTON, Lancashire.

Other associated listings :-

Looms and Jacquards	John Lamb, Comberton Hill.
Shuttles and bobbins	Irvin & Sellers, Park Wharf Mill
Rope, twine and oil cloth	Francis Frederick Jelleyman, Coventry Street.
Drysalters :	Robert Chadwick, Clensmore Julian Claudius, Vicar Street
	Geo.Holdsworth, Mill Street Watson & Son, Church Street

Carpeting America

The Americans started the carpet power loom revolution, however, they were slow to develop and expand the industry in their own country. For a period of twenty years following the Great Exhibition America provided exceptional business for the looms of Kidderminster. Perrin & Griffin were a small company in Vicar Street and in 1866 they were reported to be weaving exclusively for America. It was estimated that one-third of the town's production found its way across the Atlantic. It was not unusual for the British cargo ships to be met at the entrance to New York harbour by ferries loaded with buyers eager to place orders. Sometimes the entire stock was sold before the boat docked.

Tomkinson & Adam

From the company list Tomkinson & Adam were one of the newer and more progressive companies. William Adam knew all about the Chenille process through his association with James Templeton. In 1858 Brintons & Lewis persuaded him to come to Kidderminster to help them to set up their newly acquired Chenille Axminster plant. It was not long before he was testing the water with a small company of his own.

However, he was an engineer and not a businessman. About the same time Michael Tomkinson had a good business selling Yorkshire yarns to the Kidderminster industry. In 1869 the two joined forces. They were ideally suited. Tomkinson & Adam started in rented buildings in The Sling and Arch Hill works where they installed and operated second-hand Chenille equipment. By 1875 they had amassed enough profit to purchase the Mount Pleasant Works. However, they continued to look to the future and new production techniques.

Carpets and Rugs

Freelance Carpet Designers in 1873 and 1903

Kidderminster's Trade Directory 1873 included nineteen carpet designers. Alphonse Joannin Bouet had a studio at French Villa. Robert Christie's studio was at The Old Compass Inn, Coventry Street and a few operated from Commercial Buildings in Oxford Street. One of these was George Lees.

George Lees was the only one of the nineteen to be listed thirty years later in the *Shuttle* Industrial Supplement of 1903. By this time the majority of companies had trained their own design staff. The *Shuttle* lists only eight freelance designers. George Lees was a Carpet, Rug and Tapestry designer who had "won many prizes which were proudly displayed" at his studio in Woodfield Crescent. He was also chairman of the Kidderminster branch of the Society of Designers.

The full listing of 1903 was F.J.Mayers & G.H.Woodhouse; J.Miller Perrin; William Winbury; David Cambell; Hutton & Allen and George Lees.

However, some of the carpets woven in the town still bore the names of the nationally known designers William Morris, Charles Voysey and Walter Crane, who also illustrated children's books. In a male dominated carpet industry it was a fact that the carpet designers of the day were also male.

Caring and Sharing

The carpet industry was busy settling down to the factory system. The Manufacturers and the Weavers had established Associations and they had to abide by the rules - the emphasis was now on consultation. There was a genuine attempt by the masters to forge a bond between themselves and the workforce. The more liberated manufacturers tried to put the past behind them and, wherever possible, to show some humanity and kindness to the workforce. Yet they were also keen to demonstrate this new outlook to the town in general.

John Brinton treats his Staff

*I*n 1870 Brinton & Lewis became John Brinton & Company when John Lewis left the partnership. To celebrate John Brinton took 60 managers, clerks, designers, foremen and overlookers for a day out and evening meal.

They travelled in horse-drawn wagonettes to Witley Court where they were given the grand tour by Lord Ward. The fountains played and they were treated to an organ recital in the splendid Witley Church. The Hundred House at Great Witley was the venue for the dinner. After the food and many gallons of ale were consumed John Brinton outlined his plans and confidence in the future of the company. Once again it was a gentlemen-only occasion! The wagonettes wobbled back home with the occasional stop for calls of nature.

1870s - Growing Kidderminster

Kidderminster got its long awaited Mill Street Hospital in 1870. It was known as the Infirmary and for many years it received charitable support from the carpet industry and particularly the Weavers Association.

The carpet industry was now fully mechanised and most of the old hand looms were broken up for firewood. However, a few companies retained a small hand loom department for special orders. This gave employment to their loyal older hand loom weavers who, in the end, could not make the adjustment to the machine age.

Nationally, the carpet industry had also been doing well. But the investment in the power looms had peaked resulting in a period of overcapacity which coincided with another slump in sales bringing hard times yet again. Undaunted by the swinging fortunes of the carpet industry the Borough Council continued to improve the town amenities. A cattle market opened in Market Street and in 1873 the first sewage disposal system and mains water services were laid throughout the town.

The old Guildhall and Police Station still stood at the bottom of High Street, but not for long. The Public Reading Rooms and Corn Exchange, built in 1855 by public subscription on the site of the old vicarage, had been acquired by the Council. In 1876 the buildings were in the process of being converted into a splendid new Town Hall. This coincided with the opening of Brinton's new offices in Exchange Street.

To celebrate John Brinton commissioned a Joseph Durham to design an ornamental fountain which he proposed to put between his new offices and the Town Hall. This proposal did not go down well in the Council Chamber because they planned a statue of Sir Rowland Hill. John Brinton, therefore, reluctantly changed the design to a Gothic Clock Tower with drinking points which was located at Worcester Cross. The Town Hall opened, the old Guildhall was demolished and the statue of Sir Rowland Hill was unveiled in 1881.

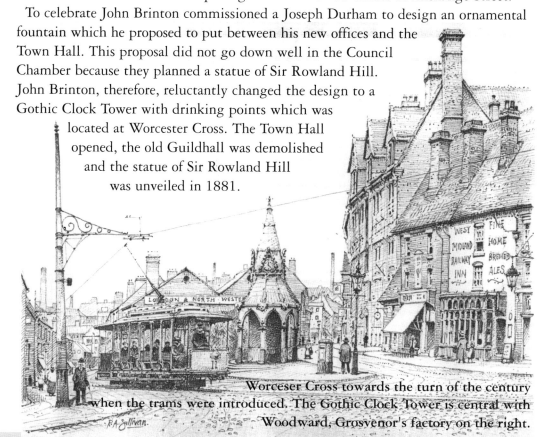

Worceser Cross towards the turn of the century when the trams were introduced. The Gothic Clock Tower is central with Woodward, Grosvenor's factory on the right.

A School of Art was founded in the early 1860s but it was not until 1879 that the
School of Art and Design was
opened in Market Street.

From this point onwards the
manufacturers could turn budding
artists into designers trained for the
carpet industry.

The design courses were eventually
moved to a new College of Further
Education built on Hoo Road.

In the 1990s, the impressive Market
Street buildings were demolished
and the site became the location of
a new Public Library.

The "Chlidema Square"

Brothers Henry and Francis Best Fawcett developed a method of weaving
bordered Wilton squares on a narrow loom with the border design
incorporated in each woven width. In this way the pile-lie or the angle of the
pile was always in the same direction throughout the carpet giving an improved
appearance on the floor. This simple idea was patented in 1882 and became known
as the "Chlidema Square". Prior to this, the square was made up by sewing a separate
border around the outside of the piece with the pile-lie in opposing directions.

No Smoke without Fire

Wool stored in the multi-storey wooden floored mills was always a fire risk
with a combination of combustible yarns and the open flames of the oil
and gas lamps. Even in the weaving sheds a spark from the machinery
could cause considerable damage. The carpet factory was designated "no-smoking".
Over the years Kidderminster has had its fair share of disastrous fires. The larger
companies employed a full time fireman whose job it was to maintain fire fighting
equipment and train the company fire-brigade who were always on call.

In 1886 Watson and Naylor's Pike Mills was gutted in a major town fire attended
by the Kidderminster Volunteer Fire Brigade, which was formed ten years earlier.
Of the many other mill fires the destruction of Broome's Castle Mill in 1927 made
the headlines when the Kidderminster and Stourbridge brigades assisted by ten
works teams fought flames reaching 70 feet above the roof. Machinery could be
heard falling through the floors of the Mill. Carpet Trades was extensively damaged
by fire during the Second World War. There were many more. On the 5th November
1959 Greatwich lost their raw material stores in Clensmore Street. No prizes for
guessing what was thought to have started the fire !

The best laid plans...

For some companies with poor order books or excessive stocks a good fire was a blessing in disguise, a view naturally not shared by the Insurance Companies. A tongue-in-cheek story has done the rounds where the Financial Director's secretary of one of the larger companies of the town rushed into the office in a flurry and pronounced, "The Warehouse is on fire" to which the director replied "Damnation ... I thought we agreed it would be _next_ Friday!".

Bruce Rainsford examines the extent of the damage to his Greatwich raw material store.

Pike Mills at the height of the blaze.

1878 Piano Destroyed by Fire

Just eleven years after it was built, Brinton's five-storey Piano Building was also gutted by fire with damage costing £30,000. Flames towered 100 feet in the air as the company's fire fighters assisted by those from neighbour Thomas Lea's Slingfield Mill and other volunteers fought the inferno.

John Brinton rode on horse back from his Stourport Estate to personally direct the 400 men tackling the blaze. At the time, the fire bell was housed on top of the nearby dyehouse drying room, the bell rang out but could not be heard above the noise of the fire.

The Chief Fire Officer of the Kidderminster Volunteer Fire Brigade missed the event and was embarrassed to find out from his milkman the following morning. This caused a rumpus. The bell was deemed useless and it was replaced by a more audible sound. This, in future years became part of Kidderminster's heritage. The new sound became affectionately known as "The Bull".

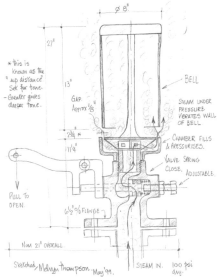

The Bull lived for 117 Years

The Bull was in fact a steam whistle of a type normally found on the funnels of the steam-ships of the day. To sound its best the whistle needed good quality high pressure steam. This was available from Brinton's supply to their giant steam engine which they called "Hercules".

On the 3rd May 1882 the fire warning was commissioned; one blast for a town centre fire, two a district fire and three blasts a Brintons own factory fire. In later years the town gained its own professional fire service and the Bull was found another use. It became the signal for the start and finish of the carpet industries' working day, with additional bellows at lunch time.

During the First World War the Town Council requested that the Bull should be available to warn the town of aircraft raids at night, the Chief Constable being the only person authorised to sound the alarm. The signal was to be four short blasts followed by a long one. At this point "all gas and electricity should be turned off at the mains and remain off for the rest of the night". Civilians were instructed not to fire guns at the aircraft. In fact the town was not seriously troubled during the war.

On 11th November 1918 the Bull declared the end of the First World War. It was also used to announce the start and finish of the one minute's silence on Remembrance Day and many other special occasions.

Over the period there were a number of steam whistles installed. At one time there were two available. The last one was reported to have come from a River Clyde steamer in the 1950s.

The closure of Brinton's town centre site brought the bellowing of the Bull to an end. On the 18th March 1999 the boilers fired for the last time. At mid-day Michael Brinton signalled three long blasts to bring the end of an era in the town. The event was extensively covered by the press, radio and television. The Bull and its predecessor, the Bell, are preserved in Brinton's archives. Yet Brinton's Bull was not unique in the industry, Worth's Bull made sure the industry in Stourport kept to time.

Name that Steam Engine

Every factory had its own steam engine. Some needed more than one for their scattered sheds. Tomkinsons & Adam had two engines which they chose to name after female members of the family. The main engine was christened Sylvia and the reserve was called Dora.

Brinton's town centre site was large with the various production sheds positioned on both sides of the river. But they devised a way of driving all their line shafting from one enormous engine including sending a drive belt across the river.

The 1,000hp steam engine was christened "Hercules" and it replaced three smaller engines. It weighed 100 tons and had a fly-wheel 16 feet 6 inches diameter which itself weighed 36 tons. The piston had a 5 foot stroke. The two main drive belts from the engine were each 34 inches wide and there was a third 30 inches wide. Hercules took eight days to install with all the associated line shafting and belt drives. The factory stopped and most of the workforce were sent home without pay during this period. Hercules was commissioned in 1879 and ran for fifty years before being scrapped in 1929. A statue of Hercules which stood proudly over the working engine is also retained in Brinton's archives. In the photograph the statue can just be seen in the top right-hand corner.

"Spit and Polish"

Steam engines of the town represented a big investment to the manufacturer. It was imperative that the engines were kept in good order to run the line shafting of the factory. Without the steam engine there was no production so they made sure that no expense was spared to achieve continuous operation. The engines had their special rooms. Some had wood panelled walls, others were tiled. Woodward, Grosvenor's Stour Vale engine room was known as "The Cathedral". With great pride, the "engineer" in charge dedicated himself to the task of lubricating and polishing "his" steam engine.

Some of the town's steam engines were given a formal christening.

Hercules takes the strain

M ary, wife of John Brinton, had the honour of turning the steam valve to officially set the mighty steam engine in motion. This was in July of 1879. The work had been completed to schedule and the directors, workforce and civic dignitaries assembled for the official opening ceremony.

In the speeches that followed a supper for the workforce was mooted as some sort of recompense for the time lost during the installation, it was a gesture of good will.

On Saturday, October 4th, the workers erected a triumphal arch between the office and the Corn Exchange and flags stretched across the road to the bank buildings. At 5pm a crowd assembled outside the Town Hall for speeches by the Vicar of St.Mary's, the Reverend Boyle, and old Mr Kiteley who acted as chairman. A weaver then presented John Brinton with an Illuminated Address depicting the buildings of the town associated with himself and two little girls, dressed in white, presented Mary with a gold bracelet set with diamonds which was a gift specifically from the female workforce. The Illuminated Address hangs proudly in Brinton's reception to this day.

John Brinton replied with a long review of the company in the past and his aspirations for the future. He thanked the 1,170 workforce and recalled their support in recent events like the fire in the Piano Building. The top floor of the restored building was decorated for the meal and gas torches provided the light. Some 900 male and female workers sat down to a dinner of 3/4 ton of beef, mutton, pork, veal, ham and lamb, 12 sacks of potatoes, cheese, 40 loaves and 2,000 rolls. The Shuttle congratulated the company for treating the female workers the same as the male. After more speeches those that could stand up went to the Corn Exchange for a dance. All at the companies expense !

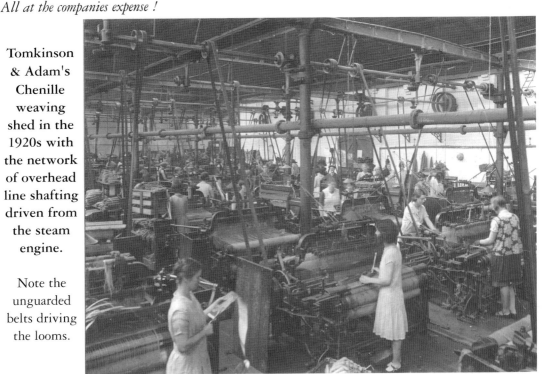

Tomkinson & Adam's Chenille weaving shed in the 1920s with the network of overhead line shafting driven from the steam engine.

Note the unguarded belts driving the looms.

The Start of "Spool" and "Gripper" Axminster

1878 - Halcyon Skinner, Spool Axminster

Halcyon Skinner was another skilled American engineer destined to add a piece to the jigsaw of the carpet industry. In 1849 he joined the rapidly-growing Alexander Smith Carpet Company in West Farms, New York.

Together they pursued ideas for weaving multi-coloured pile carpets by power loom. One of the many ideas was a "nipper" mechanism which gripped the individual tuft of yarn prior to the weaving process. However, they had better success with a principle which used yarn wound onto a spool. After considerable development **Spool Axminster** was patented in 1874. To demonstrate the principles and support the patent application Skinner made models of the nipper and the spool looms. During this development period Alexander Smith's factory was completely destroyed by fire and the model of the "nipper" loom was lost. The company was reformed in another part of New York called Yonkers. The Yonkers factory produced Kidderminster, Tapestry and the new Spool Axminster multi-coloured carpet which Alexander Smith called Moquette.

In 1878 Michael Tomkinson went to Yonkers and purchased for Tomkinson & Adam the British patent rights from Halcyon Skinner for the Spool Axminster process. Looms were brought to the Arch Hill factory and, thanks to William Adam's skill, the first carpet was produced in September of that year. They initially called the product Royal Axminster. In later years they refined the quality and it was renamed Imperial Axminster. Tomkinsons were in control of the production licence. They soon began to recoup some of their outlay by licensing Southwells of Bridgnorth, Dixons, Mortons and Woodward, Grosvenor.

The Spool Axminster process was a break through in technology. With its unlimited colour potential, it quickly became popular. The relatively light weight machinery also made it ideal for female operatives, a fact that did not go down too well with the all-male Weavers Association. Female labour was becoming the "big issue"!

It's a small World !

The working desk top model of the Spool Axminster loom produced by Halcyon Skinner for his patent application remained a treasured possession of the Alexander Smith Company. The restructuring of the American industry in the following years saw the model change ownership many times, at one time it belonged to the giant Mohasco Industries Group. Eventually the company became U.S. Axminster Inc. with its Spool Axminster plant in Greenville, Mississippi.

In May 1998 the operation was the subject of a takeover by Brintons Carpets and so, nearly one hundred and forty years after it was made the model has pride of place in the manager's office of Brintons American company - it's a small world!

Later in the chapter you will read of another connection between Brintons and Halcyon Skinner.

Spool Setting

In an operation called spool setting the "setting frame" winds the pile ends onto a spool in pattern order. In this way spool number one contains the first weftwise row of pile tufts, number two the second row and so on.

The photograph best illustrates the process - note the design point paper and the bobbins of different coloured yarn on the flat creel table.

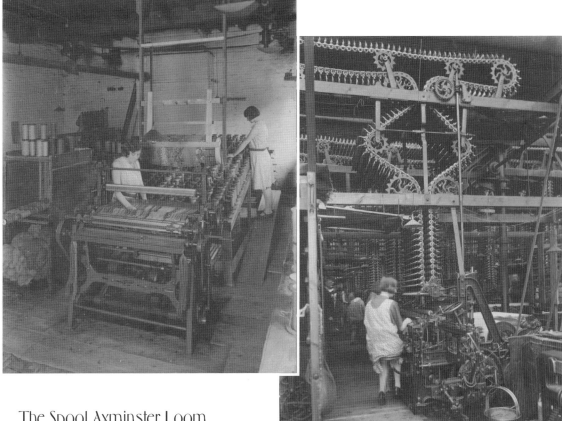

The Spool Axminster Loom

The prepared spools are held in an endless conveyor chain, the length of which represents the repeat of the pattern, or multiples thereof. The loom mechanisms index the chain to the point where the spool is removed and taken into the weaving position. The pile yarns are now woven into the carpet with a change of shedding and the insertion of the weft yarn with a travelling "needle".

The row of ends are cut from the spool with a large pair of scissor knives running the width of the carpet. The spool is then returned to the chain which indexes to the next spool and the process is repeated.

The pictures above were taken at Tomkinsons in the 1930s.

Note. The layout of the loom is based on the old hand loom principle with the backing beams to the rear and the finished cloth travelling towards the weaver where she can keep an eye on the quality. Early spool looms used the Wilton principles with the shuttle passing the weft.

More Tension with the Stouts and Specials

Power looms were more adaptable and the manufacturers experimented with the weaves and the materials to reduce costs and keep the order books full. The Weavers Association kept a watchful eye on all these developments particularly because they feared an adverse effect on the weaving rate of pay.

The cheaper form of Brussels carpet called Stouts was reintroduced and the manufacturers immediately took the opportunity to fix a lower piece rate. This did not go unnoticed. In 1882 William Green took on the Weavers Association in a battle that resulted in a four-week-long strike. After due consultation the whole issue of Stouts was referred to The Board of Conciliation. After a long deliberation, the Board decided in favour of the manufacturers and the rate was reduced.

This was just one example of a number of separate issues which brought the weavers and the manufacturers once again into bitter opposition. However, by far the biggest issue of all was the use of the cheaper female labour on the carpet weaving looms of the town.

Female Labour and the Tapestry Looms

Historical acceptance that weaving was a man's job stemmed from the hand loom period when the heavy work, the long hours and general conditions of the loom-shops made it so. But in the mechanised factory things were very different. In the North and Scotland females were already weaving on the lighter looms. It should be remembered that women were still employed in the spinning mills and in preparatory work such as bobbin winding.

The Tapestry process was new and there were no historical reasons why women could not do the work. The manufacturers saw it as the perfect opportunity to introduce female labour. The male only Weavers Association didn't agree. The fight was on! The manufacturers resolved to stand firm. In 1874 Brintons installed twenty of the latest Moxon Tapestry printing drums and looms for operation by female labour. Their male weavers strongly objected and threatened to strike. So John Brinton moved the whole operation to a factory in Leeds where female labour was accepted.

Things were made worse by a general slump in trade. Daniel Wagstaff Goodwin, the Mayor, called a meeting in the Town Hall to discuss the problem. John Brinton, Thomas Lea and the other manufacturers were called in for urgent discussions. In 1881 the Tapestry issue was so troublesome that the manufacturers got together and discussed a plan to take all their Tapestry plants to a vacant engine and waggon works in Worcester. Fortunately for the town the idea did not get past the discussion stage. The problems would not go away and so it was again inevitable that the Weavers and the Masters would yet again cross swords.

In 1884 Henry Dixon took the issue one step too far.

1884 Dixon's Strike and Riots

Dixon's Long Meadow Mills had an extensive and profitable Brussels weaving department. Henry Jecks Dixon's son Henry Jr. was expanding the family company and built a new shed to house 116 Tapestry looms. A number of the looms were earmarked for the production of a new light fabric to be known as "Medici Velvet". He promptly advertised for female labour to operate the looms. This did not go down well with veteran Noah Cooke and the Weavers Association who had 200 unemployed male weavers on their books at the time. He warned Dixon of potential problems.

Dixon was secretary of the Manufacturers Association. He felt he had some power to his elbow so he installed the first looms and in defiance of the Weavers Association hired the women weavers. This action started a chain of events that ultimately lead to serious rioting and disorder involving the 3rd Dragoon Guards and the Birmingham police. At one stage the riots involved 2,000 angry workers outside the factory gates throwing stones and missiles. Dixon's management were threatened and personally intimidated.

The Vicar of St.Mary's and the Mayor, William Green, called on Kidderminster's Member of Parliament, John Brinton, to intervene and settle the dispute. This was an odd situation for individuals who in the past had been the aggressors. However, they did negotiate a working compromise and peace was restored.

For Henry Dixon, the issue was never settled and the industrial relations remained strained until the company went out of business in 1895. This was just the tip of the iceberg. In the following years the town's female workforce, with the support of the manufacturers, very gradually gained ground.

"The Crompton Looms"

In 1884 Richard Smith & Sons obtained a licence to use the new "Crompton" Spool Axminster looms. The looms were 3/4 yard wide. They were manufactured in Massachusetts by Crompton & Knowles and were specially developed to produce a close pitch high quality Spool Axminster carpet from fine Worsted yarns. Over one hundred years later these looms are still in production, their story is told in full in chapter 5.

Dobcross make the Machinery

While Crompton & Knowles had a small share of the power machinery market in this country they were by no means the most popular loom manufacturer. That honour went to the Hutchinson, Hollingworth Company, Dobcross Works, Oldham. Through their factory gates came the finest "Dobcross" power looms for weaving Kidderminster, Brussels, Wilton Velvet and Chenille Axminster.

HUTCHINSON, HOLLINGWORTH & CO.
LIMITED,
LOOM MAKERS,
DOBCROSS, NEAR OLDHAM.
Railway Station: SADDLEWORTH, L & N. W.
Telegrams :—". FOUNDRY." Dobcross.
INVENTORS AND MAKERS OF THE
CELEBRATED "DOBCROSS" LOOM.
Awarded both GOLD and SILVER MEDALS at the Huddersfield Exhibition, 1883.

Also from the north of England John Crossley & Sons led the way with William Smith, Robert Hall, Stewart & Sharpe, A.F.Craig in close attendance. Moxon, Clayton and Fearnley provided the more productive Tapestry looms. In 1895 the Singer Sewing Machine Company introduced their first carpet joining machine.

Dobcross "Kidderminster" loom, one of many at Naylor's Pike Mills
Note the multi-shuttle box, the Jacquard cards and the extensive cordage of the "harness" from the Jacquard, also the belt drive from the line shafting.

Tapestry Weaving at Edward Hughes' Factory Mill Street

Yarn is wound on to the drum before printing across the width

Note the tubs of dye and the design pattern.

Winding the dyed yarn on to beams in readiness for the loom

The Weaving Shed

Weft looms producing Chenille fabric

Chenille Production

Steaming and
cutting the fabric into
"fur" ready for the setting loom

Weaving the
carpet on the
setting loom

Flooding is a Problem

Flooding seemed to be an annual event as the River Stour overflowed its banks. The town centre and the riverside factories always came off second best despite the many precautionary measures. The insurance companies may have suffered but the market traders had a field day with their "flood damaged stock".

The highest recorded flood was on the 14th May 1886 with over five feet in Mill Street. Things happened so quickly that Brinton's working boilers were extinguished by the rising waters. Other notable floods occurred in 1924 and 1955.

Author's memories. Carpet Trades in Mill Street could never beat the flood. I well remember the days following when it was literally all hands to the pump for the clean up, and what a smell! Wet yarn and carpet was dragged outside to dry in the open air and the electricity remained firmly off until all was safe. And no heat!

The Brinton Park

Queen Victoria's Golden Jubilee was celebrated in 1887. So John Brinton bought an expanse of land at Sutton on the outskirts of Kidderminster and presented it to the town as parkland. He had it laid out with a lake, lawns, flower beds and a number of playing fields.

John Brinton declared the park should be open every day of the week and be freely available for all. The park was named The Brinton Park after the benefactor.

"It's all for You"

A technological breakthrough came in 1885 when the town telephone exchange opened up in Worcester Street. All the carpet companies signed up for this operator-only service and soon the "tulip" telephones appeared on the desks of the sales department and the directors.

Some early numbers were -

No.1 Fire and Police	No.2 Woodward, Grosvenor	No.5 Brintons
No.6 Thomas Lea	No.7 Tomkinson & Adam	No.8 Richard Smith
No.11 Naylors	No.31 Whittall & Company	No.18 The Lion Hotel

Although conditions in the factories were rapidly improving they still lacked the basic amenities such as canteens. It was usual practice for children to bring their

THE ONLY PAPER PRINTED IN KIDDERMINSTER.

THE KIDDERMINSTER SHUTTLE,

A Weekly Journal of Local and General News, Politics and Social Progress, Art, Literature and Science, for Kidderminster, Bewdley, Stourport, and the Midland Districts.

Published every Saturday morning at the STEAM PRINTING WORKS. 13, Oxford Road, Kidderminster.

PRICE ONE PENNY.

This Paper is thoroughly independent in its opinions; liberal and progressive in politics; and thoroughly impartial. It has achieved a remarkable success among all classes in the borough and district—It is not the organ of any section or party in the community, and is much appreciated in thinking circles as a first-class family paper, treating local topics in a vigorous, racy manner. It is transmitted by post to Kidderminster men settled in all parts of the Globe as the best epitome of the passing phases of Kidderminster life and thought.

ADVERTISERS

wishing to communicate with the public of Kidderminster could not find any other medium so entirely suited to their purpose as

THE KIDDERMINSTER SHUTTLE.

parents hot lunches in a bowl, wrapped in a cloth, directly to the loom on the shop floor.

The town centre was now well lit by the Kidderminster Gas Company whose works in Pitts Lane had just been considerably enlarged, while in 1894 the free Library opened in Market Street.

The Lion Hotel at the top of High Street and the Black Horse Hotel in Mill Street were reported as being excellent commercial and posting houses. There were over 100 inns and taverns, thirteen churches and the *Shuttle* newspaper cost one penny.

The new Corporation Baths and Wash House opened in Mill Street and, in 1887, the Weavers Association moved in up the road to 105 Mill Street.

With the population well over 20,000 the house-building programme was well advanced with many terraced "Villa" developments in the areas of Park Street (photograph), George Street, Lorne Street, Offmore Road and around the Horsefair. These groups of houses today proudly display their name and date. They make interesting reading.

Brintons Invent the Gripper Loom in 1890   (Pat. No. 15,680)

Halcyon Skinner's discarded "nipper" principle intrigued the directors of Brintons. So they bought the idea, renamed it the "gripper", and started a development that led to the invention of the **Gripper Axminster Loom**.

It all started in 1884 when a tuner called Albert Dangerfield was given a room on the top floor of "The Bell Building" which was the drying room of the dyehouse. This was the very same building that housed the original fire warning bell. Dangerfield's progress was slow and so they called on Thomas Greenwood to help out. He had good experience having worked for James Holmes and Henry Dixon before joining John Brinton as head tuner in the Wilton department.

Greenwood took over and very soon he was perfecting a very coarse pitch loom. The first loom had 128 ends over the 3/4 yard width. It was built on the frame of a traditional Wilton loom with a Jacquard for colour selection and a weft shuttle. After six years the Gripper Jacquard Axminster Loom was patented in 1890.

By 1895 Brintons had four looms weaving qualities known as Beacon and Superba. The company continued with a programme of refinement and improvement. A needle motion replaced the shuttle in 1910 and the looms became wider. A finer pitch was introduced bringing the grippers closer together.

Other manufacturers were licenced to weave and when the patent ran out the Gripper loom became the most widely used for Axminster production.

Even today Brintons are still improving the looms they invented over 100 years ago.

The Gripper Jacquard Loom

The main body of the loom is like any other traditional horizontal loom. The essential difference is the way in which pre-cut tufts of pile yarn, securely held by the gripper, are presented and woven into the carpet.

A row of grippers are pitched across the loom and they draw from a "carrier" a length of pile yarn equivalent to the tuft length. The yarn is cut off and the grippers swing downward to the position where the carpet is woven. The vertically moving carriers hold all the colours available for the pattern. There are generally eight colours. The individual carriers move up and align themselves in pattern order as dictated by the Jacquard.

1930s Gripper Jacquard Loom

The Jacquard receives its instruction from a set of punched cards held in sequence above the loom. The cards index one position after each row of pile tufts is selected.

View from the rear of Gripper loom.
The bobbins of pile yarn are stacked in the colours ready to go into the "tray creel". Each tray represents a bank of the same colour: six trays are shown. The pile end yarns are drawn forward to the vertical carriers.
Note the backing material beams at the rear and the cords connecting the carriers to the Jacquard.

The Jacquard Card Stamping Operation

The punched cards are prepared in the Card Stamping Department. The plain heavy duty cardboard cards are punched with holes according to the sequence of the pattern as dictated by the design on the point paper. The "Card Stamper" reads a line of pattern and sets up the hardened steel punches in a steel plate accordingly. The plate with the punches and the card are pressed together and the card is stamped. When all the cards are stamped they are laced together in readiness for the loom. The principle of card stamping for Gripper Axminster is very similar to that needed for Wilton.

The Weaving Sheds

The Wilton and Gripper Axminster weaving sheds were busy places. These three are typical.

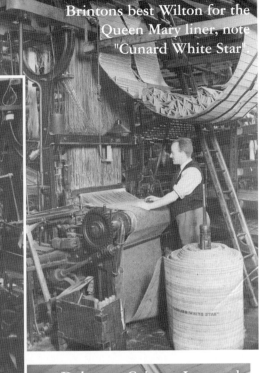

Brintons best Wilton for the Queen Mary liner, note "Cunard White Star".

Narrow Wilton at James Humphries. Row of looms with weaver and "apron".

Dobcross Gripper Jacquard Axminster broadloom at Woodward, Grosvenor. Note the creeler sitting on a steam pipe, another rewinding bobbins on the motor belts, and the lack of machinery guarding !

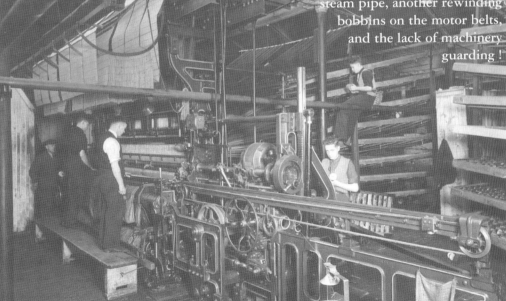

Note: The author's father is the tuner to the side with the very greasy cloth cap !

Trams and Horse Power

Between 1898 and 1929 The Kidderminster & Stourport Electric Tramway became a vital link in the transport of workers to and from the factories in Kidderminster and Stourport-on-Severn. The tramway ran from Somerleyton past Kidderminster railway station to the town terminus near Brinton's factory. It then passed down New Road through Foley Park down the Stourport Road and on into Stourport finishing by the bridge.

By 1901 electricity was available to the industry, supplied by the tramway company's generator housed at the headquarters in Tram Street, just off New Road.

Bantock's Shire horses and drays were well known around the town particularly conveying the carpets from the factories up Comberton Hill to the railway station. To give the horses a better foothold granite blocks formed the road. In the 1950s Scammell Mechanical Horses replaced the real thing.

This photograph shows a consignment of carpet leaving Brinton's main factory on the first stage of the journey to Macey's Department store in New York.

Woodward, Grosvenor take on the Tram Company

Woodward, Grosvenor were one of the first companies in town to install individual electric motors to their looms thus replacing the line shaft drives. With their two mills separated by the Worcester Cross intersection they needed to dig a duct and lay a main connecting cable across the road from their Worcester Cross Factory to Stour Vale Mills.

The Kidderminster & Stourport Electric Tramway Company got to hear of the plans and took legal action to stop the cable from travelling under the tram rails since they imagined all sorts of electrical problems. Permission was eventually given and the carpet company planned a night job when the trams were off the rails. No sooner had the task been completed than a gang of men, presumably from the tramway company, arrived and dug up the cable and cut it through. The parties returned to the courts and again they ruled in favour of Woodward, Grosvenor. The cable was successfully spliced and the electricity flowed to the mills and it is assumed that none was lost to the Tramway Company.

The Carpet Alliance & The Carpet Manufacturing Company

A former employee of Brintons called Harvey Preen set himself up in business as an accountant and independent consultant to the industry. In 1889 he conceived the idea of merging all the carpet companies into one large trading group. He put his ideas to the companies of the town.

The plans were set out in a twelve page booklet entitled -

"The Carpet Alliance"

" Being suggestions for a new Carpet Manufacturers Association."

He went on to quote the chief objectives as follows -

1. To regulate output.   2. To define and settle qualities.   3. To fix prices.

Many local discussions took place, but the principle never got off the ground.

In Kidderminster Morton & Sons and Richard Smith & Sons were two of the larger companies who were strongly in favour of the idea. They took it a stage further in 1890 when they combined to form The Carpet Manufacturing Company. Other companies were later added to the group and CMC rapidly became one of the town's leading carpet manufacturers.

The Anglo-Turkey Loom - another Kidderminster Invention

William Youngjohns was the works engineer at the Mill Street factory of Edward Hughes & Sons. In 1891 he developed and patented a powered pattern automatic knotting loom. It was a complicated piece of machinery using the principle of the Turkish Ghiordes knot. The process was slow and used for "specials" but they sold well. During the following 40 years 33 Anglo-Turkey looms were in production at widths from 3 to 15 feet.

Youngjohns and the Tuner Apprentice

William Osborne was a gardener and lived in a cottage in Habberley Valley. In 1896 he indentured his son Frederick to William Youngjohns "to learn the trade, business and craft of Loom Tuner and Machinist". The formal agreement was witnessed by H.G.Ivens, solicitor.

Youngjohns received a premium of £15 and Frederick agreed "to serve his said Master and keep his secrets ... not waste the goods, materials or tools of his said Master and not lend them to another person ... and always demean himself as a faithful, diligent and honest apprentice".

In 1901, after five years, William Youngjohns signed to say "I certify that Frederick Osborne has completeth (sic) his Term of Apprenticeship". During the apprenticeship Frederick Osborne was paid 10 shillings per week by Edward Hughes with a slight increase towards the end of his time.

Others we not so lucky !

The terms for Youngjohn's apprenticeship were not too demanding when compared with those of an apprentice from Amblecote who signed up with William Green in 1873.

He had to agree "he shall not commit fornication nor contract Matrimony within the said Term and shall not play Cards or Dice tables or any other unlawful Games" and later in the deed "he shall not haunt Taverns or Playhouses"!

A section of
Anglo-Turkey
Looms at Edward
Hughes, Mill
Street.

Hard Times Towards the Turn of the Century

Mechanisation in the American carpet factories resulted in a period of over production in exactly the same way as it did in Great Britain. In 1893 they solved their problem by dumping carpet in this country because there were no tariff barriers or trading agreements to stop them. One of the products flooding into this country was the cheaper Spool Axminster called Moquette manufactured by Alexander Smith's company in Yonkers.

The effect on the town was disastrous with many more people again out of work. For a short period the Weavers Association was able to financially support the unemployed weavers. However, they soon became critically short of funds and so the church choirs of Baxter and New Meeting volunteered to sing concerts to raise additional income. Other workers in the carpet industry had no income at all.

It was another difficult period for the carpet industry. Nine companies failed during the 1890s including William Green, Henry Dixon and Willis, Potter. However, two new companies were formed, T.& A.Naylor and The Chlidema Carpet Company. Both were destined to make their mark in the industry.

Victoria Comes by Train

In 1899 the Victoria Carpet Company of Victoria Road, Kirkcaldy, Fifeshire, decided to move south. William Green's New Road Mill was vacant so Victoria leased the Green Street factory and proceeded to relocate the whole Kirkcaldy business including some equipment and the workforce.

New Road Mill was particularly suitable for their tapestry-printing process. The whole move took two years to complete and involved the charter of two complete trains full of looms and equipment together with the families and their furniture. The story is told of some loyal workers who walked from Kirkcaldy to Kidderminster to keep their jobs.

The Spinning Mills

Larger companies continued to devote part of their manufacturing space to the spinning of the carpet yarns, but there was still good business for the independent spinner. Thomas Lea at Slingfield Mill, Edward Broome at Castle Mill and Watson & Naylor at Pike Mills all supplied the town. But there was also fierce competition from the Yorkshire yarn agents who had offices in the town.

William Rogers Moseley Greatwich decided that Kidderminster needed another independent Spinner. In 1895 he bought Caldwall Mill and installed state of the art worsted equipment. He christened his company W.Greatwich and Company Ltd. Over the following years his investments included "mule" spinning. By 1911 he had outgrown Caldwall Mill and moved to Clensmore Mill. There the company, now called Greatwich Ltd., continued to trade until 1999 when its closure brought an end to spinning in the town.

Lea, Broome and Watson & Naylor had long since ceased to exist.

Carding at Thomas Lea's Slingfield Mill in the early 1900s

Mule Spinning at Pike Mills also in the early 1900s

Brintons Spinning Mill in the 1930s

TELEGRAPHIC ADDRESS: "PLATTS, OLDHAM."

PLATT BROTHERS & Co., Ld.,

MACHINISTS,

HARTFORD WORKS, OLDHAM, ENGLAND.

MAKERS OF THE FOLLOWING MACHINERY FOR

PREPARING, SPINNING, DOUBLING

AND WEAVING

COTTON, WOOL, WORSTED & SILK,

INCLUDING

Patent Macarthy Cotton Gins, for Long or Short Stapled Cottons.
New Patent Cleaning Machines for Cotton.
Crighton's Opener with Improved Creeper Feeder.
Hard Waste Breaking-up Machinery.
Patent Burring Machines for Wool.
Condensers for Wool: Martin's, Bolette's and other systems
Combing Machines for Cotton—Heilman's Patent 6 or 8 Heads, 8 in. or 10½ in. Laps. Also Whipple's Patent.

Machinery for Carding and Spinning Silk Waste.
Combing Machines for Wool, Worsted, &c.—Little and Eastwood's Patent.
Drawing, Slubbing, Intermediate and Roving Frames.
Sizing, Dressing, Warping, Beaming, Winding, & Reeling Machinery.
Cloth Folding and Measuring Machines.
Hydraulic and Cam Bundling Presses for Yarn and Cloth.
Patent Brick Making Machinery.

MACHINERY for PREPARING & SPINNING BARCHANT or WASTE YARNS.

REVOLVING SELF-STRIPPING FLAT CARDING ENGINES,

Of Various Sections, from 67 Flats 2in. wide, 89 Flats 1⅝in. wide, to 105 Flats 1⅜in. wide.

RING SPINNING FRAMES (FOR WARP & WEFT),

To Spin on Bobbins, Pirns, Paper Tubes, and BARE SPINDLE.

PATENT SELF-ACTING MULES AND TWINERS,

RING DOUBLING FRAMES,

For Cotton, Wool, and Worsted—with Motions for making Spot, Loop, and all kinds of Fancy Yarns.

PREPARING MACHINERY for WEAVING.

POWER LOOMS,

Plain and Fancy, for Cotton, Linen, Woollen, Worsted, Jute, &c.

P. B. & CO., LD., also beg to call the attention of WORSTED SPINNERS and MANUFACTURERS to their IMPROVED MACHINERY for

PREPARING, COMBING, ROVING AND SPINNING WORSTED

On the FRENCH SYSTEM, as lately Exhibited at Manchester.

BOYD'S PATENT STOP-MOTION TWISTERS.

MANCHESTER OFFICE: 5, St. Ann's Square.
GLASGOW OFFICE: 160, Hope Street—Mr. RICHARD MURRAY, Agent.

1920s Hank Dyehouses

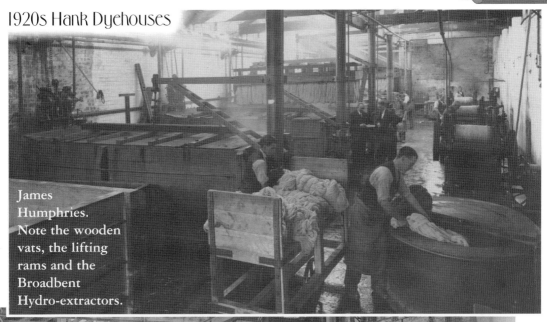

James Humphries. Note the wooden vats, the lifting rams and the Broadbent Hydro-extractors.

Large wooden vats at Tomkinsons. Note the crane for lifting the hanks

Hank drying at James Humphries. The hanks are slowly carried through the hot chamber on a brattice conveyor.

Finishing the carpet

The ladies of the narrow Axminster finishing room at Carpet Trades.

Narrow back sizing of the carpet at Tomkinsons.

Kidderminster at the turn of the Century

And so, at the turn of the century 22,000 people lived in a revitalised and modern town, new companies were emerging and they were hungry for expansion. Nearly fifty years of mechanisation in the industry had seen the introduction of a variety of new products. Kidderminster could now offer the world its own Kidderminster carpet together with Brussels and Velvet Wiltons; Spool, Gripper and Chenille Axminsters; Tapestry Velvet and Brussels and for the special orders the hand woven and knotted carpets.

Looking back, a lot of dyehouse water had gone under the bridge in a half-century that had taken the full force of the industrial revolution. Yet Kidderminster had weathered the storm and looked in good order as it prepared for the 1900s. Things could only get better !

KIDDERMINSTER AND STOURPORT

Carpet Weavers' Athletic Society's

✦ FETE ✦

And . .
Amateur

SPORTS

(AFFILIATED TO M.C.A.A.A.)

Under A.A.A. and M.C.A.A.A. Laws, Rules and Regulations, and N.C.U. Rules.

ON THE

New Athletic Grounds,

Aggborough, Kidderminster.

BANK HOLIDAY MONDAY,

AUGUST 3rd, 1908.

FIRST EVENT AT 2.15 P.M.

Programme.

OPEN EVENTS.			First, value.	Second, value.	Third, value.
1	120 Yards Flat Handicap	... ...	10 10 0	2 2 0	1 1 0
2	300 Yards Flat Handicap	... ...	6 6 0	2 2 0	1 1 0
3	880 Yards Flat Handicap	... ...	6 6 0	2 2 0	1 1 0
4	One Mile Flat Handicap	... ...	10 10 0	2 2 0	1 1 0
5	Half-Mile Bicycle Handicap	... ...	6 6 0	2 2 0	1 1 0
6	One Mile Bicycle Handicap	... ...	10 10 0	2 2 0	1 1 0
7	Half Mile Novices' Cycle Handicap	...	5 5 0	2 2 0	1 1 0

(Open to Riders who have never won a Prize in any Cycle Race other than a purely Club Event).

8   440 Yards Flat School's Challenge Cup   ...   Value Ten Guineas.

Confined to Teams of Scholars under 14 years of age, attending Schools in Stourport, Bewdley, Kidderminster and District.

Four to compete in each Team, Three to count. The Team totalling the smallest aggregate number of points to be declared the Winners. Handsome medals will be presented to the Winning Team, together with the right of the School to hold the Cup until the next Competition. Special Medal to Boy placed First. Medals to Runners-up. Entrance 1s. each Team.

Every Competitor must wear complete clothing from the shoulder to the knees (i.e., jersey sleeved to the elbows and loose drawers with slips), and in any event in which a water jump is included the drawers and slips must be dark in colour. Any competitor will be excluded from taking part in the Sports unless properly attired. A copy of this Rule, shall be placed in a conspicuous place in the Competitors' Dressing Room at every Athletic Meeting.

No Entry accepted unless accompanied by Entrance Fee.

ENTRANCE FEES —1s.6d. each. Two Events, 2s.6d. Three Events, 3s.6d., or Four Events, 4s.6d.
School Race 1/-

Starter - - - - - Mr. W. HIGGINS (Professional).

ENTRIES CLOSE SATURDAY, JULY 25th, 1908, (or First Post on Monday positive), to
W. HIGHFIELD, 4, New Buildings, Park Lane, Kidderminster.

The Track has received special preparation, and will be in excellent condition for these Sports.

DON'T FORGET OUR FAMOUS PRIZES.   TRAINS FROM ALL PARTS G.W.R

SHUTTLE PRESS, KIDDERMINSTER

Chapter 4

MERGERS, WARS AND PROSPERITY.   1900 - 1956

Herbert Smith plans the industry's future - and his own!
World Wars with regulated weaving and munitions. The industry grows and
women become equal partners. The housing boom needs carpet and man made
fibres come onto the market. The prosperous industry celebrates but the Americans are at it again.

Industry Slumps and the Engineers make their Mark.
Not a Good Start

Expectations were short-lived and in the early 1900s the industry was again in decline. The South African war was raging, taxes were increasing, the cost of raw materials soaring and cheap imports continued to arrive from abroad. The manufacturers reduced output and the workers were put on short time or had no work at all. With no state support the unemployed took to doing odd-jobs to earn "a bob or two" and the pawn shops of the town did a roaring trade. They were depressing times.

Tomkinson & Adam's
9 feet wide "Kleitos" Loom

In the Greek language "Kleitos" means renowned and Tomkinson & Adam certainly had a renowned piece of machinery in their Kleitos loom which they patented in 1902.

The whole industry could see the advantages of weaving at a broadloom width but it was not an easy step to overcome. The credit goes to the engineering skills of Gerald Tomkinson.

The Kleitos Spool Axminster loom was nine feet wide. A number of spools made up the width and the long chain carrying the spools travelled vertically through slots in four floors of their Mount Pleasant mill.

Cecil Charles Brinton, The Engineer

Over the years the carpet industry in Kidderminster witnessed some outstanding engineering achievements. William Adam, William Youngjohns, Thomas Greenwood, Gerald Tomkinson and others all contributed vital technological improvements to the carpet production machinery. But perhaps the most diverse was a young man who joined Brintons staff in 1904.

Cecil Charles Brinton, born in 1883, was the seventh son of John Brinton of Moor Hall, Stourport. Educated at Cheltenham College he went on to obtain an Honours Degree in Engineering at Caius College, Cambridge. Immediately on joining the family business he applied his knowledge to the design and development of the wider Gripper looms, while at home he used his engineering skills in a practical manner working in his own well-equipped workshop.

The "White Knight" and the "Heatherington Theatre"

Cecil Brinton was a true engineer: while others at Cambridge had bicycles, Cecil had a Rex motorcycle. In 1904, aged twenty-one, he designed and built his own two-seater motor car. The early registration was 0 (for Birmingham) 4, therefore 0 4. Not content with this achievement he improved the design for a second car in 1910 which was christened the Silver Slipper, registration SS 227.

In 1918 he built a third called the "White Knight". This got its name from the fact that it was white in colour and used a Knight Engine. After his death the White Knight fell into

disrepair but eventually it was sold to an enthusiast who faithfully restored it to its full glory. In 1988 Michael Brinton brought his grandfather's car back into the family and gave it the old registration 0 4.

Cecil Brinton never did anything by halves. When he inherited a model puppet theatre that had been in the family since 1880 he immediately set about a complete redesign of the puppets using a novel idea of his own. At his home at Yew Tree House, Belbroughton, he built The Heatherington Theatre Royal. The theatre had an entrance foyer. The invited audiences signed in for the performance

before settling into one of the 30 tip-up seats in front of a small elevated stage. This was well lit by electric light and some critically positioned moving spot lights. The three-dimensional puppets were 4 inches tall and controlled by hand-held magnets from under the stage. The bases of the puppets ran on ball bearings. The voices were spoken by the operators who were generally members of the family and other close friends. In later years the theatre was given to the Victoria and Albert Museum.

For the Cyclist

Geoffrey Tomkinson started his engineering apprenticeship in 1900 with the famous textile equipment manufacturers, Platt Brothers of Oldham.

He was a keen sportsman and, the story is told, he would sometimes cycle home at week-ends to see the family. This was a 240 miles round trip on some very bumpy roads.

More about the Companies in the early 1900s

Edward Hughes died in 1902. His sons continued to run the family company which occupied three Mill Street sites and employed over 500 workers. At the time their neighbours, James Humphries, were busy setting out a new 30-loom Spool Axminster department.

In 1903 Cooke Brothers started up at Worcester Cross Works, Oxford Street, with a Chenille plant. Later, in 1907, they leased part of their factory to a new company called The Empire Carpet Company.

Brintons were building new weaving sheds. Cecil Brinton and his team amazed the industry by constructing the 15-feet-wide Gripper Axminster loom which they called "The Majestic Loom".

At the Townshend Works in Puxton, Jelleymans were installing Chenille and Brussels looms. Greatwich became a private company at their Caldwall Mills. Meanwhile in Vicar Street, Bartons were in financial trouble.

In Stourport, Bond Worth were also investing in Spool Axminster at Severn Valley Mills. Moreover, they were looking hard at Spinning Mills in Stroud.

Victoria were settling down to life in Kidderminster. In 1916 T. & A.Naylor moved in as their neighbours with the building of Lowland Works at the Worcester Road end of Green Street.

They made Machinery

Around this time four small engineering companies provided excellent support by manufacturing textile equipment.

EQUIPMENT.

THE events of every day show that victory in the business world goes, in the long run, to the Manufacturer who, at the beginning of his career, insists on having *the very best plant* installed.

Potential Manufacturers should note that we are makers of *Dyeing and Drying Machinery* which can be thoroughly relied on.

Enquiries invited and estimates submitted.

Before starting your new business get in touch with :

S. S. PARTRIDGE & Co. Ltd., PARK MILLS, KIDDERMINSTER

Established 1886.
"Phone - 151.

Registered Tel. Address:
"Reliable, Kidderminster."

PRUNELL, LAMB & Co.
W. PRUNELL.

ENGINEERS AND MACHINE MAKERS

KIDDERMINSTER.

ALL KINDS OF SUPPLIES AND REPAIRS.

Light weight Jacquards, card stamping and beaming machines were the product of Prunell, Lamb & Company at their factory on Comberton Hill.

S.S.Partridge & Company, also on Comberton Hill and later Park Mills, made dyeing and drying machines. Mr Partridge was originally the building foreman for Woodward, Grosvenor. He advertised drying machines with circulating hot air and dyevats made from "good sound pitch pine".

In Callows Lane Phoenix Limited made Jacquards and other engineering parts. Brintons bought the business in 1924. In 1938 they moved out and sold the site to the Carpet Weavers Union. H.Robinson & Son in Fair Street made bobbins, clamps, wires, healds, grippers, dents, sleys and chenille combs and cutters.

Woodward, Grosvenor's new Sales Director

*M*aitland Kempson was appointed to his post in 1909 and he was horrified to find a warehouse bulging with carpet. Therefore, he hired the Town Hall and announced a Grand Carpet Sale. Word got around and the possibility of a good bargain created so much excitement that the Town Hall was full to capacity as auctioneer Charles Joseland quickly sold the entire stock at prices well in excess of their list value !

KIDDERMINSTER.

STOUR VALE MILLS.

⚛ CATALOGUE ⚛

OF

Important Sale of Manufactured Stock,

Comprising about

2,000 Pieces of Axminster, Wilton and Brussels

CARPETS,

750 Squares of Axminster, Wilton, Turkorah & Brussels,

Assortment of Rugs, Mats & Bedsides,

TO BE SOLD BY AUCTION BY

Mr. CHARLES JOSELAND,

(Of the Firm of NOCK & JOSELAND)

ON WEDNESDAY & THURSDAY, NOVEMBER 10th & 11th, 1909,

IN THE

TOWN HALL, KIDDERMINSTER,

By instructions from Messrs. WOODWARD, GROSVENOR & Co. Ltd.

Sale to commence each day at 10-30 prompt.

The Stock may be viewed on Tuesday, November 9th, 1909, from 2 to 4 p.m.

Admission by Catalogue only, both on View and Sale Days.

Catalogues are only supplied to recognised Carpet Dealers or their Agents, and may be obtained, on application, from the AUCTIONEER, Back Buildings, Kidderminster.

Name that Carpet

*A*ll the manufacturers tried to develop ways of making a cheaper product while retaining the appearance of the real thing. Towards the start of the First World War raw materials were again in short supply, particularly the wools. Thomas Griffin of The Empire Carpet Company hit on the idea of substituting a frame of black dyed jute into his Wilton products. He wove a sample and tested the market by showing it to a trusted friend and customer for his honest comments. The experienced buyer examined the back. He spent a few minutes feeling the pile surface before twiddling his moustache and pronouncing "It's a bloody knockout!". Empire's BKO quality sold many thousands of square yards !

Offices and Showrooms

Tomkinson & Adam's Showroom 1920s

Brinton's Marketing Office in the 1950s

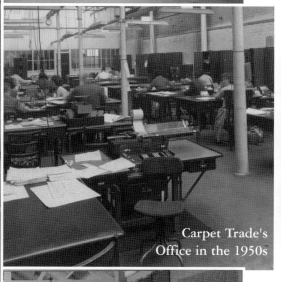

Carpet Trade's Office in the 1950s

James Humphries' Showroom in the 1920s

James Humphries' Mill Street
Design Studio

The Design Studio

Company design studios were quiet, creative areas generally situated on the top floor where good natural light was plentiful through the skylights. The studio resembled a school art room with the lines of boards and a table to the side for the pots of paint and brushes. A dirty area in the corner was the place to grind the powder paints and wash up at the end of the day.

The companies now had the ability to develop their own styles and ranges and they also kept an eye on each other as the trends changed from year to year. The designers themselves became specialists; some were good at Orientals, some Chintz and later Art-Deco and Abstract - Florals were always popular. The original artwork was transposed on to the squared point paper with a charcoal outline before the laborious task of painting in the squares began. Additional copies were needed for the factory and this was the task of the ladies or the juniors as part of the training.

The company "tuft box" contained all the standard colour ranges by number with a sample of dyed yarn for each. The colourist was responsible for these standards and he was the link between the design studio and the dyehouse.

Herbert Smith worked in such a studio at James Humphries & Sons.

Herbert Smith and the Great War

The Mill Street company of James Humphries suffered a blow when John Humphries, who was the son of the founder, died in 1901. He had three sons and they agreed to run the business between them. However, this was not a good arrangement; the turnover declined and the company floundered.

At this time, Herbert Smith was one of their carpet designers and in 1906 he was appointed General Manager. He was feared by all employees and became known as "Piggy" Smith because of his rotund appearance and his ruthless management style. But he soon got the company back on its feet with a return to profitability.

The brothers were happy to take a back seat. In 1909 they appointed Herbert Smith as the Managing Director. He immediately started negotiations to buy the company. The purchase was completed by 1914. However, Herbert Smith had other ideas. In line with the thinking of Harvey Preen and his Carpet Alliance he considered the future of the industry lay in large consortiums. Consequently, he approached the other manufacturers.

Most of the larger companies were still family owned and they were not interested

Felt making   Long Meadow Mills

in such proposals. However, his one success was the acquisition of Long Meadow Mills and the weaving business of Charles Harrison.

At the outbreak of the First World War Herbert Smith was appointed Chairman of the Carpet Materials and Rationing Committee for the whole town.

He saw another window of opportunity. Realising a war need for felt products, he took the bold step of transferring all the weaving plant from Long Meadow to Mill Street and installed new felt manufacturing equipment in its place. The sale of Long Meadow felt products made Herbert Smith a wealthy man.

Hand Knotted Carpets

Hand knotting in the style of the Turkey Work was a slow process and a job for the delicate fingers of the ladies. But the end product was a luxurious and beautifully patterned carpet that would last for years and there were people around who were prepared to pay for such luxury. In the south, the Wilton industry was doing so well that some local companies decided to give it a try.

In 1897 H. & M.Southwell of Bridgnorth started a hand-knotting section that produced some spectacular carpets over a number of years including one for Queen Victoria on the occasion of her Diamond Jubilee. The carpet contained 4,294,600 knots and measured 18 feet x 16 feet. It took 14 ladies four months to make.

In Kidderminster, Brintons had a 40-feet-wide knotting frame in their Vigornia Hand Tuft Department where they produced special orders until 1920.
Bristol Golf Club took the last delivery. However, the most notable order was the 33feet diameter circular rug for the foyer of the De Keysers Hotel in London. Before the carpet was delivered it was put on show in the Corn Exchange.

Although quality was paramount, the ladies were still paid in accordance with their output. In 1914 the rate was 3 old pence per 1,000 tufts. A good knotter would earn 14 shillings (70 pence) a week.

Author's Recommendation -
> *The Wilton Carpet Museum is worth a*
> *visit if only to see the craft of hand*
> *knotting demonstrated on a vertical loom.*

Brintons

The Renard Knotting Loom

Mechanisation in the carpet industry had many achievements. However, the one process that has tested the design engineers over the years is the tying of knots. Imagine a mechanism to recreate the workings of the fingers and thumb to produce a consistently formed and tight knot. Also, imagine the speed at which it needs to work to beat the quickness of hand operation.

This was particularly true for the finer backing materials, such as cotton, where a non-slip "weaver's knot" was, and still is, tied by hand. Yet the real test was the mechanism to replace the skill of the knotting ladies on the Turkey Work looms. The resurgence in sales of knotted carpets at the turn of the century caused the industry to look seriously for a good, productive, mechanical knotting loom.

Edward Hughes & Sons had the Anglo-Turkey looms. They were extremely slow and so Tomkinson & Adam decided to look across the English Channel. From the days of *Savonnerie*, the French had been noted for luxury knotted carpets. They had a carpet manufacturing company called Renard of Nonancourt which had perfected a Jacquard loom capable of tying knots selected from thirteen colours. Tomkinson & Adam secured the British patent rights in 1910 and set up a new department at their Mount Pleasant factory for these looms. The maximum width was five metres.

The Renard looms soon became famous for their design potential and quality. Over the years many prestigious orders were taken for the products of the "French Looms". By the start of the Second World War they were the only knotting looms left in the town. The demand eventually diminished. In 1961 the looms were scrapped to make way for the new generation of production equipment - details later.

1926 Duke of York Visits Kidderminster

In 1926 The Duke of York paid an official visit to the town and was given a guided tour of Tomkinson & Adam. He was shown the Renard knotting looms and as a momento of the visit received a very special rug produced on the loom.

The design was called "Old Hunting Carpet of Persia." It measured 27 feet x 16 feet 6 inches and comprised 2,599,836 knots. It was displayed in the Town Hall and 3,800 people paid 3d to view. All the donations were given to the Infirmary Fund.

VISIT OF
H. R. H.

THE DUKE OF YORK

on
Wednesday, July 21st.

His Royal Highness wishes to see both the workers and the works under ordinary working conditions, and no decorations must be put up inside the works.

It is requested that no weaver leaves her loom nor any worker his or her work in whatever capacity employed until the engine stops at 12.45.

The Duke will finish his tour of the works at the Knotting Loom Department.

When the engine stops all workers are asked to line up in their ordinary working clothes on either side of the yard, from the door-keeper's office up to the entrance of the Chenille shed, and then round to the door of the Knotting Loom Department. Spaces in the yard will be marked out and allotted for the various departments.

Should H.R.H. speak to any worker he should be addressed as "SIR."

To avoid confusion all orders given by the foremen and their helpers must be adhered to.

To ensure the success of the Duke's visit it is important that everything should be carried out in an orderly manner.

TOMKINSON & ADAM.

17th July, 1926.

The Royal Visit to Kidderminster, July, 1926

The Duke of York inspects the Works of Tomkinson & Adam

IT is a curious fact that, although Kidderminster is the home of the Royal Axminster carpet, it is only recently that this great British carpet centre has had the honour of a royal visit. The occasion was the opening of the new wing of the General Hospital in the town, in June last, by the Duke of York. Apart from the fact that the Duke is President of the Industrial Welfare Society, his keen interest in manufacturing was again exemplified in connection with this visit, for he included in his tour of the town a visit to the carpet factory of Messrs. Tomkinson and Adam, and was conducted over the works by the partners, Major Herbert Tomkinson, D.L., J.P., Mr. Gerald Tomkinson, Colonel William Adam, D.S.O., Colonel G. S. Tomkinson, O.B.E., M.C., and Mr. R. R. Adam, and the entire process of weaving the fine carpets, for which the firm is famous, was demonstrated to him.

PRESENTATION CARPET INSPECTED.

Kidderminster has produced carpets for nearly two hundred years. As far back as 1772 there were 250 carpet looms at work, but a great modern impetus came with the introduction of the power loom, and Messrs. Tomkinson and Adam played an important part in this development. The firm was established in 1869 with hand looms and twenty operatives. Ten years later Mr. Tomkinson visited America and brought back with him the patent rights of the first real Axminster power loom to be used in this country.

MOUNT PLEASANT WORKS.

Reprinted from THE FURNISHING TRADES' ORGANISER, *September*, 1926

Tomkinson's Heraldic Carpet

*F*ounder *Michael Tomkinson was a member of Worcestershire County Council from 1889 to 1892. His son, Herbert, was also elected from 1907. In 1949 this fact was commemorated by the presentation of a beautiful Heraldic Rug made on the company's Renard Loom. Measuring 15 feet x 13 feet 4 inches the carpet contained over 1,500,000 knots.*

The specially designed carpet was emblematic of Worcestershire. It contained the words "Worcestershire County Council" in the outer band of a circular medallion. Inside was a spray of Oak and Hops. Within the shield the River Severn was featured together with the Malvern Hills, Worcester City and the fields and orchards of the county. In each corner the County Emblem was displayed with the Black Pear tree. Herbert Tomkinson presented the rug at a ceremony at the Shire Hall in February 1949.

In 1987 the carpet was restored and hung in the County Records Office for all to see. Tomkinsons had in fact produced two of the rugs. In 1956 Sir Geoffrey Tomkinson became president of Worcestershire County Cricket Club and he had the second rug modified to refer to the club by name. It was laid in the club's committee lounge.

A Sporting Rug

*I*n 1951 a Tomkinson's customer from Birmingham, who was also a fanatical boxing fan, ordered a rug with a picture of Randolph Turpin in a boxing stance. The rug was entitled - "Randolph Turpin the World Middleweight Champion". Many more special single rug orders were manufactured.

Persian Knotted Carpet presented by the Company to the Worcestershire County Council February 28th 1949

The First World War, 1914 - 1918

Just prior to the war the carpet industry went through a period of stability. During this period negotiations took place between the Weavers Association and the manufacturers. They agreed to fix the working week at 55 hours with a normal finish at noon on Saturday.

When war broke out the companies were unsure of their future. Therefore, they all closed down totally for one week. However, a few orders trickled in so they started up again, this time for only three days per week.

The younger factory workers joined the armed forces and the union membership declined. Union reserves were drying up and it became increasingly difficult to support the unemployed. Consequently, the Mayor, Reginald Brinton, and Stanley Baldwin who was MP for Bewdley, set up a relief fund.

The industry was slow to convert to the war effort. However, Herbert Smith had led the way and soon other companies followed suit, changing Chenille looms to weave blankets and devoting factory space to engineering and munitions work. Typical of the town response was the family firm of T. & A.Naylor who quickly geared themselves up for war-blanket production at their Pike Mills headquarters.

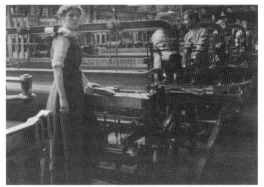

Naylors blanket weaving...

scouring...

drying...

and despatch !

Jam in Vicar Street

*V*icar Street in the late 1880s was a street of carpet factories. Near the Town Hall and Police Station (Mothercare in 2000) was The Town Hall Carpet Works. The factory had a large weaving shed at the rear near the river.

During the First World War the Government commissioned the weaving shed to store and dry out fruit grown in the area before being sent to the frontline forces abroad. The shed became known throughout the town as "The Jam Factory". After the war Brintons purchased the building and promptly christened it "J" Shed - no prizes for guessing why! After a number of other uses the building was eventually converted to the popular Brinton's Beacon Club.

Maitland Kempson swims to Order

*W*ith the war still raging Woodward, Grosvenor's sales director jumped the gun and sailed to America to keep in touch and drum up new business. With some good orders in his brief case he could not wait to get home. Unfortunately for him he chose the S.S.Lusitania for his return journey. The steamship was torpedoed and sank off the coast of Ireland. After many hours in the water he was rescued and lived to tell a remarkable tale.

The "Union" Opens its Doors

*T*he Weavers Association had always been selective with its membership. However, towards the end of the First World War they took a big step forward and changed the name to The Power Loom Carpet Weavers and Textile Workers Association. More significantly they changed the constitution. The lesson of the war years had been the need for more membership and subscriptions.

Therefore, they opened the doors to the whole industry. For the first time 800 women joined during a big recruitment campaign. This campaign also took in workers from Stourport, Bridgnorth and Stroud. In a short time the membership nearly trebled from 800 to well over 2,000. Their Mill Street office became very cramped. By 1922, with 4,000 plus members they had moved to No.8 Church Street for a yearly rent of £35 including rates. Later they invested in the latest technology with the purchase of a typewriter which cost 18/6d (92 new pence).

The Ladies get Organised

*W*ith Union backing the female workforce started to fight for their rights. On the shop floor acceptable demarcation lines between the work undertaken by women and their male "brothers" had been established and agreed. Subsequently, there were a number of disputes over women's pay and working conditions. In one such incident 22 Chenille winders of The Carpet Manufacturing Company confronted the management over rates of pay. The issue was quickly settled when the Association threatened a town strike. From this point onward the ladies played a full roll in the Union's affairs.

Back to Normal

The war ended and after a bit of wrangling the Union negotiated a substantial rise over their pre-war production rates of pay. Things slowly got back to normal. Herbert Smith again found his investment in the Long Meadow Felt operation to his advantage with a whole department making felt slippers for the housewives of the country.

The postwar recovery period also included a housing programme that benefited the industry. In those days it was common practice to have a large square rug in the main living rooms ontop of the stained floor boards or linoleum. On the stairs, a "runner", held in place with stair rods, went up the middle. The export markets

Slipper-production at Long Meadow

returned and, with a good home trade in place, the industry returned once again to profit and a period of stability.

Sir Herbert Smith Bart.

Herbert Smith was now the owner of James Humphries & Sons. He was also extremely popular and respected in the carpet industry. Just after the war he was appointed Chairman of the Manufacturers Association. In 1920 he partly achieved his ambition by bringing together a number of companies into a consortium which he called Carpet Trades Limited.

The full list started with his own Mill Street and Long Meadow Mill factories of James Humphries and Charles Harrison, to which he added his Mill Street neighbour Edward Hughes & Sons; the Slingfield Mills of Thomas Lea; two Yorkshire Spinning Companies with offices in Heckmondwike and Ravensthorpe and a German company in Weida in Thuringia.

In the same year he received a Baronetcy in recognition of his war effort. By this time his hard work and astute business deals had made him a very wealthy man. With this wealth he bought Witley Court from the Earl of Dudley.

Sir Herbert Celebrates

*S*ir Herbert Smith, Baronet "extends an invitation to his Employees to accompany him to
TEWKESBURY, on 5th August, 1920, in celebration of the Honour conferred upon him
by H.M. The King."

So read the front page of the official programme as Sir Herbert treated his 1,300 employees to a
day out by the river. Pleasure steamer rides, speeches and bands entertained the families in a field
near Tewkesbury Abbey. A sumptuous sit-down lunch started at midday and it was followed by
the toasts and presentations. Gunner H.Pheasey received the Military Medal from Sir Herbert.

For the energetic "The Athletic Sports" in the afternoon contained a mixed bag of events. Four
boxing bouts were contested for a purse of £3 to the winner. The first field event was the ladies
100 yards handicap with seven entrants, Mrs Mills had a 16 yard start over W.Bradley! Then
followed a gents 440 yards obstacle race and three flat races.

The ladies had three more events: the egg and spoon, the 100 yards skipping and a three-legged
race. The climax of the afternoon sports was the tug-of-war with a prize of £6 for the winning
team. The ladies prize was contested between the teams of Miss Cook and Mrs Harris. The men's
crown went to the winners of Lea Ltd. and Humphries Mechanics.

At 3.50pm the final of the Ladies Beauty Competition saw six unattached young ladies compete
for prizes of £5, £3 and £2. The programme clearly stated that "competitors will be requested to
lower their hair". Mr J.D.King was the lucky judge and Miss Dora Smith presented the prizes.

Author's note : My father, Cyril Thompson, was a twenty-year-old Wilton tuner at Humphries
at the time and he remembered it was a very enjoyable day out - hic! He also recalled that
Herbert Smith was well respected by the workforce and generous on occasions such as this.

Sir Herbert Retires

*I*n 1922 Sir Herbert Smith was in control of one of the town's largest companies
and all seemed set for the future. However, remarkably at the age of forty-nine,
he resigned from the board of Carpet Trades, sold all his shares and left the carpet
industry altogether. He died in 1943 and is buried at St.John's, Kidderminster.

The Carpet Trades Photographic Collection 1923

*T*he production equipment of the Kidderminster companies of Carpet Trades
Limited was photographed during 1923 at a time when the carpet industry
was in full production. There are 62 black and white photographs.

The photographs are unique because they cover all aspects of the business from
the offices, showrooms and design studio to the machinery on the factory floor. The
latter is an excellent record of life in the factory and is typical of many of the town's
other factories. Most of the carpet production methods of the day are featured
including Tapestry, Chenille, Spool Axminster, Wilton and even the older weavers
and their "specials" hand loom. These were located in the Mill Street buildings of
James Humphries and Edward Hughes. Lea's Spinning Mill is shown in great detail
together with the Long Meadow Mill felt making plant.

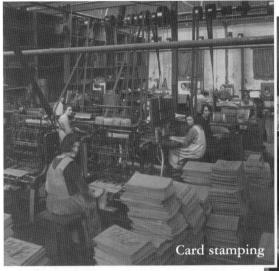
Card stamping

Hank to Bobbin Winding

Spool Axminster Setting

Narrow Spool Axminster Weaving

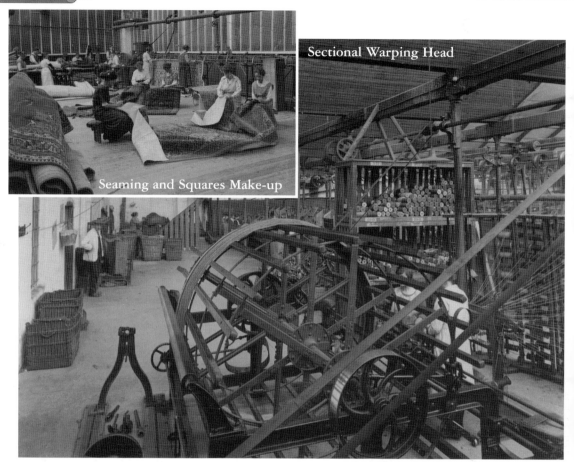

Sectional Warping Head

Seaming and Squares Make-up

The Grosvenor-Picking Loom

William Thomas Picking was a loom tuner for Woodward, Grosvenor. He was called up during the war and sent to France. There he was billeted with an old French lady who spent her spare time knitting away on an old knitting machine. He became intrigued by the knitting mechanism and identified a potential use in the Wilton weaving process. On his return to work he set about developing his idea and eventually perfected the design which was patented in 1923.

The Grosvenor-Picking Wilton Loom used hooks instead of the pile wire to form the tuft. Woodward, Grosvenor built looms for their own use and licences were issued to Brintons and an American Company. The decline of Wilton saw a general reduction in the number of these special looms. However, Woodward, Grosvenor kept faith in the process, the last looms being decommissioned as late as 1999.

St. George's Park

In 1927 the Directors of Brintons under the guidance of Dick Woodward purchased a piece of land in Radford Avenue. It was developed as a second public park and presented to the town.

The Interwar Years & The Second World War

B etween the two world wars the manufacturers and the workforce settled down to a period of stability. It was a time when the companies were encouraged to examine their management skills, their machinery and the layout of the factories. "Time and Motion" became the password to investment and reorganisation.

The design potential and production advantages of Spool and Gripper Axminster by now were well known. They rapidly became the predominant products. Wilton Velvet continued to sell well in the upper end of the price structure but there was a marked decline in the sale of Brussels, Tapestry and Kidderminster. Chenille was also losing its popularity although a few companies, particularly Naylors and The Carpet Manufacturing Company, retained faith in the product for rugs and squares well into the 1960s.

The good profits enabled the existing manufacturers to extend buildings and buy new machinery. The market was also big enough for some new companies to start up and 1927 was a vintage year of growth. In Stourport, Bond Worth built new offices, showrooms and weaving sheds. The Carpet Manufacturing Company doubled the size of Rock Works and bought Caldwall and Park Mills for their spinning operation. Also in 1927, the old established company of Tomkinson & Adam became Tomkinsons Ltd. and W. & R.R.Adam Ltd. as William and Raleigh Adam broke away to form their own company at Greenhill Works on the Birmingham Road.

In the following year Harry Dutfield and Stephen Quayle started making Chenille rugs in Franchise Street under the company name Dutfield & Quayle Ltd. Nine years later Harry Dutfield left to restart the weaving industry in Axminster. Neville Tranter became a partner and the company was renamed Quayle & Tranter.

A sad occasion for the history of the town came in 1932 when the last ever Kidderminster carpet was woven on a power loom at Naylor's Pike Mills. At the time Naylors were also expanding Lowland Works and building Foley Spinning Mill.

In 1934 A.G.Brockway moved to Hoobrook; Carpet Trades introduced their profitable Kardax Gripper looms and Jelleymans extended their Townshend Works and shipped in a plant of Crompton & Knowles Axminster looms bought from a failed American company.

In 1936 Victoria built fine new offices fronting Green Street. A few years before they had obtained the premises of the former Castle Road Motor Company for their Wilton looms, ironically to make car carpeting. Morris Carpets were busy developing their new carpet business and in 1937 a new company started with Harry Spilsbury and Bert Wilcox installing Gripper Axminster looms at their factory in Cross Street.

With all this development and expansion more workers were trained for the industry and the Union continued to gain membership. In 1938 with 5,000 members on the books they invested £6,000 in a new office and meeting room in Callows Lane. In the late 1920s two of the larger carpet companies decided to invest in their workforce and provided the first Sports and Social Clubs in the area.

Tomkinsons at Oaklands

SATURDAY, JULY 8th, 1933

Tomkinsons ltd.

FIFTH ANNUAL

Gala Day
and Sports

OFFICIAL PROGRAMME

O n May 12th, 1928 Herbert Tomkinson opened the new Oaklands Sports and Social Club to the workforce of Tomkinsons. The old "masters" house had been converted to a clubhouse and the seven acres of grounds became the sports fields. At 3 pm precisely the Mayor, Mr George Eddy, made a short speech, took off his jacket, loosened his bow tie and proceeded to partner Mr Stewart-Smith in a tennis match against Mr H. & Mr G.Tomkinson.

In a celebration opening cricket match Tomkinsons played Jelleymans in Division Two of the Kidderminster League. There were also golf and bowls tournaments.

"OAKLANDS," Chester Road

The club was popular for many years to come. However, like most others in town its popularity declined in the late 1950s against the competition of television and it closed with the land inevitably sold for a housing development.

Brintons at Spennels

N ot to be outdone, Brintons soon followed suit when in 1929 they took the unusual step of buying 130 acres of land at Spennels which they then transformed into a magnificent sports club and grounds. The large old house became the clubhouse and the grounds were developed for all the usual sports together with a putting green, a nine-hole golf course and a cycle track. Nearby Spennels Pool was available for swimming.

The club was opened on July 29th again by a busy Mayor, Mr George Eddy. The years between the wars saw many gala and sports days. They attracted good crowds - sometimes around 4,000.

Unfortunately, it was an ambitious project that was never really successful. During the Second World War the site was sold to a Munitions Company. In later years it became a Dr.Barnardo's home and then part of a housing estate.

Naylors Raise the Roof !

*I*n 1935 a tremendous feat of civil engineering was witnessed by passers by as a third storey was added to the large warehouse at T. & A.Naylor's Lowland Works at the end of Green Street near the Worcester Road island.

The work involved the raising of the whole of the existing warehouse roof including steelwork, north lights and the surrounding brickwork parapet - a total of over 1,000 tons!

A deep steel girder was put into the wall just under the roof level and then 54 screw jacks were positioned around the perimeter under the girder. With two employees to every jack, a blast on the whistle signalled a simultaneous turn of the screw and the roof was gradually raised. After six courses the matching brickwork was filled in and the slow process repeated until they had effectively raised the roof a full 15 feet.

Face to Face with the Germans !

German loom builders, Guskin, developed a Wilton weave and loom which produced two carpets at the same time. The carpets were literally woven "face to face" before being slit with a travelling knife.

In 1939 The Carpet Manufacturing Company bought two of Guskin's 3/4 Wilton face-to-face looms. Two German fitters arrived and successfully erected the first loom but they were mysteriously called back to Germany before the second was completed much to the annoyance of the CMC management. They soon found out why !

The Second World War, 1939 - 1945

At the start of the Second World War the population of Kidderminster Borough was in excess of 30,000 and the industry employed about 11,000. With the experience of the First World War under their belts the carpet companies prepared themselves for the war years. They knew what had to be done. Many skilled workers were again lost to the armed forces.

The Board of Trade pronounced carpets to be "non-essential goods" and nationally, fourteen "nucleus" carpet companies were licensed to manufacture a limited and controlled production for as long as the raw materials were available. The town's Nucleus companies included some of the larger manufacturers and also Spilsbury & Wilcox. Within their licence these companies could weave orders for the non-Nucleus companies providing the order was not for domestic use. Export was encouraged.

In November 1942 the manufacture of carpet ceased completely on the instruction of The Board of Trade. Surplus factory space was converted to government stores and the engineering workshops became vital to the war effort. Some looms were put into mothballs but others were adapted to weave war products. Chenille looms were easily converted to blanket production and Wilton looms were ideal for weaving the cotton webbing for haversacks, gun covers and tenting.

In 1940 the Government's Ministry of Supply set up a "Small Arms Ammunition Factory" unit under the control of ICI Metals. Brinton's engineering department made the tools; Tomkinsons the bullets; Carpet Trades the cases and ICI added the explosives at their Summerfield headquarters. It gave employment to between 4,000 and 5,000 people, men and women.

During the war Victoria's offices were occupied by aircraft builders Short Brothers. The Blackburn Aircraft Company took over Pike Mills and The Lockheed Hydraulic Company used Worcester Cross Works in Oxford Street.

Even the smaller carpet companies found themselves involved in some way. Kidderminster could be proud of its wartime record. As well as the small arms, jerricans, incendiary bombs, roller conveyor and the mountings for the Oerlikon gun were all produced in the carpet factories of the town. In October 1945 an exhibition was set up in the Town Hall where everyone could see exactly what had been achieved.

Oerlikon Gun

The French are Indebted to Victoria

*I*n 1940 the Victoria Carpet Company were pleased, and proud, to receive an order for the
weaving of blankets for the frontline soldiers of the French armed forces. Chenille and Tapestry
looms were quickly converted and the finished blankets were shipped over the Channel to the
battlefield. Unfortunately for Victoria, France fell to the enemy before the invoices had been paid!

The Bull Ring

Note - the converted shop window advertising "War Bonds"
- the painted kerbstones and lamppost to help see in the "blackout".
- the taped windows of Medical Hall to prevent the glass from shattering.

*At the Millennium, Baxter's Statue is near St.Mary's Church on the Ring Road, Medical Hall
is Lloyds the Chemists and Melias is the Halifax Building Society. The War Weapons shop was
roughly where the Post Office now stands.*

Brintons made
861,491 'Jerricans' and
300 miles of conveyor

Bombing off to Australia

*J*ust as the war was reaching a climax in 1944, The Carpet Manufacturing Company were
busy expanding into the southern hemisphere in partnership with the Australian company
Felt & Textiles. Important signatures were needed and it is reported that The Carpet
Manufacturing Company Chairman, E.H.O. Carpenter,
thumbed a lift in an RAF
bomber to conclude the
important deal.

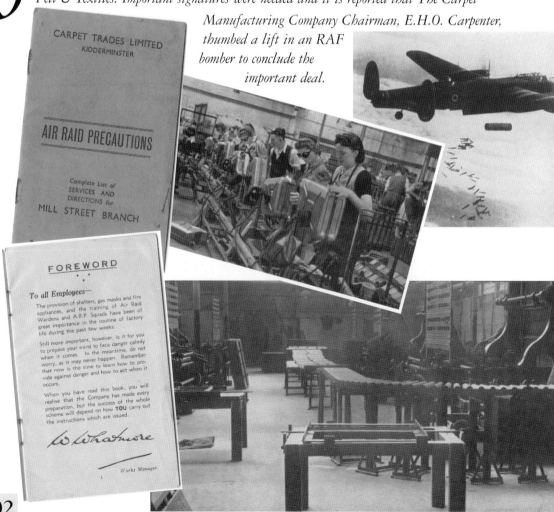

The Industry Recovers

In February 1944 the manufacturing ban was lifted and, providing the raw materials were available, the manufacture of carpets could recommence. However, the government continued to control the industry through the Board of Trade. The production licences remained together with controls on quality and price. All carpet woven during this period had a distinguishing red line woven into the warp backing. Remarkably these controls remained until 1951.

Immediately after the war the companies had the difficult task of returning their factories back to carpet production. Raw materials continued to be scarce and the workforce returning from the war had to be integrated with those who had remained during the war. The town was also host to 1,200 Polish ex-service men who had fought in North Africa and Italy and found themselves in the camps at Summerfield, Drakelow, Mustow Green and Burlish. Lady Eddy chaired a committee to help find them jobs and many chose the carpet industry.

The essential jute for the carpet backing was particularly in short supply. This brought out a series of substitutes including "bump" cotton, Fibro and Kraft paper made into a yarn. Ardil was the name given to a fibre made from ground nuts! The recovery was slow and hard work. Two years after the war only 6,000 workers had been re-employed.

However, the carpet industry could see better times ahead as the building industry got to work. In the late 1940s a number of companies were formed. William Hill built the Worcester Road factory; Bouchers introduced Carpet Products (CP) to Abercynon in South Wales and Carpet Weavers set up in Lye. But, perhaps the best known name to launch a business at that time was Lionel Rowe who, together with partners Bert Beams and Bill Hopkins, set up the Minster Carpet Company in Orchard Street.

Federation of British Carpet Manufacturers and the NJC

During wartime the manufacturers worked well together planning and sharing the limited production. Herbert Tomkinson had been chairman of the Carpet Manufacturers Association (CMA) since 1921 and during the war he was appointed chairman of their Executive Committee. This high profile group represented the whole industry and was the industry's link to the Board of Trade.

Sir Stafford Cripps, chairman of the Board of Trade, came to Kidderminster in January 1946 to discuss proposals for a working party to settle the needs of the carpet industry. Cyril Newton showed him around Carpet Trades. This was followed by a lunch and a conference at the nearby Black Horse Hotel in Mill Street. These talks resulted in the formation of the National Joint Committee. The NJC formulated pay and conditions for the carpet industry and it included representatives from all the manufacturers, the trade unions and the Ministry of Labour.

In 1948 The Federation of British Carpet Manufacturers replaced the CMA.

Bouchers Build the Looms

BOUCHER & COMPANY LTD
TEXTILE MACHINERY MANUFACTURERS

STOURPORT ROAD, KIDDERMINSTER
TELEPHONE : KIDDERMINSTER 4711 (10 lines)   Telex: 338278

Established 1836

The origins of the Boucher Engineering Company date back to the pioneer company Prunell, Lamb & Company who were founded in 1836. After the war Bouchers were renting buildings near Carpet Trades in Mill Street. John Wilkinson was in charge and he started to expand the operation cashing in on the post war growth and the desperate need for textile parts. They initially took a good order for the refurbishing of Jacquards for The Carpet Manufacturing Company. This provided the finance for the development and manufacture of their first narrow Wilton loom in 1951 which was sold to Steeles of Banbury for £200, including the Jacquard.

By 1950 Bouchers, having outgrown the Mill Street factory, rented part of Pike Mills from the Borough Council. As general engineers they built tyre-making plant for the world. As textile engineers they developed a range of equipment for the carpet industry including Wilton and Gripper Axminster looms, card stamping, spool-threading machines and beaming machines. Yet they probably became best known for their press work making Axminster spools and tube-frames.

In 1968, with Pike Mills due for demolition, they built a new factory on Stourport Road. The needs of the carpet industry, however, were rapidly changing as new processes were introduced and Bouchers found it difficult to remain in touch. In 1972 they decided to reduce in size and concentrate on what they could do best. They sold the Stourport Road factory to Brintons and moved to Chlidema Mill to concentrate on the spool and tube-frame production. John Wilkinson also set up a second-hand machinery business.

"CONSOLE" HIGH SPEED
CARD CUTTER

Easier to use than a typewriter ! Operator can be trained within an hour. Quick and simple method of colour selection only 1½ inches from the design paper. Automatically stops when card is cut, automatic numbering device, centralised lubrication system, high cutting speed and rapid conversion to other card sizes. Operator fatigue reduced to a minimum for the machine takes care of the Brainwork.

Author's Note: My father, Cyril Thompson, worked for Bouchers in the boom years. He built the looms in Mill Street and at Pike Mills and then travelled to the customer for the erection and commissioning. He was always the "first weaver". I remember him spending many weeks away from home in most parts of Great Britain and Ireland. He was even responsible for starting up a brand new factory in Iceland! When the new College of Further Education opened on Hoo Road one of the town's companies donated a Wilton loom and my father had the job of setting it up to weave. He persuaded me to help him out as "part of my education". I spent many hours leaning into the loom passing the warp ends through. He earned 5/- (25p) an hour and I earned 2/6d (12.5p). After this part of my "education" I decided to stick to my day job, Engineering.

HYDRAULIC
BEAMER

Boom Time in the 1950s

Can't make enough !

With the manufacturing restrictions removed the companies geared themselves up for a boom period as raw materials became available. The country did its best to regenerate business with the staging of many fairs and exhibitions.

In 1951 at the Festival of Britain, loom makers Platt Brothers exhibited a working Spool Axminster loom with female weavers from Carpet Trades. Two years later at Belle Vue, Manchester, The International Textile Machinery Exhibition brought the latest technologies to the United Kingdom. The British Industries Fair at Castle Bromwich was for many years a shop window used by the town's manufacturers. Earls Court became the venue for the annual carpet fair. In later years the fair was transferred to Harrogate in Yorkshire.

The big wide world had also been starved of the British Carpet and the export markets reopened with a vengeance. The housing boom got into full swing as new housing estates were built for the councils and the private sector. In Kidderminster alone 3,400 Council houses were built between 1945 and 1973. New estates developed at Birchen Coppice, Franche, Habberley, Comberton, Hurcott Road, Rifle Range and Hoobrook. Moreover, in keeping with a national trend five tower blocks of flats were added in the 1960s.

Kidderminster's building programme was reflected throughout the country and the carpet industry was one of the many to prosper in the following years. The carpet companies were again recruiting and by the mid-1950s the Union membership was approaching a record level at 5,000 members.

"Wall to Wall"

New houses were different; they were "modern". The rooms were bigger and the old standard of the carpet square on the "lino" was out of date. These new houses needed a fitted "wall-to-wall" carpet.

This was good news for salesmen as the orders rolled in. However, the production departments were not so happy because the weaving width of the looms on the shop floor was still predominantly narrow, although there were some wider looms including the old nine foot standard. Most rooms were based on the 12 foot width although there was a demand for 15 foot. This was a challenge the engineers could not afford to miss.

"I have wall-to-wall carpeting."

Boom Time for the Engineers

Brintons had always designed and manufactured their own looms and continued to do so. However, they were not the only ones in town with good engineering facilities. Russell's Foundry in Clensmore provided many of the castings needed for the looms under construction in the engineering machine shops at the larger carpet companies.

The general equipment suppliers also enjoyed this period of prosperity. For the manufacture of Axminster looms, David Crabtree & Sons of Bradford made Gripper Jacquard while Platt Brothers of Oldham cornered the Spool sector with their faster "split-shot" Looms. Splitting the two weft shots gave better productivity and was the idea of Arthur Davis who was Works Manager for Bond Worth. Crabtree also combined the two with their Gripper-Spool loom, the spool system gave the option of unlimited colours to the Gripper weave.

There were a number of Wilton loom manufacturers including Bouchers, Robert Hall, Craig of Paisley, Smiths and Crossleys but the most progressive at the time was Wilson and Longbottom of Barnsley. With the accent now well focussed on speed of production Wilson & Longbottom were developing their own range of "face-to-face" looms. Carpet Trades, and others, worked closely with them on these developments. Patterned face-to-face carpet provided the biggest challenge.

From abroad, the Belgian Wilton loom maker Michel Van de Wiele was the choice of The Carpet Manufacturing Company at their New Road factory.

The investment continued in the spinning mills and the dyehouses. Petrie & McNaught, Knowles, Longclose, Samuel Pegg all became well-known nameplates on the wet equipment of the dyehouses. Broadbent made a large spin dryer to extract water from the hanks before drying. After the weaving process the industry looked to Sellers of Chapel Hill, Huddersfield, to supply the equipment to apply the latex backing and shear the top of the carpet level.

More Changes and Man-Made Fibres

Patterned borders were unnecessary in wall-to-wall carpets and therefore new disciplines were introduced into the design studio. Inspiration was derived from abstract items such as leaves, bubbles, shadows, cobblestones and even the ski-run. Plain carpet also became very popular with some special effects created on the Wilton wire looms. These included a mixture of cut and uncut pile. Carpet Trades introduced a luxury long shag pile carpet which, when woven in the natural colour, resembled the actual sheep skin. The product was called "Peerless" and Elizabeth Taylor was said to have carpeted her yacht with it!

The methods of production changed as the looms produced long rolls of carpet instead of a succession of squares. Warehouses needed to be extended and equipped with special racking and handling equipment for these large and heavy rolls. Customers ordered carpet to fit the size of the room. Manufacturers installed special machines to cut the carpet to length and automatically pack for immediate delivery.

It was not only the nature of production, however, that was changing, the materials available were also the subject of considerable research and development. In the early 1950s natural fibres dominated production. Pure wool was used for the pile with jute and cotton forming the backing materials. The supply industry had to gear themselves up to satisfy the demand. For example, such was the volume of jute consumed in the town that the jute industry in Dundee ran a special "Jute Express" train from Dundee to Kidderminster station every Sunday. Orders placed by the Friday would ensure the jute was available at Kidderminster station on the Monday.

The huge demand also created the opportunity for companies such as ICI and Courtaulds to invest in the development of synthetic fibres. In America the familiar name of DuPont was already a leader in the field. "Man made fibres" was a new phrase to the industry as fibres with names like Evlan, Rayon, Acrilan, Courtelle and Bri-Nylon became the subject of loom trials.

The distribution network also worked overtime to deliver the orders around the country and to the dockside. The railway system had long since replaced the canal as the major distributor. Many rolls of carpet were hauled up Comberton Hill (Station Hill) to the goods yard and, for a while, Carpet Trades had its own rail carriage converted into a showroom. There was a lot going on with employment for all.

Crossleys Come to Town - again !

Somehow the Halifax firm of John Crossley & Sons has always managed to influence the carpet industry in Kidderminster. Gone were the days when the Kidderminster industry bought their looms and gone were the days when they ran a company of their own at Worcester Cross Works.

In 1953, they took another significant step forward and joined forces with Carpet Trades to form a large and powerful consortium which was known as John Crossley-Carpet Trades Holdings Ltd. The new group had the range of products, and the buying power, to beat all comers. Both companies benefited.

Herbert Smith would have certainly have given this marriage his blessing!

107

The Workforce Thrives

And so to summarise the position:

The manufacturers had full order books and were making a good profit.
The companies were investing in new buildings and improved equipment.
The industry had taken on-board the needs of wall-to-wall carpet.
The product development teams were looking at the materials of the future.
But, to quote an old saying, "What about the workers ?".

They knew the score. With full order books and deadlines to meet the Union grasped the opportunity to negotiate some exceptionally good wages and agreements. On their part the manufacturers put up a token resistance but the odds were firmly in the favour of the shopfloor workforce. The industry was still very labour intensive and whole families worked in the factories, often for the same company, just as they had done in the days of the hand loom. Family life was good and workers had money in their pockets. People smiled a lot and the whole town benefited.

At the workplace the Government turned the screw a little insisting on better conditions and standards of guarding under the Health and Safety at Work Act. Meanwhile, the companies did their bit with subsidised canteens and other benefits including the sports and social facilities. Tomkinsons still owned Oaklands; Carpet Trades developed White Wickets on the Franche Road and Brintons were neighbours to The Carpet Manufacturing Company at Oldington. Victoria provided an excellent sports ground in Hoobrook. Their social club was in the upper rooms of the former Castle Road Motors in Pump Street. In Stourport Worth's facilities were in Mill Road.

In these halcyon days before television the annual company sports day was a gala event for all ages. Carpet Trades brought bus loads of families from their Yorkshire Spinning companies for the annual bun feast. Many employees qualified for the Long Service Award and they could still have chosen a gold pocket watch!

The local sports leagues contained a predominance of carpet works teams. Rivalry between the companies was good natured and good for the sport and the town. The traditional Carnival was revived and the companies' individual departments worked hard to decorate the "float" ready for the big day in August. It was remarkable what could be achieved in a short time as people worked together.

Each day the factory "Tannoy" system was tuned into "Music while you work". The larger companies hosted BBC Radio's popular "Workers Playtime" which was a daily lunch-time half hour variety show live and direct from the works canteen. The annual Industrial Church Service was another opportunity for the workforce to put on a display. Brintons "Beacon" and "Tomkinsons Times" were typical of the company magazines of the day. Company newspapers and Societies all reflected the prosperity and the feeling of comradeship that existed in the carpet industry.

Carpet Trades Operatic Society took over The Playhouse on Comberton Hill for their annual production on more than one occasion, while every Friday the town followed the progress of "Walter the Weaver" in the *Shuttle.*

WALTER THE WEAVER – PUBLIC SERVICE

Vernon Davis '55

Carnivals over the Years

The tradition of carnival has produced some remarkable results. Ageing photographs in Tomkinson's archives feature the theme of the countryside with a horse-drawn cart loaded with hay and people! Greatwich transformed an early solid white-walled tyred car into a slipper for their Cinderella presentation. But one of the most imaginative came from the Frank Stone Company who provided the Carnival Queen in 1936. Frank Stone, son of the founder, was a keen beekeeper. It was therefore not surprising that he chose the "bee theme" for his carnival entry. The picture shows the Carnival Queen Bee, Miss Margery Wharton, seated with her attendants to her side. Frank Stone is standing behind, his wife is the lady with the hat. Leonard Brooks of Station Hill took the photograph in Stone's showroom.

Author's Note : My Aunt, Margery Wharton, now in her late eighties, celebrated the Millennium with her husband, family and four great-grandchildren at their home in Oldswinford and she still looks as good as she did in 1936!

109

TUC Conference in Stourport ?

*A*t the Union AGM the Chairman reported that, as usual, he and the secretary would be attending the Annual TUC Conference in Blackpool. Some wag at the back shouted "If the meeting had been in Stourport I suppose me and the bloody sweeper could have gone!". This was typical of the humour of the day.

Author's Memories. - No apologies for this pure nostalgia !

*C*arpet Trades in 1952 was one of the biggest firms in town and I was an innocent sixteen-year-old engineering apprentice starting my working life as a very small fish in an extremely large pool. I was grateful to John Grant, their Chief Engineer at the time, for giving me the opportunity. However, little did I know that my education was just starting !

Carpet Trades was a typical company of the day; everybody seemed to know each other and be working for a common cause. There was a lot of "leg pull" and people smiled a lot. The managers were all promoted from the ranks; they knew their job and were well respected. I soon found my way around the factory and observed that each department had a characteristic of its own.

Narrow Spool weaving, spool setting, picking and the winding were very feminine domains with a lot of chatter. The Tannoy was always tuned in to the latest "top-ten". By complete contrast the Wilton sheds, male only, were very serious and industrious. The "House of Lords" was a noble place where the rich weavers wove fine Worsted Squares on the Roma looms. They came to work in their Sunday best and donned their hessian aprons. They earned good money and were known to give their creelers a tip if they cleaned the loom well at the end of the week. Strangely, the looms didn't seem to have a number or location, they were just known by the name of the weaver.

In summer, the finishing room was sticky with the hot-air dryers adding to the ambient temperature and this produced the annual demand to paint the roof lights and install fans. The warehouse was the ideal place to work with few people around and it was generally cool and quiet. The place to be avoided was the dyehouse - always hot, steamy and smelly. For eyeing-up the girls, spool setting provided the best selection, they seemed to be more my age. I cycled to work on my drop handle-bar bike generally just beating the Bull. The bike sheds were full and the odd Wilton weaver's Ford Cortina or Austin Seven looked lonely in the car park.

In the machine shop there was always banter as the apprentice was sent to the stores for "the big stand" or the "long weight". I remember the tea breaks when we all queued up at the boiler with our grubby cups. The canteen did a good lunch. However, many had sandwiches and then played darts, or went for a "wander up town", or just sat on the large picture window ledge facing Park Butts and watched the world go by! The window always displayed the companies' beautifully designed products: often a Persian design Ambala Square.

Engineering apprentices in the carpet industry were not well paid. I remember my girl friend, Shirley now my wife, was a picker at Brintons and she always earned twice my weekly wage packet. She liked the "top ten" and bought a "78" gramophone record every week from Allens music shop in Blackwell Street to play on her new record-player. Big Bands were all the rage and we enjoyed the occasional Sunday evening Jazz concert at the Playhouse on Comberton Hill.

When we went to the Futurist Cinema in Vicar Street, if she was paying it was upstairs but downstairs if it was my turn! We met all our friends at the Florence Ballroom in Blackwell Street at the Saturday-night dance, always best suit and black polished shoes.

In return for a day at "Tech" (in my case the School of Science in Market Street) I had to work Saturday morning for nothing and provide all my books and stationery. As part of my training I was sent to Russell's Foundry in Clensmore, near the Navigation public house, to work on the iron casting of heavy loom-sides and spike-rolls, all important parts for the company's own produced Wilton and Gripper looms.

Towards the end of my apprenticeship I moved into the drawing office where things were cleaner. The engineering fitters called our drawings "comics" and when we were out on a survey measuring up in the sheds we often were called "the Undertakers" - amongst other names!

One of the perks of the job was a day out at the Yorkshire Spinning Mills or the loom makers, also in Yorkshire. In the days before the motorways, the old Morris Oxford company car would wend its way to Buxton for bacon sandwiches and coffee, then on over Holme Moss and into the northern towns. On rare occasions I stopped the night at the George Hotel in Huddersfield. Otherwise it was the long flog back with a dinner break in Stone and home by midnight.

The carpet factory has its own language. There are cops and cordage; heals and heddles; lacings and lingos; combs and comber boards; shedding, harness and the good old jumbos. Individuals in the factory were known by nick names: "Sausage" had been a butcher; "Co-op" was a grocery delivery boy. Other names were more descriptive and not so kind!

I played tennis and table tennis for the company teams. I even made one appearance in a football team at Mullers (they were short and after the event I knew why). I never played again! All in all, my apprenticeship was good and I was grateful to those who helped me through those informative years in the 1950s at Carpet Trades in Mill Street.

All Square at the Cricket Ground

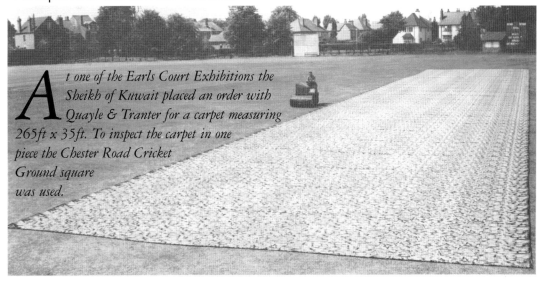

At one of the Earls Court Exhibitions the Sheikh of Kuwait placed an order with Quayle & Tranter for a carpet measuring 265ft x 35ft. To inspect the carpet in one piece the Chester Road Cricket Ground square was used.

Gilt Edge
'Canal Shed'
Face-to-Face

The Author's wife (nearest) picking a
carpet for the Queen at Brintons in 1957.

Gilt Edge
Narrow Jacquard
Face-to-Face

Around the Corner

And so, in the mid-1950s Kidderminster was a good place to live and work. The town was rich and prosperous, and in the carpet industry things had never been better. There was a general air of contentment.

Yet across the Atlantic the American engineers were not resting on <u>their</u> laurels! In Georgia, two brothers had developed a new carpet producing machine that had the potential to shake the foundations of the whole carpet industry. The word was around that the machine was so productive that it would spell the end of the weaving loom. It is ironical that about 100 years before, another American, Erastus Bigelow, had posed the same sort of threat to the industry with his power loom. The Kidderminster carpet masters ignored him. What would they do this time?

TUFTERS, TECHNOLOGY AND DECLINE. 1956 - 2000

The industry welcomes tufting but Kidderminster is cautious.
The town gets its first Tufter but the big boys plump for Kosset.
Tufting the pattern is a problem so they try printing the finished carpet.
The computer age makes its mark as the industry tightens its belt.
Mergers, failures and the inevitable redundancies decimate the carpet industry.

Chapter

5

The Advent of Tufting

The Cobble Brothers invent the Carpet Tufting Machine

In 1940 brothers Joe and Albert Cobble had a small engineering workshop in Dalton, Georgia, and it was there that they made parts for the first carpet tufting machine. The "Tufter" was erected in a local garage. Developments stopped during the war period but resumed immediately after. By 1946 they had produced a broadloom tufter at 5/8 inch gauge (pitch of the needles).

Like all good inventions, the basic concept is very simple and dates back to the Tudor period when poor folk made rugs by hand "podging" strips of rag or thick woollen yarns into a coarsely woven backing. American history records that in the colonial years Welsh immigrants to North America also made rugs in this way. But towards 1900 the principle had been adapted for bedspreads, bathmats and scatter rugs and the term "Candlewick" became the popular name.

The Candlewick industry built up around the town of Dalton where the Cobble brothers lived. Early products were hand made. However, in the 1930s, to satisfy an increasing demand, they successfully converted old single-needle sewing machines to speed up the operation. The single needles became multi-needles and they experimented with carpet yarns and so it was that the first generation of Carpet Tufting Machines came on to the market.

By 1950 the Cobble Brothers were producing these very basic machines at 9 feet and 12 feet width. True to form the engineers in the North of England immediately got interested. This time it was the Lancastrians.

The Tufting Process

In its simplest form, the principle involves a bank of needles secured in the "needle bar" which spans the width of the carpet. The needles are threaded with a continuous supply of yarns from bobbins on a creel. The needle bar reciprocates up and down at speed and the needles penetrate a pre-woven sheet of primary backing.

At the bottom of the needle stroke a "looper" catches the yarn and holds it down until the needle has withdrawn. In this way a loop is formed on the underside. The looper then releases in readiness for the next needle insertion and so on. The tuft can remain as a loop. Alternatively a knife mechanism working in conjunction with the looper cuts the end of the tuft. Therefore, the carpet can be either cut-pile or loop-pile in the style of Brussels.

113

The Pros and Cons of Tufting

Although the end product looks very similar on the floor the principles of tufting and weaving are very different.

The loom literally weaves the whole carpet securely binding the pile tufts in position with the backing yarns. Intricate multi-coloured patterns can be created with the aid of the Jacquard or the Spool. In comparison, the tufting process needs four elements to achieve the same result.

Firstly, the roll of "primary backing" material has to be produced. This is slightly wider than the finished carpet. In the early days a woven jute hessian was popular but in later years the man-made fibre industry produced many alternatives. Secondly, the Tufter produces the carpet as previously described. Because the yarn through the needle is continuous it is virtually impossible to change its colour on the run. Therefore, generally speaking, the carpet from the tufter is plain. Thirdly, on a large Backing Plant a "secondary backing" is stuck on to the underside to give the carpet some body and more importantly to lock the pile tufts in position. There are a variety of secondary backings which can be woven jute or man-made. At the cheaper end of the tufted market a latex foam is spread and cured instead of the secondary backing.

The fourth element is the pattern. The creation of the pattern is the one stumbling block that has ultimately stopped the tufting process from defeating the weaving loom. Later in this chapter reference will be made to some of the many attempts to recreate the multi-coloured patterns in the style of the woven Axminster.

The quality of a tufted carpet is determined by a number of criteria:
- The gauge of the needles, ie. the pitch of the needles in fractions of an inch.
- The depth of penetration of the needle through the primary backing, ie. pile height.
- The throughput speed of the primary backing in relation to the needle cycle, which determines the rows of tufts per inch in the warp direction.
- The quality of the pile yarn material, which can range from the best pure wools to the cheapest man-made fibres.

The major advantage of the tufting process is purely and simply the speed of the tufter. Today, the average broadloom Axminster loom can produce between 15 and 20 rows of weft-wise tufts per minute. A normal tufter can achieve over 1,000. There are many considerations which come into the final equation, including quality and efficiency. But considering all things it is a fact that the tufting process is significantly faster and more productive than weaving and it is therefore, cheaper.

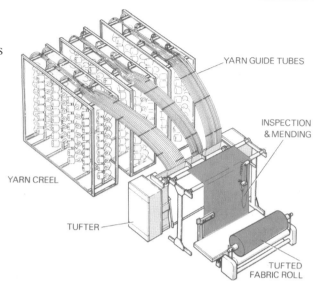

YARN GUIDE TUBES

INSPECTION & MENDING

YARN CREEL

TUFTER

TUFTED FABRIC ROLL

Tufting Comes to Blackburn

Stanley Shorrock and B.Mercer made British history when, in 1953, they formed British Tufting Machinery Limited in an old mill in Blackburn. The company became better known as BTM. They offered cut-pile or loop-pile tufters in 3/16 and 5/32 inch gauge and in widths of 5, 9 and 12 feet. The tufting machines came complete with the primary backing feed and a creel.

The business expanded. In 1956 BTM moved to larger premises and started to manufacture the long backing plants for applying secondary and foam backings. About the same time they took a licence to manufacture the Mohasco pattern attachment. These attachments provided very simple ways of creating a variation to the plain colour pile surface.

The Cobble Brothers also set up a company in Gate Street, Blackburn. In 1960, the mighty American Singer Group acquired an interest in Cobble and the company became Singer-Cobble Ltd. At the time, BTM were their main British competitor and so, in 1961, Singer-Cobble bought BTM.

The demand for tufters was growing, both in this country and in Europe. Soon the more ambitious employees of Singer-Cobble were leaving and forming their own companies: 1962 Ellison Tufting, 1964 Edgar Pickering and in 1966 the Universal Tufting Machinery Company or UTM. Blackburn was now firmly established as the centre of the European tufting machinery manufacturing industry. The developments in man-made fibres also helped the growth of the tufting industry. The fibres were stronger, slicker and ideally suited to the faster tufting operation. The tufter soon established a good reputation at the cheaper end of the market with plain and textured carpet to suit the wall-to-wall needs of the housing boom.

ellison
ELLISON TUFTING MACHINERY LTD.
Eclipse Mill, Feniscowles, Nr. Blackburn

Pattern Scan ... System!

COBBLE
Designs for Indu...

SINGER-COBBLE LTD.
GATE STREET   BLACKBURN   ENGLAND

COBBLE BROS. MACHINERY CO.
RIVERSIDE DRIVE • PHONE OX 8-3481 • CHATTANOOGA, TENN, U.S.A.
GATE STREET WORKS • BLACKBURN, LANCASHIRE, ENGLAND

Write for illustrated literature
Universal Tufting Machinery (Lancs) Ltd
George Street West, Blackburn, Lancashire
Telephone: 0254 53681 (3 lines)

EDGAR PICKERING [Blackburn] LIMITED
Whitebirk Drive : Blackburn : England. Tel: Blackburn 57811 (6 lines).
Telex: 63260. Cables: Pickering, Blackburn.

What about Kidderminster ?

Kidderminster was a weaving town steeped in history and tradition. The noises and smells of the carpet factory was part of life. Weaving was a craft handed down over many years. The weaving loom was an intricate piece of machinery. The Tufter was just "a big sewing machine!". More to the point, the industry was doing well and had never employed so many people. So, what was Kidderminster's reaction to this "new kid on the block" ?

You'll find Quality in The World of Kosset Carpets.

Kosset

KOSSET CARPETS LIMITED, BROOKFOOT, BRIGHOUSE, YORKSHIRE.

In those days the Kidderminster manufacturers were not gamblers when it came to big investment and they took a long and hard look at what was going on in Georgia and Blackburn.

A working party representing the town's larger companies went to America to assess the potential for Kidderminster's future.

They observed that the tufting factories were very different from the weaving sheds, not only in the style of machinery but also the skills needed on the shop floor. Therefore, to invest in tufting, the manufacturer needed capital to finance, not only the machinery, but also buildings and the necessary services. They needed a workforce with new skills that, ideally, were not governed by the restrictive practices of the weaving operation which had become part of the Union's demands.

With these factors in mind, Brintons, John Crossley-Carpet Trades Holdings, The Carpet Manufacturing Company and Templetons of Glasgow pooled their resources and in 1955 set up The Kosset Carpet Company at Brookfoot Mills in Brighouse, Yorkshire. T.Bond Worth were a little cautious and took a half share. In this way four major local carpet companies held a stake in this new developing tufting market without affecting the status-quo in Kidderminster.

The northern companies took a totally different view and made a considerable investment in tufting. Cyril Lord became a household name as he flooded the country with his direct-sale, cheap tufted carpet. Indirectly, this was good for the weavers because it clearly labelled "tufted" as cheap and of questionable quality.

The Empire Strikes First

But it was not only the big boys who were looking at tufting. In 1956 The Empire Carpet Company booked their place in local history and became the first Kidderminster company to install a tufter at their Foley Park factory. The new BTM tufter was 5/32 inch gauge, 12 feet wide and produced a cut-pile carpet.

Author's comment : My father knew the Griffin family, who owned Empire. He was given a quick look one Sunday morning just after the tufter was installed and he took me along. It was the first tufter I had ever seen and my lasting impression was the incredible speed at which the carpet was produced.

The Companies of the 1960s

The red Carpet Annual is a good reference book for the whole of the industry. It listed the companies, the agents, the suppliers and it provided good statistical data for carpet sales. The 1965 Carpet Annual gives us the following information:

The Kidderminster Carpet Companies

W. & R.R.Adam Ltd.	Green Hill Works
Brintons Limited	Exchange Street
Brockway Carpets Ltd.	Hoobrook
The Carpet Manufacturing Co. Ltd.	New Road
Carpet Trades Limited	Mill Street
Chlidema Carpet Co. Ltd.	Green Street
The Empire Carpet Co. Ltd.	Foley Park Works
Greatwich Ltd. (Spinners)	Clensmore
Hardwick & Austin Ltd.	Fair Street
William Hill (Kidderminster) Ltd.	Worcester Road
Jelleyman & Sons Ltd.	Townshend Works
The Minster Carpet Co. Ltd.	Orchard Street
Morris & Co (Kidderminster) Ltd.	Viaduct Works, Hoobrook
T. & A.Naylor Ltd.	Lowland Works, Green Street
Quayle & Tranter Ltd.	Franchise Street
Frank Stone (Kidderminster) Ltd.	Green Street
Tomkinsons Limited	Duke Street
The Victoria Carpet Co. Ltd.	Green Street
Woodward, Grosvenor & Co. Ltd.	Stour Vale Works
T.Bond Worth Ltd.	Severn Valley Mill, Stourport on Severn

Others - local or owned by the above.

Carpet Products Ltd.	Abercynon, Glamorgan
Carpet Weavers Ltd.	Lye, Stourbridge
Kosset Carpets Limited	Brighouse
I. & C.Steele & Co. Ltd.	Banbury
The Warwick Carpet Co. Ltd.	Warwick

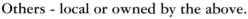

The main U.K. and Ireland competitors

Associated Weavers	Bradford	John Lyle & Co.	Glasgow
Axminster Carpets	Axminster	Hugh Mackay & Co.	Durham
Birstall Carpet Co.	Batley	A.F.Stoddard & Co.	Elderslie
Blackwood, Morton Co. (BMK)	Kilmarnock	James Templeton	Glasgow
T.F.Firth & Sons	Brighouse	H.Widnell & Stewart	Bonnyrigg
William Goodacre & Sons	Kendal	Wilton Royal	Wilton
William Gray & Sons	Ayr	Naven Carpets	Naven
Lancaster Carpets	Denton	Youghal Carpets	Cork

The Swinging Sixties

For those who worked on the shop floor the salesmen were seen as the elite. They had the palatial offices, the company car and the expense account. But in the sixties they earned their corn.

The postwar boom years produced some spectacular sales figures. CMC sold over a million square yards of their Axminster Globe quality "Skaters Trail". Carpet Trades did the same with "Goya" woven in Jasonia and Guildhall qualities. Brintons were one of the first to introduce the 80% wool 20% nylon blends with their Regina 82 Axminster. It was an instant success with "Watergrass", later, another big seller "Greensleeves" added Evlan to the blend in the Candia 442 quality.

Quayle & Tranter's beautiful deep pile Norsk rugs were in great demand and Woodward, Grosvenor, in 1966, reproduced the "Ardebil" design as a Wilton Grosvenor square. The original Ardebil, hand knotted in 1540, hangs in the Victoria & Albert Museum. One of the reproductions was presented to the County Museum at Hartlebury Castle where it takes pride of place near the entrance. Tomkinson's Royal Gobelin, Victoria's Super Argus, Bond Worth's Trio quality "Persian Garden" and Naylor's Translea all sold well adding to the company profits.

Goya design created by Heather Willis, winner of the Royal Society of Arts Carpet Bursary in 1962.

(Goya was a Spanish artist in the 18th century)

118

BY APPOINTMENT
TO HER MAJESTY THE QUEEN
CARPET MANUFACTURERS
THE CARPET MANUFACTURING COMPANY LTD.

GLOBE *Axminster*

Meriden *Wilton*

3C's *Wilton*

superb carpets by fine craft

Karan *Axminster*
Super *Wilton*
Vanessa *3-shot Wilton*
Kariba *Wilton squares*
Impney *3-shot Wilton*
Claverly *Wilton*
Pennant *plain Wilton*

CMC

showrooms

THE CARPET MANUFACTURING COMPANY
KIDDERMINSTER *Telephone 2271 (4 lines)*

LONDON 5 Newgate Street EC1
Telephone City 7911
MANCHESTER Clydesdale House
27 Turner St 4 *Deansgate 5271*
LEEDS 17 Wellington Street 1
Telephone Leeds 25613

GLASGOW 49 Queen Street C1
Telephone City 4794
SOUTHSEA 106 Palmerston Road
Telephone Portsmouth 24681
BRISTOL 68 Park Street
Telephone Bristol 28524

BROCKWAY'S

"KIDDERMINSTER" CARPETS
(guaranteed all-wool pile)

in *Wilton and Axminster*,
Squares, Rugs, piece goods

A . G . BROCKWAY LTD . KIDDERMINSTER
TELEPHONES: 4076-4077, 3728

Regina 82

REGINA 82
the new BRINTONS Axminster carpet range, gives *four times the wear of* an all wool carpet of equivalent quality. Regina 82 is a combination of *something old and something new.* 80% warm wool and . . . 20% strong, resilient BRI-NYLON.
That's how it gets its quite unique qualities—more resilience and longer life; more brilliant colours that remain faster to sunlight or cleaning; keeps clean longer because the backing contains stainless jute. Regina 82 is available as Body carpet—22½", 27" and 36" wide, Broadloom—7'6", 9'0" and 12'0" wide, all widths designed to lie together.

*Regd. Trade Mark of British Nylon Spinners Ltd.

REGINA 82
Gripper Woven Axminster is made by
BRINTONS LIMITED of KIDDERMINSTER
Makers of fine carpets since 1783
Showrooms: London, Manchester, Newcastle-on-Tyne, Glasgow, Bristol, Leeds, Cambridge(Dist. Centre.)   Agencies: In all parts of the world

Roulette
the latest
addition to
the **"NORSK"**
rya rug
collection

"NORSK"
RYA
Made in England

Quality
in **ABUNDANCE!**

CARPET
FRINGES
SOFT
FURNISHING
FRINGES
WILTON
AND
HAIRCORD
CARPET
F.S.K.

Manufactured by
FRANK STONE
(Kidderminster) LTD.
Phone 2177   'Grams 'Stone,Kidderminster'

ROYAL GO...
IMPERIAL
PIECE GOODS

ROYAL GOBELIN
KLEITOS & BOUDOIR BROADLOOM
KLEITOS SQUARES

Imperial and Rite Rugs
Anglo-Persian &
Anglo-Smyrna Carpets.

TOMKINSONS
LIMITED
P.O. BOX No. 11, KIDDERMINSTER
WORCS.

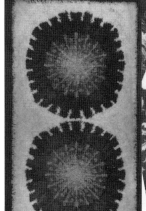

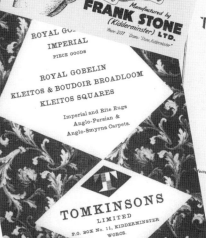

T. & A. NAYLOR LIMITED
KIDDERMINSTER

Telephone:
KIDDERMINSTER 2261 & 2262
Telegraphic Address:
"NAYLOR, KIDDERMINSTER"

LONDON OFFICE:
19/20, OLD BAILEY, E.C.4
Telephone: City 2445/6

...facturers
of

"ROYLAN", "NAYLON" & "BULWARK"
Axminster Broadloom and Body

"TANSLEA"
Axminster Broadloom and Squares

"LORAYN"
Axminster Broadloom, Body and Stair

"TANKARA"
Axminster Body and Stair

"TANSMERE"
Rugs, Sofas and Corridors

Candia 442 'Greensleeves'
designed by David Seager

Thomas Bond Worth
AND SONS LIMITED
MANUFACTURERS OF

High Grade Carpets

Spool Axminster Seamless Squares, Piece Goods and Rugs.
Wilton Seamless Squares, Piece Goods and Rugs. Chenille
Axminster Seamless Squares.

Overseas Representatives

MEXICO. Allied National Corporation Ltd., Anco House, Buckingham Gate, London. S.W.1. SOUTH AFRICA, Atkinson & Joscelyne (Pty.) Ltd., 301 Birmingham House, 108 President St., Johannesburg. Atkinson & Joscelyne Buildings, 32 ...

Greig Bros. (Agencies) Pty. Ltd., 1st Floor, Brisbane Arcade, Queen Street, Brisbane. MAURITIUS Mercantile Bureau, 5 Box 24, Port-Louis. Ltd., Cambrian Buildings, Nairobi. ... 167 Mgr. Hoyek ... 34a, ... kirkegaten 32, Oslo. 116 Main Street, P.O. Box 1471.

DISTINCTIVE CARPETS

- Grosvenor and Kemnor seamless
- Wilton squares and Rugs
- Grosvenor Broadloom
- Grovax
- Grovax Broadloom
- Imperial, Gobelins and Aubusson piece goods
- Wilton piece goods

Seamless Axminster squares and Rugs

THE ABOVE ARE ALL-WOOL PILE. MIXTURE PILE ALSO AVAILABLE

Woodward, Grosvenor

& Company Limited Kidderminster Telephone 2202

SHOWROOMS: LONDON: 2-4 Little Britain E.C.1. MANCHESTER: Clydesdale House 27 Turner Street. LEEDS: 8 York Place. NEWCASTLE: Room 6 Dial House Northumberland Street. GLASGOW: Mackenzie Bros. 200 St. Vincent Street C.2.

MORRIS Carpets

WILTON PL...
FIGUREL...

Agents at

...ALIA: Bottomley Bros. Pty. ... Lane, Melbourne. Bottomley ... 4-156 Clarence Street, Sydney.

...EALAND: Bottomley Bros. (N ... G. Buildings, Elliott St., Auck...

...SIA: J. W. Stratton (Agencie ... Box 2392, Salisbury.

Det Norske Oceankompa... Oslo.

...vitex, Klara, Norra, Kyrko... C.

Wilh. Hansen, Osterbrog...

Ypsilantis, P.O. Box N...

Reissman, 64 Wellingto...

...ice, 41 Donegall Place

MANUFACTURERS of
Axminster Broadloom Body, Squares
and Rugs

MINSTER
CARPET COMPANY LTD.

FIGURED AND PLAIN WILTONS
SEAMLESS AXMINSTER SQUARES
9ft. AND 12ft. BROADLOOM
3/4 AND 4/4 RUGS AND BODY
ALL WOOL
ALL ARE MOTHPROOFED

of orchard street
kidderminster

Manufacturers of
WILTON &
AXMINSTER
CARPETS

The CHLIDEMA CARPET Co.LTD

ESTABLISHED 1807

Retail Representation,
19 & 20 Old Bailey, E.C.4 City 2445-6
London Wholesale and Export,
4, Snow Hill, E.C.1 Central 8334

KIDDERMINSTER
Telephone: 3435 & 3436

Everybody loves a Kosset carpet!

Kosset carpets have become the most popular branded carpets in Britain. Their outstanding quality, wealth of beautiful plain colours, mixtures and patterns, and excellent value at every price level please both the trade and the public.

For the latest information write to: Kosset

Behind Kosset Carpets Limited:
Brintons Limited
The Carpet Manufacturing Company Limited
John Crossley Carpet Trades Holdings Limited
James Templeton and Co. Limited
T. Bond Worth and Sons Limited
Carpets, Brookfoot, Brighouse, Yorks.

Design No. 28/225 - Gold/Green Aubasson - also in Fawn/Blue & Fawn/Pink

W. & R. R. ADAM LIMITED
GREENHILL WORKS · KIDDERMINSTER · ENGLAND

The Industrial Chaplains

The Bishop of Worcester, Robin Wood, was a great believer in bringing the Christian message to the workplace. To this end the Kidderminster Industrial Chaplaincy was formed in 1959 with Roger Howes as the first Industrial Chaplain. "Jolly Roger" was an instant success in the factories and the public houses of the town which he referred to as "his Church". His booming voice could be heard the length of the picking room.

A number of other well-respected chaplains followed but in 1978 the town gained another character in the form of Bill Hopley. Bill was a lad about town. A keen sportsman, he became a good friend to the industry. He was featured in the 1983 BBC Songs of Praise television production filmed at St.Mary's Church and Brinton's Carpet factory.

Author's Note - The work of the Industrial Chaplains was co-ordinated through a committee representing all the town's companies. I represented Carpets International on that committee for many years. For a time Kidderminster's Churches were sponsors of a Youth Training Scheme (YTS) housed in the Youth Centre.

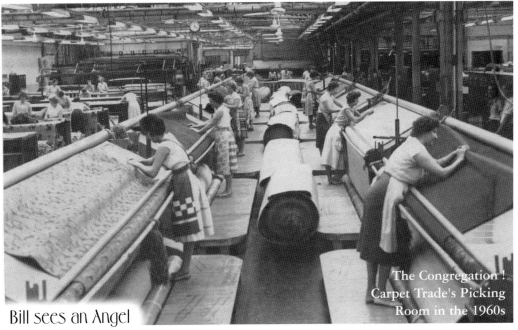

The Congregation !
Carpet Trade's Picking
Room in the 1960s

Bill sees an Angel

Bill Hopley ultimately became Chaplain to the Birmingham Police Force but he retained special memories of his time in the Kidderminster Carpet industry. He regarded it as a privilege to work in the factories and meet the workforce, management and directors on what he called a "level playing field". But the playing field he likes to remember most is Twickenham, where he was entertained to a boozy day out with one of the companies.

They had plum seats down at the front. The Rugby was good but the highlight of the day was the appearance of streaker Erika Roe in her well-reported and photographed dash across the field. Bill told the story many times "She was a big girl and truly an Angel on the Field ! ".

The Manufacturers Spend the Profit

The boom period of the postwar years continued well into the sixties with most companies ploughing some of the profit back into the business. Brintons accelerated their loom building programme, put their money into an Australian factory in Geelong and started to plan factories on the Stourport Road. Tomkinsons expanded into Wilton with the acquisition of the Banbury company I.& C.Steele. They also started to think about new offices. In 1963 Bond Worth, now under the direction of Dr Murray, bought the Townshend Works and Jelleymans amongst other companies. The Carpet Manufacturing Company set up the Debron process at their Bridgnorth factory, while Carpet Trades continued to expand their Mill Street operation which included an impressive new three-storey office block.

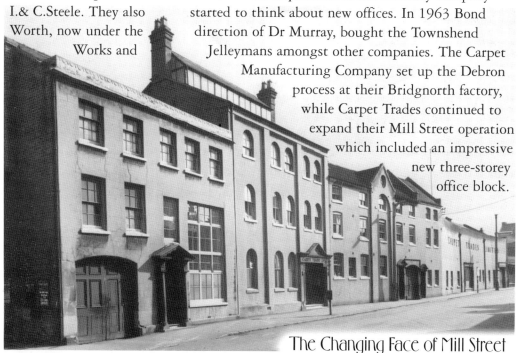

The Changing Face of Mill Street

Mill Street was to carpets what Fleet Street was to the newspaper industry. Long before the canal was built many of the town's principle companies lined the appropriately named street with their houses, offices and show rooms at the front and their weaving sheds and dyehouses, on the river, at the rear. Before the power loom, the Lea family, Richard Smith, Edward Hughes, James Humphries and even William Brinton traded from premises in Mill Street.

But, one by one they were taken over or moved to other parts of town until there were only the companies of Edward Hughes and James Humphries remaining, they had become Carpet Trades in 1920.

Carpet Trades was one of the town's largest companies. It occupied 37 acres of land between Mill Street and a boundary formed by the canal and the river. Just after the Second World War they even diverted part of the river to release more land for production sheds.

The offices and showrooms fronted Mill Street. For many years one of the landmarks of the town was the very large "picture window" which so prominently faced the road junction where Park Butts joined Mill Street.

The window was a prize advertising location and Carpet Trades missed no opportunity to display their best designs and rugs to good effect. In 1961 John Mellor, their Director of Design, organised an International Design Competition and the winning designs were proudly displayed in the window for all to see.

Sadly, in 1962, the picture window was literally shattered as the bulldozers moved in to demolish the old frontage and make way for a state-of-the-art new Administrative Block. The building quickly became a landmark in its own right if only for the modern design and the prominent 62-feet - high clock tower which was faced with Serpentino Santa Maria Italian Black Marble slabs. But little did the company, or the town, know that this prestigious building would stand for less than 30 years, considerably less than the jumble of frontages it replaced including the famous picture window. Details are given later.

1963 Statistics Tell a Story

Kidderminster was still a weaving town. However, in the north, investment in Tufting appeared to be paying off as vast quantities of tufted carpet were sold in the market place. The town's main stake in this business was Kosset. A survey by The Carpet Annual gives a good indication of the growth of tufting:

UK Production in 1963	sq.yds	£ /sq.yd
Wool Pile Gripper and Spool Axminsters	30,033,000	1.64
Wool Pile Wiltons	9,670,000	2.21
Chenille, Tapestry and Hair carpets	827,000	1.77
Tufted.carpets, mainly plain and textured surfaces	27,000,000	0.89

Note: The costs given above are the ex-works production costs. The 1962 figure for tufted carpet was 15,000,000 square yards which means that production nearly doubled in the following year!

The Tufter is here to stay

The writing was on the wall for all to see and some of the Kidderminster companies who were not involved with Kosset took immediate action. Following the lead given by Empire, Victoria bought their first tufter in 1956 and after successful trials made plans for their Worcester Road tufting factory which opened in 1963. In 1964 Tomkinsons introduced their tufted products under the banner of Ludlow Carpets and in the same year Bond Worth pulled out of the Kosset consortium and bought a tufting company in the north of England.

In the following years other companies invested in the new technology; Naylors 1965, Quayle Carpets 1965, Greatwich-Georgian 1966, W. & R.R.Adam 1970 and

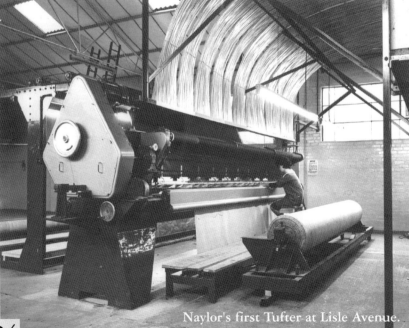

Naylor's first Tufter at Lisle Avenue.

Brockways soon afterward. New technology replaced old as Naylors broke up the last chenille looms in town to make way for the tufters. During 1961 Tomkinsons scrapped their unique French Renard knotting looms for the same reason.

QRY Year

Q uality and Reliability Year started in 1967. It was a time when the whole industry pulled up its socks.

Is in Quality YOUR Hands

THIS IS NOT THE END, BUT THE BEGINNING!

Everybody got involved with the many projects, committees and competitions. The suggestion schemes for reward brought some interesting and novel ideas. Not all of them were practical.

Approaching the 1970s - A Time for Change !

C arpet Trades became Gilt Edge in 1967. However, totally against the trend, The Empire Carpet Company called in the receivers, while Chlidema bought their Beauchamp Avenue factory and the equipment.

While most companies had a finger in the tufting pie in one way or another Brintons took what seemed to be an unusual step by selling their interest in Kosset. This action demonstrated their faith in their own engineering skills to develop faster and more productive weaving looms. They were effectively committing themselves to a smaller sector at the upper end of the woven market. Meanwhile, in 1969 Tomkinsons set up Mid-Wales Yarns as their spinning company.

The big event of the year, however, involved two of the town's establishment companies. Over the years Kosset had not been as successful as many might have imagined, probably because it was owned by a consortium with too many cooks in the kitchen. Brintons withdrawal actually left John Crossley-Carpet Trades Holdings and The Carpet Manufacturing Company as the only remaining stakeholders. In 1969 these two merged to form Europe's largest carpet manufacturing group which they called Carpets International Ltd. If the earlier men with vision, Harvey Preen and Herbert Smith, had been alive at the time they would surely have cracked open a bottle of champagne in celebration of a dream come true.

Carpets International was large with many factories in Kidderminster, Bridgnorth, Halifax and other parts of Yorkshire including Kosset in Brighouse. They also owned established companies in Commonwealth countries. In the following years they set up enterprises in developing countries using the technical expertise of their own staff and some of the looms and equipment from the town's factories, a fact that did not go unnoticed at the Union Headquarters in Callows Lane.

Yet all in all Kidderminster was still on course. The companies had invested and there was a good feeling amongst the many employees still passing through the factory gates. The industry was fighting fit as it entered the seventies.

125

The Seventies and the Carpet Printers

Non-Wovens and Carpet Tiles

The oil crisis of 1972 started a rise in production costs and the carpet industry again felt uncertain about its future. With the accent on quality and durability the industry examined a number of alternative floorcoverings based on the principle of sticking precut tufts of yarn on to a primary backing material coated with an adhesive.

Two local companies were particularly successful in this field. The Carpet Manufacturing Company had their "pleated" Debron product and Bond Worth developed and patented the Bondax Process. Bondax was novel since it had the same pattern potential as the woven carpet using the Spool or Jacquard system.

There were other techniques. For example, Gilt Edge introduced Endura in 1968. Endura was a hard wearing synthetic needle-punch material which was used extensively for sports surfaces including the football pitches which had a degree of popularity at the time. Some companies also wove green polypropylene artificial grass for pitches. Collectively, these alternative floor coverings were called "non-wovens" and in general their sales became restricted to the contract market.

The use of PVC as a hard backing promoted the development of carpet tiles. These proved to be very popular with the growing computer market which needed quick access to the mass of underfloor wires. Most of the larger companies experimented by converting their standard woven ranges into tiles. Not all were successful.

Patterned Tufting

Competition between the weavers and the tufters remained with the woven sector continuing to dominate the quality end of the market. Up to this time the tufters had failed to reproduce the intricate designs of Axminster. Still determined no matter what the cost, they invested in a number of developments designed to solve the problem once and for all. Two early attempts involving Kidderminster companies reflect the thinking logic of the day.

Firstly, in 1973 Tomkinsons built a new factory in Clensmore Street and set up a subsidiary company called St.Mary's Carpets. There they installed a state of the art warp printing system called the Crawford-Pickering Process which was manufactured and marketed by Edgar Pickering's tufting company in Blackburn. The process recreated the obsolete Tapestry principle where printed beams of yarn were produced prior to the tufting operation. It was an involved system using dye-saturated pads to print the individual sections as the multi-bank of yarns travelled through the machine. The patterned product was good but the process contained insurmountable technical problems and was eventually withdrawn. Carpets International had a similar plant at their Kosset factory but the problems were inherent to the design and it also failed.

Carpets International were also involved in the second development which linked them with the Ellison Tufting Machinery Company in an idea conceived by pioneer Stanley Shorrock. The process was nicknamed the "Blackburn Rivet".

126

A special tufter was built with hollow needles and a huge creel containing eight sets of colours. A mechanism selected a colour and fed the yarn forward by one tuft length. The tuft was cut and blown down a tube and into the needle at the point of insertion into the primary backing. On withdrawal of the needle the single tuft remained in the backing like a rivet, hence the nickname. Again the development was dogged with technical problems and eventually ran out of money.

The potential of this equipment was sufficient to worry the large Spool Axminster loom maker Platt Bros. of Oldham and so they bought into the development and for a while continued the work. Eventually the Platt-Ellison partnership ceased production. The whole development was scrapped just before it was due to be installed in the Mill Street weaving sheds. These two developments demonstrated the tufting industry's determination to pattern the product and although they failed, they did provide valuable experience and a pointer to the next course of action.

The Shaky Seventies

Woodward, Grosvenor had, in recent years, been associated with Grays of Ayr and in 1970 the two companies became part of British Carpets Ltd., which was controlled by the giant Guthrie Corporation. As part of a programme of rationalisation the company consolidated all production in Stour Vale Mill and sold the historic Worcester Cross Factory to the Town Council.

At the same time Chlidema vacated their Green Street Mill and moved to the old Empire factory in Foley Park. Two new companies started up with Chanter Carpets in Alveley and David Bayliss on the Sandy Lane Estate in Stourport.

Although the industry was still buoyant there was an air of uncertainty around and perhaps this was the reason for the Union to record its highest membership ever at 6,683. The uncertainty became a reality and by the mid-1970s the recession was getting a firm grip on the carpet industry. Medium-sized companies seemed to come off worse and we saw the demise of four well-known names in the town: 1976 T. & A.Naylor, 1978 Morris Carpets, which, at the time were known as Morris-Gloucester under the ownership of the Irish company Youghal, 1979 Quayle Carpets who were closely followed by Chlidema.

Smaller companies also suffered. 1979 was the end of the road for the Oldington Trading Estate based P.J.Hopkins which started in Green Street in the 1950s. Around this time Bond Worth was in trouble and, after a period in receivership, they were bought by a consortium of Middle Eastern businessmen. Greatwich-Georgian became part of the Bowater Corporation together with Minster Carpets which had earlier taken over Spilsbury & Wilcox. William Hill's factory on the Worcester Road also ceased operations.

The changes and failures were a warning to the industry. The surviving companies started to retrench and consolidate. Many more jobs were lost during this period. For a while the looms stood idle in the empty unheated factories. However, a few brave employees took the opportunity to have a go and start up on their own.

Changing Industry - Changing Town

With the population nearing 50,000 the sixties and seventies was a time of change all round. Kidderminster was a very prosperous town and so, in keeping with a national trend, it felt the need to "modernise".

For many years the traffic travelling through the town centre was controlled by a policeman who stood at the bottom of High Street sheltered from wind and rain by a concrete "pulpit". In 1962 he waved his arms for the last time and the pulpit was demolished. This action started a town-centre redevelopment programme that appears to have been going on ever since.

It was sad to see the first of the old historic carpet mills of the Industrial Revolution being demolished. These included Pike Mills, New Road (1968), Imperial Mill in Mill Street (1976) and the Park Wharf Mill buildings in Park Butts (1980). The town centre, itself, went through a period of upheaval with the transfer of the Cattle Market from Market Street to a new site at the top of Comberton Hill. This was followed by the gradual construction of the ring road in a number of phases.

An out-of-character Crown House was built. The old Victorian indoor market was lost to the bulldozers as the town gained the Swan and later the Rowland Hill Shopping Centres. Three multi-storey carparks provided the parking spaces. Woodward, Grosvenor's old Worcester Cross Offices became the Law Courts and the weaving sheds at the rear were transformed into an indoor market.

However, although the lost mills were significant, the town retained its carpet factory image. A walk down Green Street, Mill Street, Corporation Street or along the canal towpath would confirm the fact. In summer, through the open windows and the half-open doors the clatter of the looms could be heard. The distinguishing smell from the dyehouses and the timely sounding of Brinton's Bull was a constant reminder that Kidderminster was still a carpet town!

The Tufters get printing

The Crawford-Pickering and the Blackburn Rivet had fallen by the wayside and so the industry turned its attention to printing the pile surface of the plain tufted carpet. The European cloth print-line manufacturers modified and adapted their flat-bed and rotary-screen printers for the carpet industry. These were large and costly machines requiring very special steam, water and drainage facilities. Furthermore, each individual pattern needed a set of delicate and expensive screens. These lines were really intended for the bulk producers. A number were installed in the north of England and other centres but none in Kidderminster.

However, there were alternatives and, in the late 1970s, two local companies tested the water. Victoria opted for the smaller well-tried Stalwart Printer at their Green Street factory. But Carpets International put their faith in an Austrian engineer from Kufstein called Peter Zimmer. He was pioneering a totally new concept which he called The Chromotronic Jet Printer.

Screen printing had an inherent problem of pile deformation and the "bleeding" of dyes where the screens contacted the pile surface of the carpet. However, Zimmer's Chromotronic was designed to eliminate these problems. A plate containing a number of jets passed over the surface of the carpet without physical contact. The jets, containing fluid dyes under pressure, opened and closed on the instruction of a master computer which was programmed for the pattern. Eight colours could be printed at four metres width. At 400 feet (122 metres) in length Chromotronic was one of the longest continuous production lines in the industry.

The multi-million pounds investment was a "first for the industry" and Carpets International chose to install it at their Mill Street site during the late 1970s. It was big investment with building extensions and the purchase of the first tufters for CI's Southern Division. Chromotronic had considerable problems that had to be solved on the run. Eventually though, it produced many of miles of printed carpet. The print definition was significantly better than the screen printers but, again, not good enough to worry the Axminster woven market.

In 1987, with the company in the throes of change, the line was decommissioned, broken up and sold at scrap value, less than ten years after it was built.

In the following years the American tufting machinery manufacturers turned their attentions back to the tufter. A number of developments followed all designed to directly tuft a pattern at the production stage. The simpler tufters created small geometric patterns by sliding the needle bar sideways; the more advanced tufters established ways of changing the coloured yarn ends in the needle.

Ironically, these variations have significantly slowed down the production rate to the point where output is not much more than that of the faster weaving looms! Some of these advanced tufters have been installed in Kidderminster.

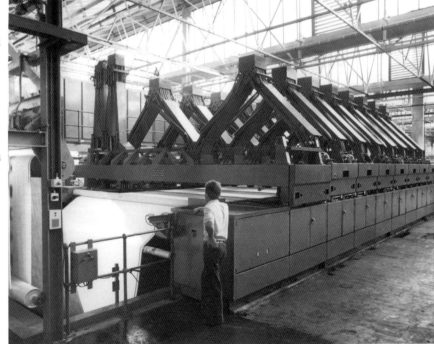

The Zimmer Chromotronic Jet Carpet Printer.

129

1980s Mergers, Takeovers, Rationalisation and Failures

Trading in the eighties was difficult as the imports continued to adversely affect the industry. The glut of American imports of the 1970s had been superseded by a predominance from our European neighbour, Belgium.

Most companies were finding it difficult to break even. Some of the larger companies were content to trade in the red for a while in order to weather the storm. It became a boom time for the management consultants who were set loose on a very suspicious workforce. The failures of the 1970s had halved the Union membership.

In 1982 Woodward, Grosvenor changed hands as a group of managers became the owners. Two years later Melton-Meades bought the Clensmore mills and factories of Greatwich and Georgian. The mighty Carpets International was sold to the John Crowther Group in 1985 and in 1988 it changed hands again becoming part of John Ashcroft's Coloroll empire. After two years of good investment at Mill Street the company was ready for the future challenge but John Ashcroft had overstepped the mark and, in June 1990, the receivers were called in. The quest for a buyer was fruitless and so the gates were finally closed early in 1991. This was a major blow to the town with the loss 1,100 jobs including another 890 Union members.

The foundations of the Kidderminster carpet industry started in Mill Street and near-by Church Street and Vicar Street. Mill Street, therefore, became the last of the trio to sever its connection with the carpet industry when Coloroll closed. Good production equipment left the factory on the low-loaders bound for the north and developing companies abroad, these are potentially the town's real competition! The landmark office block, with its marble tower, was demolished in 1993 together with the weaving sheds and warehouses as manufacturing reluctantly gave way to the superstores. And so began the construction of Crossley Retail Park.

Author's comment - I have remarked earlier that the Halifax name of the Crossley family keeps managing to influence Kidderminster. Would it not have been more in keeping with the historical background of the site to have chosen a suitable local name?

Computers in Design Studios, Dyehouses and Sales

With a greater proportion of the market share now available the surviving companies realised they had to embrace the rapidly developing computer technology to remain efficient. Computers were common place in the company offices but it was not until the seventies that they were commercially available to recognise colour. This was a big step forward and, in the following years, it revolutionised the design studio, the dyehouse office and, ultimately, proved to be a valuable asset to the salesman on the road.

In the larger companies the nineties design studio became like any other office. Gone were the rows of designer's boards and in their place was the computer. In a complete reversal of needs these terminals are shielded from the natural light!

Architect's sketches could be instantly scanned and turned into the design format for discussion. Colours could be changed at the touch of a button. The old design papers were photographed and stored in a central computer library. In this way the customer could very quickly see a full range of possibilities.

The close relationship between the design studio and the dyehouse became a thing of the past as the dyehouse office was rearranged to house its own computer. The dyeing sequence was controlled by computer and the final colour was no longer passed by the "dyer" using the standard "tuft box" and his many years of experience.

The travelling salesmen were issued with "lap-tops" to show the customer what the company had to offer. These techniques were particularly suited to the contract market where the sales force needed to convince architects and interior designers. A declining home trade had prompted the larger companies to extend their effort in

the export contract market. The well-trodden decks of the cruise liners and continuous pounding of agitated feet on the floors of the casinos of Las Vegas provided good business for the weaving looms of Kidderminster.

Big Brother and the EJ.

The use of computers grew rapidly and from the mid-90s onwards they became part of the furniture on the shop floor. Looms were fitted with monitoring systems. These sophisticated systems allowed the company to remotely monitor the production of each loom and to analyse the reason for stoppages and delays. Management could now, instantly, assess the performance of loom, the materials not to mention the weaver.

The value of the computer was also recognised by the equipment manufacturers. Traditional Jacquards have been part of the loom since 1825 but towards the end of the 90s the electronic Jacquard became available. The "EJ" was fitted directly to the loom where it replaced the old pattern-card selection system. It was quicker to programme and it eliminated the laborious card stamping operation and the space consuming pattern-card stores.

In both weaving and the tufting sectors of the carpet industry the computer was well and truly gaining control.

Towards The Millennium

At the start of the 1990s things were a little more settled as the industry surveyed what was left and set about a recovery. The number of employees working in carpets had dropped drastically and the carpet industry was still losing much of its history. The loss of the historic Mill Street weaving sheds was closely followed by the demolition of the Library and School of Science and Art.

Brintons and Victoria began to look closely at their ageing town-centre factories. The river and the canal were no longer needed and the jumble of buildings were expensive to maintain and inadequate for the needs of a modern carpet factory. Thus, following the lead given at Crossley Park, the developers became hungry for more. Perhaps it was inevitable that both companies would grasp the opportunity to sell up and consolidate their business away from the town centre.

Victoria made plans to transfer their Green Street business to the Worcester Road factory. This involved the building of a new dyehouse, further building extensions at the rear and new offices at the front. The company also planned to vacate their Wilton section which was housed in the former Castle Road Motors factory.

Over the years Brintons has become an international company and part of their production has been transferred to Portugal and a new factory in India. The remaining equipment was relocated at the Telford and Stourport Road factories. In 1998 they bought U.S.Axminster Inc. of Greenville, Mississippi. The origins of this company date back to Alexander Smith and Halcyon Skinner.

Carpets of Worth were also cutting back at their Stourport factory with some of the equipment transferred abroad and to their Kidderminster factory in Puxton. Tomkinsons joined forces with the Lancashire based company Gaskells and the last spinning mill closed as the old established Greatwich Company sold up in 1999.

The late 1990s were depressing times as the companies and their equipment moved out. The whole situation was summarised at noon on the 18th March 1999 when Michael Brinton pulled the lever to signal three final blasts of Brinton's Bull.

The Crompton Looms at Park Wharf

Sultana is the Fruit of the Much-Travelled Looms

One small item of good news for the area involved Richard Smith's 100-years-old Crompton Looms. In 1997 the Sultana Carpet Company was set up on the Sandy Lane Industrial Estate in Stourport. Sultana being the trade name of a high quality deep-pile Spool Axminster product marketed only in narrow widths to designs that date back to the 19th century. The "Crompton" looms on which the carpet is woven form an important part of the town's carpet history.

In the late 1880s American loom manufacturer Crompton & Knowles of Worcester, Massachusetts, patented the looms and granted a license to Kidderminster's Richard Smith & Sons. They installed a plant of looms at their Park Wharf factory. During the last 100 years these looms have had a charmed life. They have been bought and sold a number of times, each time involving a major transfer of location. They first wove in Kidderminster and have ended up in Stourport but the journeys in between make a good story.

The first journey involved the delivery of the looms from Massachusetts to the Park Wharf factory in Kidderminster. Licenses were also granted to other companies including John Crossley & Sons of Dean Clough Mills in Halifax. It was Crossleys who introduced the quality known as Sultana. Richard Smith & Sons became part of The Carpet Manufacturing Company and at some time ceased production on the Crompton looms. The looms were sold to Crossleys, and so, in a second journey the looms travelled north to Halifax.

In 1969 The Carpet Manufacturing Company joined forces with John Crossley-Carpet Trades Holdings to become Carpets International. In 1982 a major restructure of the group saw the closure of the weaving sheds at Dean Clough. However, Sultana was still a viable product and so, when Dean Clough closed, the looms made their third journey from Halifax back to Kidderminster.

The looms were installed at the Mill Street factory which was just over the road from Park Wharf where they started their working life. Carpets International became Crowthers then Coloroll. In 1990 when Coloroll failed the looms were bought as part of a northern management buy-out. And so they were travelling north yet again, this time up the motorway to a new Kosset company in Bradford. This was their fourth journey, but not the last!

The Bradford company was sold to the American group Shaw Carpets who, in 1996, decided to sell all their Axminster plant. A consortium of local businessmen got together, formed the Sultana Carpet Company and bought the looms. Back down the motorway came the Crompton Looms, this was their fifth journey.

At the Millennium the much travelled looms were still in good working order weaving the Sultana product.

133

The 1999 Yellow Pages List the Companies as follows:

Adam Carpets, Birmingham Road
Brintons, Exchange Street
Brockway Carpets, Hoobrook
C.P.Carpets, Green Street
Carpets of Kidderminster, Wilden
Carpets of Worth, Severn Valley Mill
Contract Carpet Weavers, Green Street
Enterprise Weaving Co., Firs Ind. Est.
Georgian, Goodacre, Clensmore

Master Weavers, Franchise Street
Frank Stone, Green Street
The Sultana Carpet, Stourport
Tomkinsons Carpets, Duke Place
Traditional Weavers, Beauchamp Ave.
Valetta Carpets, Lisle Avenue
Victoria Carpets, Green Street
Woodward, Grosvenor, Stour Vale
Saxon Carpets, Wilden Lane

The British Carpet Manufacturers Association, Castle Mill, New Road.
The Power Loom Carpet Weavers & Textile Workers Union, Hurcott Road.

Woven or Tufted - The Debate Continues

It is an historical and statistical fact that the tufter won the production volume battle against the weaving loom. In most retail shops today there is a predominance of tufted carpet. Unfortunately, a lot of it is imported! The American carpet industry rather jumped the gun when, in the 1950s and 60s the majority of their weaving plant was scrapped in favour of the tufter. We were not so hasty in this country, especially in Kidderminster.

The town has always regarded itself as, first and foremost, a weaving town. The local newspaper is named after the weaver's shuttle and the Union is generally referred to as the "Weavers Union" or more correctly the "Power Loom Carpet Weavers Union". The early masters may have been reluctant to adopt the power loom but over the years their successors have been slow to let go!

Brintons and Woodward, Grosvenor are profitable and they only have a weaving plant. Their decision to concentrate on the loom has paid off. On the other side of the coin companies like Victoria and Tomkinsons have successfully mixed the two.

The real issues have been debated earlier in this chapter with the examination of the tufting industry's attempts to create a pattern with the definition and quality of a woven carpet. Had they been successful things would have been very different. Perhaps it was not by chance or good salesmanship that the architects selected a Kidderminster woven for the cruise-ship Oriana; the arduous traffic of Terminal Four at Heathrow or the largest order in history, Hong Kong's new Chek Lap Kok airport. These applications are ideally suited to the weaving process and the skills of the town.

And so, to summarise, until an alternative floorcovering comes along to challenge the carpet industry both the tufters and the weavers have established their position in the market place.

Millennium Roundup

During the final decade before the Millennium the heart went out of the industry as more than a thousand people trained for the carpet factories had to adopt new skills; many took early retirement. The industry as a whole had suffered, even the National Joint Committee, set up after the Second World War, was disbanded in 1992. The NJC had for many years provided a yardstick for pay rises in the town. What remained of the textile department of Kidderminster's College on Hoo Road took the final blow as it lost the successful and prestigious B.A.(Hons) Design for Floorcoverings & Interior Textiles course.

Around the town centre the sights and sounds of the carpet industry have gone. The walk along Mill Street, Corporation Street and Green Street tells a totally different story from what it did ten years ago. Brinton's town centre factory is empty and boarded up awaiting the developers. Victoria are busy moving their equipment out of the Green Street site that has been their home for 100 years and Rowe Carpets and the industry at the Lowland Trading Estate are preparing to vacate. At Clensmore Mill the Greatwich spinning equipment is for sale and the Union, with a membership of less than 2,000, now has its offices in Hurcott Road.

Yet the town still has a thriving carpet industry, the establishment names of Brinton, Tomkinson, Victoria, Adam, Worth, Brockway and Woodward, Grosvenor together with others continue to play an important part in the town's economy.

The river and the canal have long since lost their usefulness to an industry that could not have been established and flourished without them. However, the town still has a few of the old mills left to tell the tale. At the moment the Piano Building is to be saved from the bulldozer, Stour Vale stands unscathed at the top of Green Street and the New Road Mills of Victoria are for sale. On the canal side, Lea's Slingfield Mill is a listed building and will remain. But what a different view Thomas Lea would have were he able again to climb to the top of the square boilerhouse chimney to survey his mill and the town.

The surviving hand loom-shops of the Horsefair and Mount Skipet serve as a reminder of the town's heritage. The carpet industry, started over 250 years ago by John Pearsall and John Broom has had a chequered history. Over the years the message seems to have been that change is inevitable. Every time the industry settled down to a period of stability something happened to upset the apple cart.

And so, I sincerely hope you have enjoyed the read. I am sure you will be in no doubt about my feelings for the town and its carpet history and I can think of no better way to end than to quote a modified version of the old 1886 weaver's toast:

" May the trade of Kidderminster <u>continue</u> to be trodden under the feet of all nations " Cheers !

Meanwhile the Carpet Museum Trust, under the leadership of Richard Pugh-Cook and Charles Talbot, are working hard to preserve some of the treasures for a Museum of the Carpet Industry in one of the historic old carpet factories in the town centre.

Chapter 6

COMPANY REVIEW.

This chapter briefly reviews the carpet companies in Kidderminster together with those in Stourport, Bridgnorth, Bewdley and the West Midlands.

Acknowledgement

Research into the history of the many companies has been very time consuming and I am grateful to a number of people who gave me free access to their own documents and experience.

In particular to Peter Legat who, a few years ago, chose to study the Kidderminster carpet industry for a college course. His research resulted in the production of an extensive document which is retained in the Kidderminster Reference Library. Considering that Peter had not worked in the industry his understanding of the subject was remarkable and I am grateful to him for allowing me to use his work as the starting point for my own research.

Brinton's archives and the research of their former archivist Jack Smith provided a lot of detail. From the industry, the BCMA, the Union and local knowledge I am particularly indebted to - David Adam, Terry Allsop, Roy Annable, Stewart Anton, David Bamford, David Bayliss, Jim Bennett, Trevor Brandon, Chris Brighton, Michael Brinton, Frank Cavendish, Alan Crewe, Derek Crowther-Green, Dave Everett, Sylvia Fairbrother, John Fudge, Don Gilbert, Heather Goodwin, Geoffrey Head, Bill Hopley, Lou Isaac, Adrian Johnson, Misses E.J and M.Lea, Mr and Mrs Andrew Marsden-Smeadley, Roger Mathews, Derek Mead, John Mellor, Mrs Barbara Naylor, Ewart Osborne, Arthur Pagett, Richard Pugh-Cook, Ernie Pyke, Cedric Quayle, Tony Roden, Gordon Rudd, Roger Sly, Yvonne Smith, Robert Spilsbury, Charles Talbot, David Thompson, Ron White, John and Michael Wilkinson and Bob Worboys.

Geoff Neal and Anna Carter of Stourport, Charles Purcell of Bewdley and Derek Crockson of Bridgnorth. Also John Burrows of Massachusetts, USA.

The Staff of Kidderminster Reference Library and Shane Downer at the County Records Office. Kidderminster Shuttle & Times.

I am also grateful to my brother, Barry, and many others who have provided snippets of information that have contributed to make up the full story.

Maps and Locations

The following street plans have been reproduced from 1924 Ordnance Survey maps held in the County Records Office at County Hall and I am indebted to them for permission to reprint the relevant sections.

Using Mill Street as the starting point I have tried to follow a logical order of development through the town and so on to the districts. Companies that have combined have been kept together to show their true origins.

Note :   *The map references, e.g, { Map A.6 }, refer to the <u>location</u> of the company.*
            The outline of the buildings were ever changing over the years.

Accuracy of Information

Every care has been taken to ensure the accuracy of information contained in this publication but no liability can be accepted for any errors or omissions.

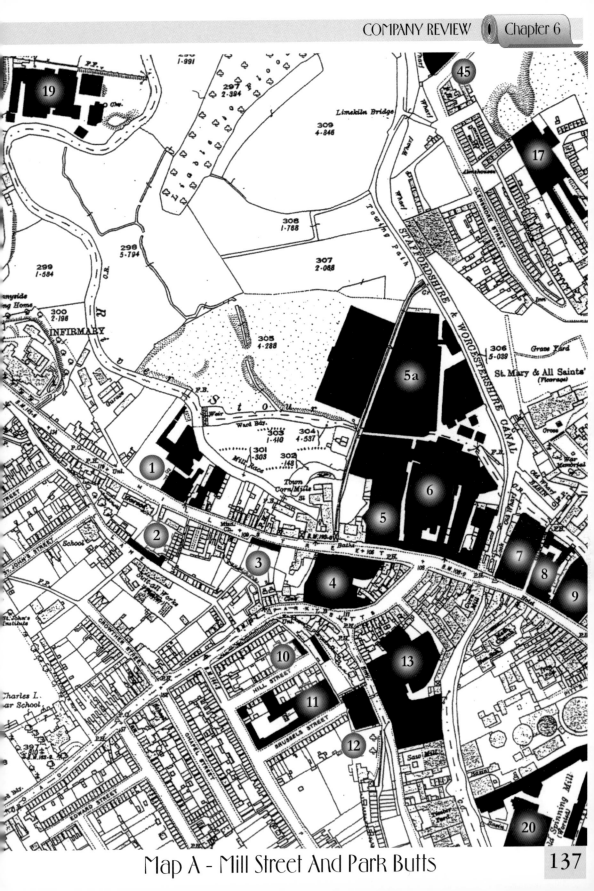

Map A - Mill Street And Park Butts

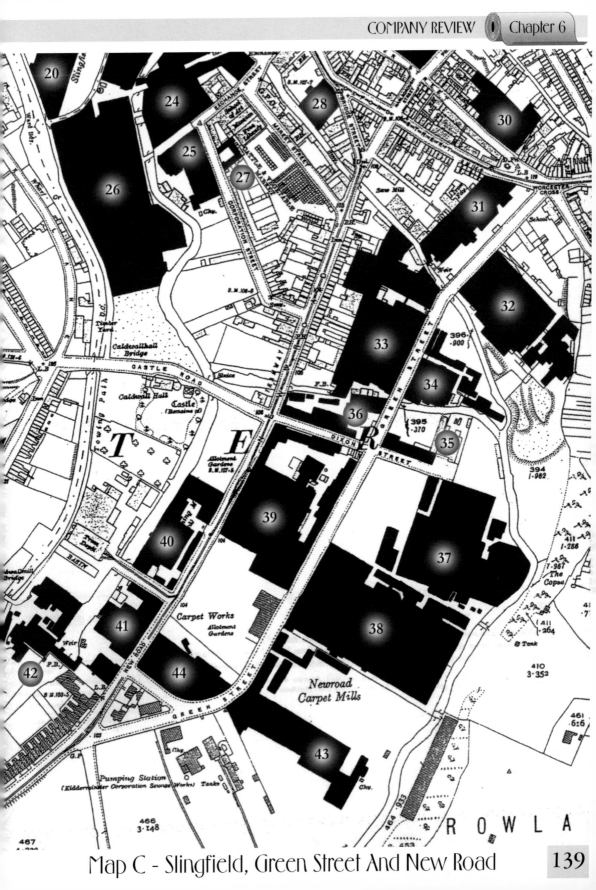

Map C - Slingfield, Green Street And New Road

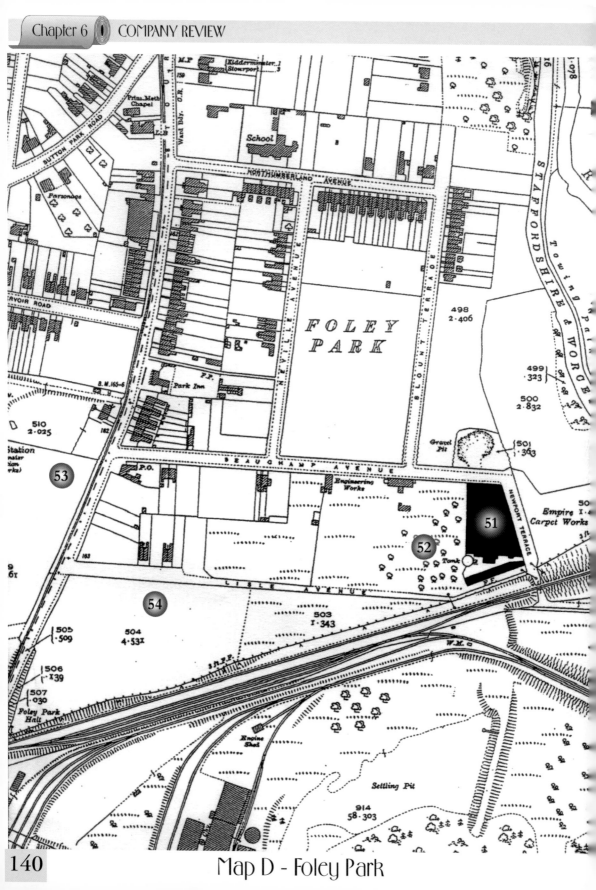

Map D - Foley Park

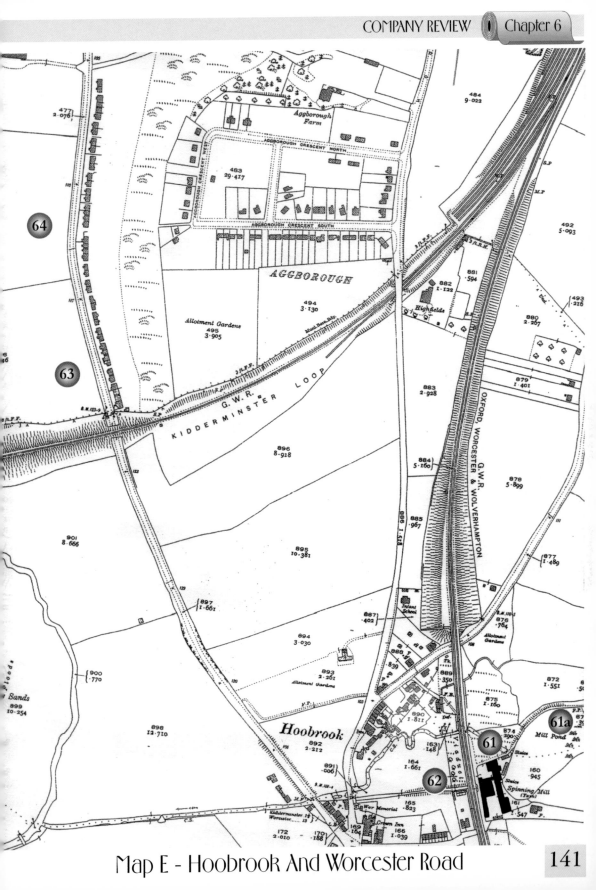

Map E - Hoobrook And Worcester Road

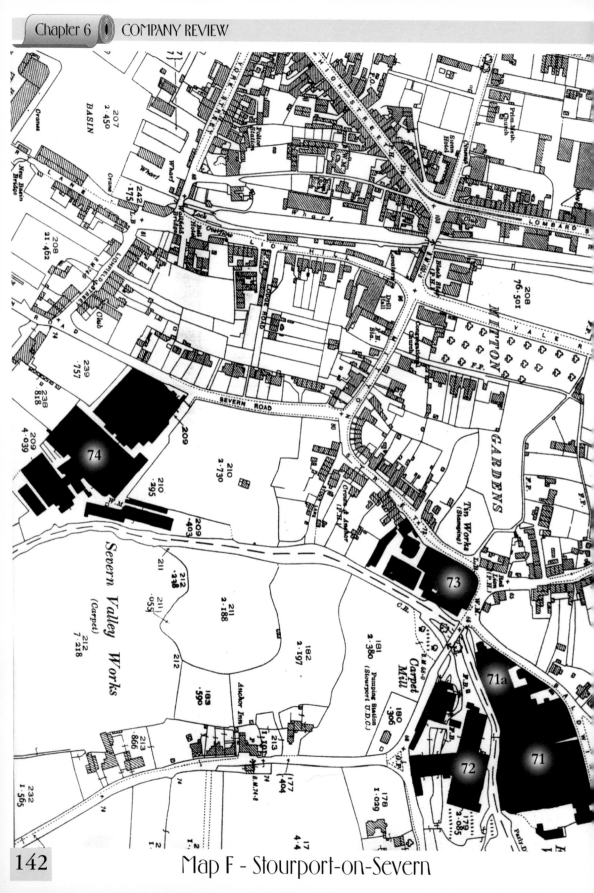

Map F - Stourport-on-Severn

MOUNT SKIPET, MILL STREET AREA
Pearsall and Broom {Map A.10}
John Pearsall and John Broom were cloth and "Stuff" weavers at Mount Skipet.

1735 They were the first weavers of "Kidderminster" double carpet.

1749 John Broom introduced the Brussels weave.

For a time John Pearsall was in partnership with his son as **John Pearsall & Son.**
John Broom & Sons {Map A.10}
1760 John Broom had sons Joseph and John Jr. in the business.

1777 John Broom Sr. died and Joseph took control of the company. Sometime later John Jr. bought the Pearsall company and joined his brother in partnership.

1811 Joseph Broom died and brother John Jr. became the sole owner.

Over the following years the company gradually developed into a large concern with spinning, dyeing and nine factories in the Mill Street and Park Butts area. They also owned the mill in Hoobrook {Map E.61} and the original buildings on Mount Skipet. In addition there were many small loom-shops and house locations around the town.
Broom, Sons & Horne
c1820-29 John Broom was joined by a Mr Horne who provided financial help.

1825 John Broom successfully adapted the Jacquard to the Brussels loom.

1828 The troublesome times around the general strike seriously affected the profits.

1832 John Broom's company was bankrupt, he ceased production and sold up.

1836-38 For a while John Broom leased the Worsted Spinning Mill at Drayton.

MILL STREET
The Talbot Family
1760s onward Samuel Talbot was a cloth and Bombazine weaver in Mill Street.
He was associated with the Lea family by marriage and in business. The family history records association with the companies **Lea & Burford** and later **Humphrys & Talbot** and it is probable that Samuel and his sons George and Henry worked with these firms. Samuel died in 1783.
Lea, Humphrys & Talbot
1788 George Talbot and Abel Humphrys were in partnership until 1795.
George Talbot
1795 George Talbot was a "Manufacturer of Bombazines and all sorts of silks and worsted stuffs" while George's brother Henry was a salesman for the company.
George and Henry Talbot
1801 Over the following years the Mill Street company prospered and developed into a large concern with other locations and property around the town. They had over 150 hand looms and 300 employees weaving Brussels, Kidderminster, Venetian carpet and some cloth, including Bombazine.
George and Henry Talbot & Sons
1818 George's and Henry's sons, both named after their fathers, joined the company.

1831 George Sr. retired from the business and five years later Henry Sr. also retired.

George Talbot & Son

1847 George Jr. became the owner, he brought in his sons Alfred and Pemberton. Later George retired, Alfred left the business and Pemberton took sole control.

Pemberton Talbot

1854 The town was rapidly converting to power loom and so Pemberton Talbot licensed and bought Crossley's Bigelow-Collier Brussels power looms. Unfortunately, he allowed the license to lapse and Crossleys took him to court. He lost the case and was forced to sell up in 1861. Pemberton Talbot continued in a very small way but was never again successful in the industry.

Penn Family

1776-1801 Henry Penn had a carpet factory in Kidderminster and later a spinning mill in Wolverhampton. William Penn, possibly son of Henry, wove carpet and Bombazine in Kidderminster until about 1815.

CALLOWS LANE, BRUSSELS STREET AREA, MILL STREET, WORCESTER ROAD

The Lea Family

The Lea family were involved in the spinning and cloth industry in the 1600s. Around 1650 a Stephen Lea wove Kidderminster "stuff" in Callows Lane. *{Map A.7}* There are also references to **Lea and Burford** and later **Lea, Burford and Talbot**. By the mid-1700s a Francis Lea was a leading cloth and Bombazine manufacturer in the town. He had two sons, John and Thomas.

Francis Lea and Son

1781 Francis Lea and his son John were partners. They introduced carpet weaving.
1793 Francis retired, John became the sole owner and around 1800 he built the Brussels Street factory *{Map A.11}*. He was now a major employer in the town. Around 1815 John Lea brought his son, Thomas Simcox Lea, into the partnership.

John Lea and Sons, Town Carpet Mills, Mill Street *{Map A.7, A.8}*

1818 The company moved to the Mill Street premises and for the next twenty-five years expanded to over 200 hand looms and a workforce of more than 450. During this time William Brinton Sr. was the Works Manager and his son Henry was a travelling representative for the company.
1843 John Lea died and the company passed to his son Thomas Simcox Lea. As Thomas Simcox Lea grew older he looked to the family for help in the business. His son Frederick became a Church Minister and so he took into partnership his nephew George Price Simcox. In 1850 Thomas Simcox Lea retired.

George Price Simcox, Beaver Works, Worcester Road

1850 George Price Simcox was now in control and over the following years he invested in a number of pioneering experiments. These included early power looms, a block carpet printing system and the manufacture of a cheap Brussels quality called "stouts". Considerable money was lost in these enterprises and the business suffered. Six years after he took over he was bankrupt and ceased trading altogether.

CALLOWS LANE, MILL STREET & SLINGFIELD MILLS, THE SLING

Francis and Thomas Lea

1793 Francis Lea, having retired from his partnership with son John, decided to set up again, this time with his other son Thomas. Together, they started a worsted spinning business in Callows Lane and around 1800 they introduced carpets.

1792 Francis Lea's daughter, Elizabeth, married a William Butcher and they had a son named George. George Butcher, when he was old enough, came into the family business and they decided to separate the carpet interests from the spinning.

Butcher, Worth & Holmes *{Map A.7}*

1831 George Butcher took over the carpet production and went into partnership with William Henry Worth and James Holmes to form a new company in Callows Lane. Four years later Thomas Lea gave his spinning business to George Butcher. In order to retain the family name George Butcher changed his name by Royal Licence to George Butcher Lea. By 1838 they had 108 looms and 214 employees.

1844 The Butcher, Worth and Holmes partnership broke up and George Butcher Lea decided to concentrate on the spinning company. George had a son called Thomas Lea who grew up in the business and eventually took control at a very young age. (William Henry Worth went on to form a new company with his sons.)

1857 The Callows Lane and Mill Street buildings were sold to Edward Hughes.

Thomas Lea, Slingfield Mills, 1864 *{Map B.20}*

Thomas Lea expanded worsted spinning and in 1864 he built Slingfield Mills. As the business grew he bought other adjacent properties on The Sling cartway. These included the failed Kidderminster Cotton Spinning Co. *{part Map B.21}*.

1885 A single floor factory building was built on to the side of the main mill. Thomas Lea had become the Liberal Member of Parliament for Kidderminster and he developed other interests away from his spinning business. Thomas had a son named Sydney and his brother, Judge George Harris Lea, had a son called George Percy.

1891 Sydney and George Percy Lea joined the company.

Lea Ltd. *{Map B.20, part B.21}*

1892 The company was restructured with Sydney and George Percy in control. Thomas Lea became Sir Thomas Lea Bart. for his service to the town. He died three years later. The early 1900s were troubled times for the whole industry.

1920 Lea Ltd. was sold to Herbert Smith and became part of Carpet Trades Ltd.

1948 Carpet Trades transferred the spinning equipment to Castle Mills and sold the Slingfield complex to Brintons for their spinning operation.

1990s The main Slingfield Mill, the boilerhouse and the square chimney were designated a Grade II listing. At the Millennium the Slingfield Mill buildings were empty awaiting the town centre development.

See page 46 for a more detailed history and description.

VICAR STREET, MILL STREET, LONG MEADOW MILLS
Cole and Bowyer {Map B.23}
1803 Joseph Bowyer was in partnership with James Cole in Vicar Street. In 1819 James Cole left. Bowyer continued until 1829 when he sold out to Henry Brinton.
Bowyer and Dixon
1830 Joseph Bowyer and Henry Jecks Dixon formed a partnership. Their factory and offices were in Mill Street and they had 70 hand looms around the town.
1838 Joseph Bowyer died and Henry Jecks Dixon bought his interests.
Henry Jecks & John Dixon
1838 Henry Jecks and his brother John continued to operate from the Mill Street factory. At the advent of the power loom they purchased land at Long Meadow on the Back Brook branch of the River Stour and built a new modern mill {Map C.37}.
1854 Long Meadow Mills opened. The multi-storey mill, weaving sheds and a dyehouse were purpose built for their 60 Brussels power looms.
1878 Henry Jeck's son Henry Jr. joined the company. They continued to invest with new buildings for Royal Spool Axminster and later the latest Moxon Tapestry plant.
1884 The Dixon's strike and riots were caused by the employment of female labour.
Henry Jecks Dixon & Sons Ltd.
1889 They became a limited company but the troubles and a downturn in orders resulted in the company going out of business six years later.

LONG MEADOW MILLS, DIXON STREET
Charles Harrison & Sons, Stourport
1896 Charles Harrison & Sons of Lower Mitton bought Long Meadow Mills.
Charles Harrison, Kempson and Company Ltd. {Map C.37}
1896 The Harrisons went into partnership with Maitland Kempson, together they bought Long Meadow Mills and the equipment from Henry Jecks Dixon & Sons.
Charles Harrison & Sons Ltd.
1909 Maitland Kempson left to join Woodward, Grosvenor leaving the Harrisons in control. Herbert Smith, owner of James Humphries & Sons, provided some financial help. In 1914 Smith took full control of the company. He transferred the carpet machinery to his Mill Street factory and installed a felt manufacturing plant.
1920 Charles Harrison and Sons Ltd. became part of Carpet Trades Ltd.

CHURCH STREET, MILL STREET
Lea and Newcomb, later Joseph Newcomb & Son {Map B.14, A.3}
c1800 Joseph Newcomb and William Lea had a factory in Church Street and loom-shops in Mill Street with over 50 hand looms. During the following thirty years the company doubled in size and became one of the town's larger companies.
1830s William Lea retired. Joseph Newcomb continued until 1861.
Much later the Mill Street buildings became part of the Edward Hughes company.

Edward Hughes *{Map A.3, A.6, A.7}*

Edward Hughes was born in 1814. He was a draw-boy at the age of seven.

1850 Edward Hughes and his brother Joseph started their own business in Orchard Street. By 1855 they had 40 hand looms at three locations around the town.

1857 The company bought the Town Carpet Mills in Mill Street from Thomas Lea.

1867 They added 85 Brussels power looms.

1874 A new Tapestry section opened with 25 Moxon looms.

Edward Hughes & Sons

1875 Edward Hughes sons, Frederick Charles and Joseph Edward joined.

1891 William Youngjohns patented the Anglo-Turkey Knotting Loom.

1902 Edward Hughes died, Frederick Charles became Managing Director and two more sons, John William and William John, joined the company.

Edward Hughes & Sons now had 500 employees on three Mill Street sites including a small hand loom section which remained well into the 1900s.

1919 Frederick Charles Hughes died and the company was sold at auction to Herbert Smith who was the next door neighbour at James Humphries & Sons.

1920 The company became part of Carpet Trades Ltd.

NEW ROAD

E.A.Broome & Company Ltd., Castle Spinning Mills, New Road *{Map C.40}*

1877 Edward Broome left Brintons and built the five storey Castle Mills near the river for Worsted Spinning. In later years he was succeeded by his son Neville.

1947 Castle Mills and the spinning business was sold to Carpet Trades.

1963 Carpet Trades sold the Mill to Brintons who extended the buildings.

1980s Brintons moved out and the Mill became part of a small Industrial Park.

MILL STREET

The Humphries Family

Benjamin Humphries was a hand loom weaver in the late 1700s.

He had three sons John, Thomas and James. They all became carpet manufacturers.

1825 John Humphries was in business in Mill Street. The company failed in 1830 and he took the Brussels looms and the weavers to Massachusetts. The American company became very successful and President Martin Van Buren awarded him two silver medals. Thomas Humphries started a company in Dudley Street.

1828 Benjamin and his son James were partners at a factory in Vicar Street.

1841 Benjamin left and so James continued on his own.

Thomas Humphries took over the Vicar Street site and in 1855 moved to the Lord Ward Shed at Stour Vale Mills. The company ceased when Thomas died in 1865.

John Humphries & Company

John was a cousin of James Humphries. For a while he was in partnership with Joseph Kiteley in Vicar Street. Around 1845 he left and went to work for James Humphries in Mill Street.

James Humphries & Sons *{Map A.5}*

James Humphries was the most successful member of the family in Kidderminster.

1841 Together with his sons, George Hallen and John, he formed a company in Mill Street. John married the daughter of George Collier, Crossley's chief engineer.

1852 Cannons were fired as the foundations were laid for a large new weaving shed to house Bigelow-Collier Brussels power looms *{Map A.5a}*.

1860 James Humphries retired and his son John became Managing Director.

George Hallen left and ran a small factory in Mill Street until it failed in 1870.

For the remaining part of the 1800s James Humphries & Sons was a prosperous company benefiting from its connection with America where they made good sales.

James Humphries and Sons Ltd.

1891 The business became a limited company as John's sons Walter, Sydney and James joined. The introduction of Spool Axminster by other companies was adversely affecting their Wilton and Brussels trade and they began to lose money.

1900 Humphries invested in 30 Spool Axminster narrow looms.

1901 John Humphries died and so the control passed to his three sons. The business declined. At the time Herbert Smith was a designer in their design studio.

1906 Herbert Smith was appointed General Manager. Three years later he was appointed Managing Director and in 1910 he started proceedings to buy the company. By 1914 he was in control and about the same time he bought Charles Harrison & Sons Ltd. at Long Meadow Mills.

1918 At the end of the First World War Herbert Smith started negotiations to purchase other companies in the town.

1920 James Humphries & Sons became part of Herbert Smith's Carpet Trades Ltd.

James Humphries & Sons

Note :   The company logo contains Herbert Smith's mark which looks like the American Dollar. Because of this he was sometimes known as "Dollar Smith".

MILL STREET, DIXON STREET, THE SLING

Carpet Trades Ltd. *{Map A.5, A5a, A.6, B.20, part B.21, C.37}*

1920 Carpet Trades Ltd. [CTL] became the group name with six companies under Herbert Smith's control. They were James Humphries & Sons and Edward Hughes & Sons, both of Mill Street; Charles Harrison & Sons, Long Meadow Mills, Dixon Street; Lea Ltd., Slingfield Spinning Mills and two Yorkshire spinning companies, Pyrah & Sons of Heckmondwike, and Robert Squire & Sons of Ravensthorpe.

1920 Herbert Smith became Sir Herbert Smith Bart. in recognition of his war work.

1920 A German company was also bought at Weida in Thuringia, it was sold in 1932.

1922 Sir Herbert Smith, aged forty-nine, resigned and sold his CTL shares.

1934 The Kardax Gripper Axminster quality was introduced and became a best seller. The first looms came from America but the majority were developed and manufactured in the company's own workshops. Kardax weaving ceased in 1970.

1936 Carpet Trades was restructured and became a public company under the Chairmanship of Sir Guy Garnet.

CARPET TRADES LIMITED
KIDDERMINSTER

DIRECTORS:
THE HON. M. F. P. LUBBOCK
(CHAIRMAN)
THE HON. A. W. BALDWIN
C. L. DALZIEL
SIR W. GUY GRANET
SIR T. SYDNEY LEA, BART.
A. J. PYRAH
E. READ

GENERAL MANAGER: C. S. NEWTON.

SECRETARY: J. B. HILL, F.C.I.S.

WAREHOUSES & AGENTS:
LONDON, MANCHESTER. GLASGOW. BELFAST,
AUSTRALIA, NEW ZEALAND. U.S.A., CANADA,
SOUTH AMERICA. SOUTH AFRICA. SCANDINAVIA,
HOLLAND, GERMANY. SWITZERLAND, EGYPT, KENYA,
UGANDA, ZANZIBAR, BELGIAN CONGO.

TELEGRAMS & CABLES: "CARPETRADO, KIDDERMINSTER"
TELEPHONE: 500 (5 LINES).

MANUFACTURERS OF
ALL GRADES OF
MACHINE MADE CARPETS
PIECE GOODS AND RUGS
MECHANICAL FELTS AND
UNDERFELTS.
SPINNERS OF WORSTED
WOOLLEN AND HAIR YARNS
FOR BOTH DOMESTIC AND
EXPORT MARKETS.

1938 Sir Guy Garnet resigned and the Hon.M.F.P.Lubbock took control.

1939-45 The company played an important part in the Second World War effort producing blankets and ammunition. They were part of a town consortium working for the Ministry of Defence.

1946 The river was diverted within the factory to increase the production shed area.

1947 Carpet Trades bought Castle Mills from E.A.Broome and Son who were Worsted Spinners. Shortly afterwards they sold Slingfield Mill to Brintons. After the war Cyril S.Newton became Managing Director.

John Crossley - Carpet Trades Holdings Ltd.

1953 The two companies formed a partnership. The Hon.M.F.P.Lubbock was Chairman with C.P.Crossley as Executive Vice Chairman. Both had overseas interests.

1955 Crossley-Carpet Trades became part of the consortium in Kosset Carpets Ltd.

1957 **Long Meadow Felt Company** became a wholly owned subsidiary.

18th September 1962 A new £350,000 front office block was officially opened.

Gilt Edge Carpets Ltd.

1967 Carpet Trades changed its image and traded under the title Gilt Edge Carpets.

Gilt Edge Carpets

1968 The hardwearing Endura non-woven product was launched. The company received the Queens Award for Industry for this technical innovation in 1973.

1969 John Crossley-Carpet Trades Holdings merged with The Carpet Manufacturing Company to become Carpets International Ltd.

PARK BUTTS, PARK LANE AREA

Park Wharf Factory, Park Butts {Map A.13}

Towards the end of the 1880s a number of companies occupied parts of the Park Wharf Factory. They included Samuel Brighton Palmer, F.J.Sellers and Edward Perrin Griffin, but the best known name was Richard Smith & Sons.

1877 Richard Smith & Sons bought Park Wharf.

1890 Richard Smith & Sons became part of The Carpet Manufacturing Company.

1980 Park Wharf was demolished.

Lower Park Works, Park Lane

1875 **Greaves, Fidoe & Co.** John Frederick Greaves and Thomas Fidoe started the company. Thomas Fidoe left and the company became **J.F.Greaves and Company.**

1889 Richard Smith & Sons bought Lower Park Works.

1890 Richard Smith & Sons became part of The Carpet Manufacturing Company.

149

The Rock Building, Park Lane *{Map A.12}*

1884 Rock Works was built by Richard Smith for the latest power Chenille looms.

1890 Richard Smith became part of The Carpet Manufacturing Company.

1902 A bridge across Park Lane connecting Rock Works to Park Wharf was added.

1927 Rock Works was extended towards Park Butts and the steps to Mount Skipet relocated. The Rock buildings have a unique set of tunnels into the sandstone rock. At the Millennium the buildings are empty and derelict.

Imperial Mill, Mill Street *{Map A.4}*

1864 Imperial Mill was built for the **Edwin Shaw Company**. It was later owned by **W.J.Bannister and Company**, 1884 and **F.Cole & Company**, 1890.

1898 Imperial Mill was bought by The Carpet Manufacturing Company.

1976 Imperial Mill was demolished.

MILL STREET, PARK BUTTS AREA

Richard Smith *{Map A.2, A.10, A.11}*

1855 Richard Smith began in a very small way in a leased factory on Primrose Hill, Mill Lane *{Map A.2}*. There he produced Chenille hand loom rugs. In 1868 he purchased the factory and expanded his business considerably over the next few years.

Around 1870 he bought Lea's Brussels Street factory *{Map A.11}* and the Mount Skipet factories *{Map A.10}*.

1875 Richard Smith died and the business was taken over by members of the family.

RICHARD SMITH & SONS

THE CARPET MANUFACTURING COMPANY LIMITED,

Offices and Warehouses :

78, Mill Street, KIDDERMINSTER.

Works:

Mill Street, Park Wharf, Imperial Works, Brussels Street, Coventry Street, Mill Lane, Hall Street, Hill Street, KIDDERMINSTER.

Richard Smith and Sons *{Map A.1, A.13, B.18}*

1875 William Henry and Edward Smith became joint Managing Directors. The company continued to expand with factories near the Shakespeare Inn, Coventry Street, *{Map B.18}*, a factory in Hall Street and another in Waterloo Street.

1877 The Park Wharf factory was purchased *{Map A.13}*.

1884 A large new factory with offices was built in Mill Street *{Map A.1}*. The Park Wharf factory was extended. The Chenille hand looms were replaced by weft and setting power looms under licence from William Adam. The company also obtained the licence for the "Crompton " fine-pitch Spool Axminster looms.

1890 Richard Smith & Sons merged with Morton & Sons in July to form The Carpet Manufacturing Company.

VICAR STREET, STOUR VALE, NEW ROAD
Woodward & Morton
1809 John Woodward from Evesham and James Morton started weaving Bombazine at a factory in Vicar Street. Later they wove carpet.
James Morton & Son
1829 John Woodward resigned and James Morton's two sons, William and Edward, joined the company. Bombazine was discontinued but they expanded the hand loom carpet weaving operation to over 100 looms during the following ten years. They wove Kidderminster and Brussels carpet and employed over 200 people.

1855 James Morton & Sons were one of the first tenants of the Stour Vale Mill Company {Map C.32}. They had two units for their Bigelow-Collier Brussels looms. The Vicar Street premises were retained for offices and warehouse. Around 1860, James and son William both died leaving Edward in control. The company prospered and with the need to expand bought open land in New Road.

Morton and Sons {Map C.39}
1869 Edward took his son Edward James into the business.

1870 Thomas Tempest Radford became a partner in the company.

1870 Morton's Factory in New Road was built to the designs of J.G.Bland. It was a complete factory with a three-storey office block, weaving sheds and a dyehouse.

1872 Edward Morton died leaving Edward James and Tempest Radford in control.

1878 The company obtained the licence to install Royal Axminster Spool looms.

1890 Morton & Sons merged with Richard Smith & Sons to form The Carpet Manufacturing Company.

NEW ROAD, MILL STREET, PARK BUTTS, PARK LANE, STOURPORT
The Carpet Manufacturing Company {Map A.1, A.4, A.11, A.12, A.13, C.39, F.72}
1890 The Carpet Manufacturing Company (CMC) was formed with the merging of Morton & Sons of New Road with Richard Smith & Sons of Mill Street. The companies continued to trade under their own names

until 1919. Morton's offices in New Road became the headquarters and Richard Smith's son William Henry Smith was the first Chairman.

1894 Anderson, Lawson and Company were sponsored in Stourport {Map F.72}. Edward James Morton became Chairman. He died in 1914 and was succeeded by Alexander Smith (no relation to Richard Smith) from Glasgow. Alexander Smith fully integrated the two companies into the CMC name.

1914-18 During the First World War they wove army blankets on Chenille looms.

1924 Alexander Smith died and William Henry Smith's son William Henry Stewart-Smith took control of the company.

1927 CMC bought the Kidderminster Spinning Company and the Caldwall and Park Mills in New Road {*Map C.41, C.42*}; these became CMC's spinning operation.

1931-34 The Anderson Lawson company was transferred to Kidderminster.

1937 W.H.Stewart-Smith died and E.H.O.Carpenter became Chairman.

1939 At the start of the Second World War the company was one of the "Nucleus" companies who were allowed to continue some carpet production. They also converted looms to blanket production and installed equipment for armaments. Imperial Works, Mill Street, was used by Accles and Pollock and part of the New Road Mill became a Ministry of Supply stores. At the end of the war CMC bought all the Chenille plant they could find including a plant of the latest Fielding automatic weft looms. This investment proved to be very profitable.

1944 In a partnership with Felt and Textiles of Australia Ltd. they set up three overseas companies. These were

The British-Australian Carpet Manufacturing Company Ltd.

The Carpet Manufacturing Company (New Zealand) Ltd.

The Carpet Manufacturing Company (South Africa) Ltd.

1944 H.M.Southwell of Bridgnorth became part of CMC.

1955 CMC became part-owners of The Kosset Carpet Company. W.P.W.Anderson, Vice Chairman of CMC, was appointed Chairman of Kosset.

1963 The company started to develop the Debron non-woven process at Bridgnorth.

1967 E.H.O.Carpenter retired and was succeeded by W.P.W (Peter) Anderson.

1969 The Carpet Manufacturing Company and John Crossley-Carpet Trades Holdings merged to become Carpets International Ltd.

KIDDERMINSTER LOCATIONS, BRIDGNORTH, YORKSHIRE, OVERSEAS

Carpets International Ltd.

1969 John Crossley-Carpet Trades Holdings merged with

carpets international UK

Carpets International (U.K.) Limited P O Box 15 Mill Street. Kidderminster Worcestershire DY11 6XE
telephone (0562) 3434 telex 338488

The Carpet Manufacturing Company and all subsidiaries to form the manufacturing group Carpets International. As its name implied it was a large international company with factories in Kidderminster, Yorkshire and a number of countries abroad.

In Kidderminster, the group had many sites principally the main Mill Street complex of Carpet Trades, Morton's New Road factory, Caldwell and Park Spinning Mills, Park Wharf factory, the Rock Buildings and the Park Street Warehouse, Imperial Mill, Mill Street and Long Meadow Mills, Dixon Street.

In Bridgnorth were the Friars Works of the former company H. & M.Southwell.

In Halifax, Dean Clough Mill was the hub of business but there were other sites in Yorkshire including Kosset, the Illingworth Felt Company and Croslee Yarns.

Abroad they retained factories in Australia, New Zealand, South Africa and in the following years invested in Thailand, Malaysia, the Philippines and the USA. The group manufactured a wide range of products including Wilton, Spool and Gripper Axminster, Gripper-Spool Axminster, Tufting and printing, Felts for all uses and a range of non-wovens including Endura, Debron and carpet tiles.

1971 Carpets International created two divisions, North and South. Kidderminster became the base for the Southern Division with offices in New Road.

1972 Long Meadow Mills and the felt production were sold to Bury-Masco.

In the following years the company reduced the number of individual factories in Kidderminster and eventually consolidated on the Mill Street Site {Map A.5, A.6}. By now the factory buildings had spread to cover most of the land towards Townshend Works {Map A.19}.

1972 **Carpets International, Georgia, Inc.** was set up for the manufacture of contract carpet tiles. Carpets International UK were half owners. The venture was profitable and eventually was bought out and became known as Interface. In the following years the whole group struggled and, despite major restructuring, Carpets International became unprofitable and the share value decreased.

John Crowther Group

1985 Carpets International was bought by the Yorkshire-based John Crowther Group. More rationalisation took place following a consultant's report.

Coloroll Group

1988 The Crowther Group sold the carpet companies to John Ashcroft's Coloroll. Coloroll commenced a major investment programme at the Mill Street site with

new machinery and a complete refurbishment of the 1960s office block. Kidderminster became the weaving division and was given the name Crossley. In the spring of 1990 Coloroll was bankrupt and the receivers, Ernst and Young, took over the running of the factory in the hope of a buyer.

Carpet Division – Crossley

In December 1990 the company ceased trading altogether and the equipment was sold or scrapped. The majority of the Mill Street buildings were subsequently demolished and Morton's New Road Mill became an industrial estate.

PUXTON

F.F.Jelleyman *{Map A.19}*

1866 Frederick Francis Jelleyman came to Kidderminster from Stratford-on-Avon to make ropes, twines and tarpaulins. His first factory was in the Clensmore area.
1874 He relocated his business to the Townshend Works at Puxton on the river. Subsequently, he became involved in the expanding carpet industry.
1890 Townshend Works was considerably enlarged for the carpet machinery.

F.F.Jelleyman & Sons

1898 Francis Jelleyman's two sons Frederick John Robert and Sydney Francis joined the business and they started weaving Chenille and Brussels Wilton.

TELEGRAMS:"JELLEYMAN,TOWNSHEND, KIDDERMINSTER."
TELEPHONE:-72.

LONDON, 8.LOVELL'S COURT, PATERNOSTER ROW,E.C.
TELEPHONE:-12576, CENTRAL.

JELLEYMAN & SONS LTD.
CARPET & RUG MANUFACTURERS.

Townshend Works,
Kidderminster,

Jelleyman & Sons Ltd.

1910 The business became a limited company and by now Townshend Works was complete with offices, design studio, weaving and finishing sheds and a dyehouse.
1911 The founder died and the two sons became joint Managing Directors.
1934 The company expanded further with new weaving sheds and the purchase of Crompton & Knowles narrow and broadloom Spool Axminster Looms from the Philadelphia Carpet Corporation in America which had gone into liquidation.
1939 Frederick John Robert and Sydney Francis Jelleyman died within six months of each other. They both had sons who continued to run the company.
1939-45 During the Second World War the Chenille looms wove army blankets and the dyehouse was converted to making gun mountings. The Ministry of Works used part of the factory to store gas masks for the Ministry of Home Security.
The company continued to develop and invest during the postwar boom period.
1963 T.Bond Worth & Sons bought the company. For the following ten years Jelleymans retained its own identity with a separate office and sales force.

Bond Worth Holdings Ltd.

By the mid-1970s the company had been gradually integrated with Bond Worth and the Jelleyman name became obsolete.
1977 Bond Worth went into receivership and was bought by a group of Middle Eastern businessmen.

Carpets of Worth Ltd.

1979 The new owners reduced capacity and generally restructured the whole company. Townshend Works effectively became a satellite weaving factory.
At the Millennium, Worths were actively moving equipment from Severn Valley Mills in Stourport back to the Townshend Works at Puxton.

The Puxton Manufacturing Company

A small company operated from a weaving shed in Puxton Lane between 1965 and 1975. Initially with a Wilton plain loom they developed into Spool Axminster.

MILL STREET, VICAR STREET, WORCESTER STREET, NEW ROAD

James Hooman and Company and Joseph Pardoe and Company

Around 1800 James Hooman and Joseph Pardoe ran companies in the town.

Hooman and Pardoe

1805 Hooman and Pardoe formed the company with an office in New Road.

Hooman, Pardoe & Hooman

1809 Another member of the Hooman family joined the firm.

1820s Both founder members retired and they were replaced by their sons.

Pardoe, Hooman & Pardoe

1829 Thomas and James Pardoe together with George Hooman built up a very successful company. Within three years they had 130 hand looms and had moved the main office to Oxford Road, now Oxford Street {Map C.28}.

By 1840 the company was the largest in town with 242 hand looms weaving mainly Brussels and Kidderminster carpets. They also owned three spinning mills including one in Caldwall Mill {Map C.42}. For a time they owned the factory in Bewdley. Many of the looms were located in loom-shops in Worcester Street {Map B.29}.

1847 The company bought land in The Sling just off Mill Street {Map B.21} and built a factory for 110 Tapestry Brussels looms and the associated printing drums.

With the conversion to power the company decided to concentrate production on the Tapestry process, all the old Brussels hand looms were scrapped. This decision proved to be their downfall and in 1858 a recession in the Tapestry business brought an end to the company. The effect on the town was devastating as 800 people were put out of work. James Pardoe later became a director of John Crossley & Sons.

PITTS LANE, MILL STREET, CHURCH STREET, STOURPORT

Thomas & James Bough

In the early 1800s brothers Thomas and James Bough established a company with Brussels hand looms and loom-shops located in Pitts Lane, Mill Street and Church Street where they also had a dyehouse. The partnership failed in 1848.

Thomas Bough

For the next six years Thomas Bough retained more than 70 looms controlled from an office in Mill Street. He did not convert to power and went out of business.

James Bough

James Bough continued to operate from the Church Street factory. He later became a tenant of Worth's at Severn Valley Mills, Stourport.

Joseph Baker and Son

About 1780 Joseph Baker built up a business with over 40 Brussels looms. In 1832 he was joined in business by his son. The company ceased trading three years later.

Bayliss & Wagstaff

Around 1812 Thomas Bayliss went into partnership with Daniel and Samuel Wagstaff in Mill Street. The company failed after 12 years.

Joseph Hiles 1825-1840s A Mill Street company with 34 Brussels looms.

CHURCH STREET, STOUR VALE MILL

Robert Shirley

1803 Robert Shirley became a carpet manufacturer. In 1820 he was declared bankrupt but by 1822 was back in business. At one stage he owned 56 hand looms. In the mid-1820s he had premises in Lower Mitton, Stourport. The company failed around 1837.

George and Henry Robinson

In the 1790s George Robinson started a carpet business in Church Street. The hand loom business continued to be run by the family until it closed in 1861.

Dobson Companies.

A number of Dobson companies were registered, 1776 **Butler & Dobson,**
1809 **Timothy Dobson & Co.**, 1820 **Timothy Dobson & Son**

James Dobson and Son

1832 The company had an office, dyehouse and counting house in Church Street. The hand looms were around the town in Queen Street, Clensmore and New Road.

John Lloyd Dobson

1840s James retired and his son John Lloyd Dobson took over the company.

1855 After a period in partnership with Edwin Shaw, John Lloyd Dobson became a power loom weaver at The Stour Vale Mill Company.

1864 John Lloyd Dobson died and Edwin Shaw took over his section at Stour Vale.

Edwin Shaw

Edwin Shaw was a manufacturer in partnership with John Lloyd Dobson.
He also had his own company in Mill Street.

1864 Edwin Shaw operated from The Stour Vale Mill Company until 1884.

James Cole and Sons

1803-19 James Cole was in partnership with Joseph Bowyer in Vicar Street.

1819 He formed a company with his sons in Church Street.

1821 James Cole's son, James Jr, took control of the company.

Barber and Cole

Around 1825 James Jr. and John Sutton Barber were partners with 70 hand looms.

Atkins & Naylor

1878 Frederick Atkins and George Whitfield Naylor had an office in Church Street and rented part of Stour Vale Mill. In 1880 the company became **Naylor & Lloyd.**

John Woodward & Company

1829 Following the dissolution of his partnership with James Morton, John Woodward set up on his own at a factory in Church Street. The business was reasonably large with more than 50 Brussels hand looms. In later years others joined and the company was known as **Stoddard & Woodward** and **Woodward & Gandell**, both around 1838. The company had ceased trading by 1850.

Harvey & Company

1865 Harvey & Company were in Church Street with a small Brussels hand weaving loom-shop at premises to the rear of The Shakespeare Inn in Coventry Street.
In 1875 the company became **Broom, Harvey & Company.**

THE SLING, ARCH HILL, MOUNT PLEASANT, CHURCH STREET

William Adam, George Race & Company

William Adam was an engineering apprentice with Templetons of Glasgow. He became a skilled engineer specialising in the Chenille process.

In 1858 he came to Kidderminster to help Brinton & Lewis set up their newly acquired Chenille Axminster plant. He was ambitious and so, with Brinton's job completed, he joined George Race, who was Brinton's accountant in a business in Coventry Street making Chenille rugs. The company failed in 1863 and was bought out by H.R.Willis & Company. William Adam continued as their Works Manager.

Michael Tomkinson

Michael Tomkinson was an agent supplying Yorkshire yarns to the carpet industry.
1861 He bought Pemberton Talbot's complete rug stock and sold it for a good profit.
1869 Michael Tomkinson and William Adam combined to form their own company.

Tomkinson & Adam

1869 Tomkinson & Adam were registered with a capital of £1,000, ie. £500 each. William Adam looked after engineering and production and Michael Tomkinson was the salesman. They started in rented property in The Sling {Map B.21}

and at Arch Hill Works {Map B.15} where they installed second-hand Chenille hand looms purchased from the Willis company.
1875 Tomkinson & Adam were profitable and they bought premises at Mount Pleasant {Map B.17}. About this time they purchased the whole of Brinton's Chenille rug making plant in an agreement which saw Brintons marketing the production.
1878 Michael Tomkinson went to New York to purchase the British patent for Spool Axminster. The original quality was only 5 pitch x 5 rows per inch using the thicker woollen yarns, but by 1892 it had improved to 7 pitch, which is the current standard. William Adam also developed and patented the first powered Chenille Setting loom. Tomkinson & Adam held the manufacturing rights for these two processes and were able to control the licences. It was a good commercial position for the company. Royal Axminster production thrived enabling the company to extend Mount Pleasant and purchase the Arch Hill factory outright. The Arch Hill factory was known around the town as "The Fish Factory" {Map B.15}.
1879 No.6 Church Street {Map B.14} was bought for offices and showrooms.
1887 The "Jubilee" shed was built at Mount Pleasant together with a boilerhouse, dyehouse, warehouse, preparatory and finishing. In 1897 they added another production building along Churchfields and, in 1902, a warehouse extension.
The company continued to develop the Spool process and in 1896 they introduced an American patent for the production of Axminster squares on a 9 feet wide loom.
1898 William Adam died when only 58 years old.

William Adam was succeeded by his sons Peter, the Head Designer, and William Jr. Michael Tomkinson's sons Herbert, Gerald and Geoffrey also joined the business.

1900 Geoffrey Tomkinson started his engineering apprenticeship with the large textile engineering company Platt Bros. of Oldham. They later became the builders of the Spool Axminster looms.

1902 The "Kleitos" 9-foot-wide Spool Axminster loom was patented.

1910 Tomkinson & Adam bought the British licence for the French Renard loom.

1914-18 The company had limited production during the First World War.

1921 Michael Tomkinson died aged eighty-one.

1926 The Duke of York visited the factory.

1927 The families of William Adam and Michael Tomkinson decided to end their association. The Adam family moved to a new factory at Greenhill on the Birmingham Road, while the Tomkinson family retained the existing factory sites.

Tomkinsons Ltd. *{Map B.14, B.15, B.17}*

1927 Tomkinsons Ltd was registered, Herbert Tomkinson became the first Chairman.

1939-45 During the Second World War Tomkinsons played a major part in the town's effort making over a quarter of a million blankets and tarpaulins on the Chenille looms. Together with ICI, Brintons and Carpet Trades they were involved with small arms ammunition. They were also partners with Albright and Wilson in the filling and assembly of phosphorus mortar bombs and grenades. Geoffrey Tomkinson was Regional Officer for The Ministry of Supply. The company quickly resumed production after the war.

1955 Geoffrey became Sir Geoffrey Tomkinson for his war services.

Tomkinson Holdings Ltd.

1959 The company continued to grow and Norman Lancaster became Group Chairman succeeding Sir Geoffrey Tomkinson. In the same year they became part owner of **Overseas Carpets Ltd.** Christchurch, New Zealand.

1960 **I.& C.Steele & Co. Ltd.** Steele's Wilton plant at Banbury joined the group.

1961 Tomkinson's first tufters replaced the Renard Knotting Looms.

1963 **Mount Pleasant Spinning Co. Ltd.** was set up within the main factory to produce some of the company's yarns.

1964 **Ludlow Carpets Ltd.** was the name given to the Tufted Division. The original plan was to build a new factory in Ludlow but they could not get planning permission from Shropshire County Council.

1965 Tomkinson's new office block was built at Duke Place. Later the Church Street offices were sold to the District Council. The location of the Mount Pleasant Spinning Company created space problems on the shop floor and they decided to expand and relocate. At the time the Town Council were not permitting industrial development within the town and so Tomkinsons chose a green field site in Wales for a their spinning company.

1969 **Mid-Wales Yarns Ltd.** Llandrindod Wells, was set up to spin the companies total yarn requirement. They considerably expanded over the subsequent years.

1973 **St.Mary's Carpets Ltd.** A purpose-built factory was built in Clensmore Street to house the new Crawford-Pickering yarn printing equipment. The process was unsuccessful and so the factory was sold to Stalwart (Kidderminster) Ltd. in 1975.

In the years following Tomkinsons rationalised its production and equipment. In Kidderminster they concentrated on Spool Axminster and Tufted.

The Ludlow Carpets name was dropped in 1980. Tomkinsons prospered and modernised in the 1980s. During the 1990s discussions were held with other manufacturers with a view to a merger.

Mr.Tomkinson

1999 Tomkinsons joined **Gaskells plc.**, the Lancashire based company, to form the third largest carpet manufacturing company in the country.

GREENHILL WORKS, BIRMINGHAM ROAD
W. & R.R.Adam Ltd.

1927 The company was set up by William Jr. and Raleigh R.Adam after the partnership with Tomkinsons ended. They built the Geenhill Works. Their first product range

was exclusively Spool Axminster rugs and carpet.

1938 The production buildings were extended. These included a new Setting Shed.

1940 William Adam Jr. died and Raleigh ran the company until his retirement in 1969. In the 1970s the company invested in American-manufactured wide Wilton looms and purchased their first tufting plant.

Adam Carpets Ltd.

1983 The private company was restructured under the direction of Raleigh's son David Adam. Jim Bennett also became the sales Director. The business was condensed into the main weaving sheds and the surplus buildings became industrial units.

Spool Axminster and Wilton was phased out and the company invested in a new tufting plant. The dyehouse was retained and run for commission work.

At the Millennium the company continues to develop and expand.

MILL STREET, WORCESTER CROSS, NEW ROAD

Potter, Walford and Company

Thomas Potter and Samuel Walford were officers of the Friendly Society of Operative Carpet Weavers during the Weavers Strike of 1828.

1830 They became manufacturers. After fours years the company was growing with over 20 hand looms but Samuel Walford left the partnership for America.

Potter & Duckham

Thomas Potter took a new partner and they built up the company to 36 looms. Around 1840 the company ceased trading.

Edmund Potter

Thomas Potter's son Edmund started as a draw-boy working for Charles Harrison in Stourport. He worked his way up to become their travelling representative.

H.R.Willis, Potter and Company {Map C.31}

1869 Edmund Potter was in partnership with Henry Richard Willis at Worcester Cross Works until 1878.

NEW ROAD AREA

Caldwall Carpet Mill, New Road {Map C.41}

E.Potter and Company

1878 Edmond Potter borrowed £10,000, formed his own company and built Caldwall Carpet Mills in New Road. The main production was Axminster.

Potter & Lewis

1883 John Lewis, who had previously been with Brintons, came into the company.

1892 The business failed and the mill and equipment was sold to G.M.Whittall.

G.M.Whittall and Company

1868 Moses Whittall became a weaver of Brussels and Wilton in Park Butts. His three sons Arthur, George Mathias and Matthew were also in the business. (Matthew later emigrated to Worcester, Massachusetts, and became a large manufacturer in America). Around 1876 the company relocated to Stour Vale Mills. Ten years later Moses Whittall died and his sons carried on the business.

1892 They bought Caldwall Carpet Mill and the equipment from Potter & Lewis.

G.M.Whittall & Co.Ltd. {Map C.41}

1899 The company became a limited liability company and two years later was sold to Clement Dalley and Aaron Price. In 1906 the Axminster plant was sold to Chlidema and the Caldwall Mill buildings to the Kidderminster Spinning Company.

Kidderminster Spinning Company {Map C.41}

1906 The Kidderminster Spinning Company bought the mill and converted it into a large Spinning operation.

The Carpet Manufacturing Company {Map C.41, C.42}

1927 The Carpet Manufacturing Company bought the business and later combined it with Caldwall Spinning Mill to become the Spinning Division of CMC.

NEW ROAD, CLENSMORE MILL
Caldwall Spinning Mill, New Road *{Map C.42}*
There was originally a corn mill on the site.

1829 **Pardoe, Hooman & Pardoe** were Worsted spinners at the mill until 1858.

1877 **William Birkett**, spinner and yarn agent, occupied the mill.

1895 **W.Greatwich** bought the mill for his spinning company.

Clensmore Mills, Clensmore Street *{Map A.45}*
1823 Right Hon.Thomas Foley sold freehold land at Clensmore near the canal to a Civil Engineer who built a windmill and buildings for corn milling.

Best & Collins
1838 William Butler Best and Charles Collins leased the buildings and started a Worsted spinning business.

1863 Clensmore Mill was built on the site and a 30hp steam engine installed.

C.E. & H.Jeffries
1866 Charles Edward and Henry Jeffries installed 20 Brussels power looms in Clensmore Mill. Twenty years later the company failed and the looms were sold.

Roger Brinton & Company
1896 Roger Brinton, from Bridgnorth, ran a Worsted spinning operation until 1907.

Greatwich Limited
1911 Greatwich Ltd. bought the freehold of Clensmore Carpet and Corn Mills.

CROSS STREET, ORCHARD STREET
Spilsbury & Wilcox Ltd.
1937 Harry Spilsbury, his son also Harry, and Bert Wilcox started Gripper Axminster weaving at premises in Cross Street. For part of the war they were a "Nucleus" company. In 1961 the business was merged with The Minster Carpet Company.

The Minster Carpet Co. Ltd. *{Map B.16}*
1947 Lionel Rowe, Albert (Bert) Beams and William (Bill) Hopkins set up the company in Orchard Street. Starting with narrow Wilton they later added Gripper Axminster.

Minster Carpet Company Ltd.
1961 Spilsbury & Wilcox and The Minster Carpet Company merged.

1970 A new shed was built in Clensmore Street for Gripper Axminster production.

1976 The company became part of the Bowater Corporation and the Orchard Street factory was sold.

Figured and Plain Wilton
Richtone · Rushock
Radnor
(Mothproofed)

Axminster Squares
3/4 and 4/4 Body
Winchester · Beckford
Bransford
(Mothproofed)

THE MINSTER CARPET CO.
ORCHARD ST. : KIDDERMINSTER
Telephone 3312

CLENSMORE STREET
Stalwart (Kidderminster) Ltd.
1975 At the failure of Tomkinson's St.Mary's Carpets, Stalwart took over for a short time. In 1979 they sold the buildings to Bowater's Georgian Carpets.

CALDWALL SPINNING MILL, CLENSMORE MILLS

W.Greatwich and Company Ltd. *{Map C.42}*

1895 William Rogers Moseley Greatwich started Worsted spinning at Caldwall Mill. In the following years he expanded and invested in Woollen Spinning.

Greatwich Ltd.

1901 Greatwich became a private limited company. By 1918 the founder's son, H.J.L.Greatwich was in control together with Harry Westcott and George Rainsford.

TELEGRAMS:
GREATWICH, KIDDERMINSTER.
TELEPHONE NOS. 2287
(2 LINES)

ALL COMMUNICATIONS TO CALDWALL MILLS.

Caldwall Spinning Mills,

GREATWICH LTD., *Kidderminster,*
WOOLLEN SPINNERS.

BRANCH WORKS:
CLENSMORE.

They purchased more land adjacent to the Clensmore site and considerably extended the buildings. After the Second World War production was consolidated on the Clensmore site and later Caldwall Spinning Mill was sold to The Carpet Manufacturing Company.

1952 Bruce Rainsford, George's son, joined the company and in 1964 he became Chairman. They had a dyehouse to support the core business of Woollen and Worsted spun yarns. Greatwich was one of the first companies to spin viscose rayon pile yarns for the carpet trade, also blends of wool and nylon.

Georgian Carpets Ltd. *{Map A.45}*

1966 Greatwich Limited went into Tufted carpet manufacture with the

Georgian Carpets Ltd
Clensmore Mills, Kidderminster, Worcs. Tel: Kidderminster 2287-8 & 3659

formation of a separate company on the Clensmore site.

Bowater Corporation

1976 Greatwich and Georgian became part of the Bowater Corporation together with Goodacre & Sons of Kendal and tufting manufacturers Bolton Carpets.

The neighbouring Minster Carpet Company also joined the group. In Bradford, the group owned Carlton Spinning which was run by Bruce's son Francis Rainsford.

1977 In a rationalisation plan the Minster weaving plant was transferred to the Goodacre factory and Georgian received the tufters from Bolton.

1979 Georgian bought the premises vacated by Stalwart Ltd. in Clensmore Street for additional warehouse capacity.

Georgian, Goodacre Ltd. (Melton-Meades Ltd.)

1984 The Bowater Corporation sold out to the Nottingham company Melton-Meades who renamed the group Georgian, Goodacre Ltd. In this arrangement Greatwich, Georgian and Goodacre returned to trading under their own brand names.

1999 The Greatwich spinning operation ceased production and the spinning and dyeing equipment was offered for sale. At the Millennium, Georgian continues to produce the tufted ranges but the Spinning sheds are empty.

CALDWALL ROW (MARKET STREET), VICAR STREET

Wright, Gower and Gough

1807 Charles Wright, George Gower and John Gough formed a company to continue an established hand weaving business in town. Later Gower and Gough withdrew and Charles Wright's nephew, George Crump, became a partner.

Charles Wright & Nephew

The company had many loom-shops around the town including New Road, Queen Street, Mount Pleasant, Crabtree Close, Silver Street and Worcester Street.
The headquarters and factory was in Caldwall Row later called Market Street.

Wright and Crump

1838 The company was renamed, they owned 67 looms with a workforce of 140.

Wright, Crump and Crane

1850 Thomas Edward Crane joined the business and within five years he was in control together with John E.Barton. Barton had been a London-based salesman.

Crane and Barton

1856 A factory was built on the river in Vicar Street for Brussels power looms.

John E.Barton & Sons {Map B.22}

1864 Thomas Crane died and John E.Barton became the owner together with his two sons Everard and Charles. In 1872 they built a new multi-storey office, showroom and warehouse fronting onto Vicar Street. In 1885 John E.Barton died and in 1905 the company ceased trading and closed.

From this time onwards the multi-storey buildings became the frontage of the Vicar Street shops at the ground floor. There were offices on the upper floors.
At the Millennium the upper part of Barton's Mill frontage can still be seen.

Cox & Daughtrey

1825 Around this time John Daughtrey and William Cox had a factory in Caldwall Row. By 1830 they had 38 hand looms. In earlier years William Brinton had been apprenticed to James Daughtrey as a Brussels weaver.

Thomas Hopkins

1829 Thomas Hopkins manufactured carpets and rugs in Vicar Street. Within ten years the company had 93 Brussels hand looms and 183 employees.
The company failed in the late 1840s.

MILL STREET

John Gough and Sons

Around 1820, having left the partnership with Wright and Gower, John Gough was in business on his own in Mill Street. His sons George and Edgar later joined the company. They had over 50 hand looms but by 1840 the company had failed.

VICAR STREET, BACK MARKET STREET (CORPORATION STREET)
Cole & Bowyer, Vicar Street *{part Map B.23}*
James Cole and Joseph Bowyer had a factory at the rear of the Vicarage (now the Town Hall) near where the river Stour splits to form Back Brook at a weir.
Joseph Bowyer
1819 Joseph Bowyer was the sole owner and Henry Brinton leased part of the factory. Within four years Bowyer had enlarged the buildings and Henry Brinton took even more of the factory space. He bought the whole factory in 1829.
Palmer Brothers
1854 William and Samuel Brighton Palmer were manufacturers in Church Street.
Palmer & Radford of Waterside Mills *{Map C.25}*
1862 William died and Samuel went into partnership with Thomas Tempest Radford and they built the Waterside Mills in Back Market Street.
1864 George Gower Woodward joined and the company became **Woodward, Palmer & Radford**. Two years later Palmer left and the title changed again to **Woodward & Radford**. The company title eventually became **The Waterside Mill Company** but in 1882 it failed and the Waterside Mill buildings were purchased by John Brinton.
Crabtree & Palmer, Town Hall Carpet Works, Vicar Street *{part Map B.23}*
1877 James Crabtree and Samuel Brighton Palmer formed a company and built the Town Hall Carpet Works, behind the Town Hall with the frontage on Vicar Street.
The Brussels Carpet Company
1884 The company was renamed and John Stooke became a partner replacing Samuel Palmer. Two years later the business failed and the buildings were bought by **W.B.Purdey & Company**. By 1890 **Whittall Brothers & Company** were the owners.
1896 The company was sold up. The frontage became The Kidderminster Cycle Company and the weaving sheds to the rear were bought by Brintons. The weaving shed area became known as the "Jam Factory" and later Brinton's Beacon Club.

THE BRINTON FAMILY of HILL POOL, MILL STREET, VICAR STREET
Around 1770 John Brinton settled in Belbroughton. A Thomas Brinton also came to the area. John's grandson William and Thomas's son Samuel were about the same age and they became involved with the rapidly growing carpet industry.
William Brinton, Hill Pool
1783 William Brinton started a Worsted Spinning business at Hill Pool Mill near Chaddesley Corbett. William also rented premises near the canal in Mill Street where he had a dyehouse and did some carpet and cloth weaving.
Green & Brinton
Richard Green was related by marriage to the Brintons and he was also a carpet manufacturer in town. In 1783 he went into partnership with Samuel Brinton to form a small carpet company. In 1790, when the company failed, they only had 7 Brussels hand looms. Samuel Brinton later ran a small business in Blackwell Street.

William Brinton from Dudley

1784 William Brinton, aged 14 years, came from a branch of the family in Dudley to learn the carpet trade. He was a weaving apprentice to James Daughtrey, a clerk with William Penn and finally joined John Lea in Mill Street *{Map A.7}*.

1793 William joined his relation William Brinton at his Mill Street factory. William, from Dudley, married and had three sons Henry, William Jr and John.

Thomas Cooper

1750 Thomas Cooper was a weaver of the town, he had two sons John and Joseph.

Coopers & Brinton

1800 John Cooper and William Brinton from Dudley went into partnership to manufacture carpet and cloth. William's son Henry worked in the company learning weaving, spinning, dyeing and he also gained sales experience. In 1817 the partnership was dissolved and William returned to Lea's factory in Mill Street as the manager, Henry became their travelling representative.

Henry Brinton had four sons and four daughters, two of his sons worked in the industry and two of his daughters married into the industry. One married Francis Crossley of Halifax and a second was married locally to Edward Broome. Henry was ambitious and friendly with another manufacturer, Joseph Bowyer.

Henry Brinton & Company *{Map B.23}*

1819 Henry Brinton started his own business by renting part of Joseph Bowyer's factory in Vicar Street. Four years later Bowyer expanded and Henry was able to take even more buildings to install Brussels hand looms. By now Henry also ran William Brinton's Mill Street factory. The business was expanding and so, in 1828, Henry brought his father and brothers into the company.

1829 Joseph Bowyer sold his Vicar Street factory to Henry Brinton. In comparison with other companies the site was large at over 4,000 square yards and included dyehouse, drying room, winding and weaving sheds, a counting house and also two houses. The hand looms wove Brussels, Wilton, Venetian and "town made" rugs. Henry Brinton was expanding and he bought other factories in town which he leased out. By 1836 he had more than 100 looms around the town. He started to expand his Vicar Street site to bring these looms into the one location, this policy was to pay off later with the necessary conversion to power loom weaving.

1845 Henry purchased adjoining land on the other side of Back Brook and built additional sheds and a Mill. The address of his factory was Vicar Street but the development would have been to the rear of the Vicarage along what we now call Exchange Street.

H. BRINTON & SONS,
MANUFACTURERS OF PATENT
TAPESTRY & BRUSSELS CARPET,
AXMINSTER CARPETS & RUGS,
KIDDERMINSTER;
AND
WORSTED SPINNERS,
HILL POOL MILLS,
CHADDESLEY CORBETT.

Henry Brinton & Sons *{Map B.23, C.24, C.26}*

1848 Henry's two sons, Henry Jr and John, aged twenty-one, became partners in the business. In the following five years he bought more town-centre land towards the canal and made improvements to the Hill Pool Spinning Mill.

1855 The hand looms were being phased out and replaced with Tapestry and Brussels power looms. The first full-time American salesman was appointed.

1857 Henry Sr. and Henry Jr. both died within a few months of each other and John Brinton took control of the company at the age of thirty. He needed help.

Brinton & Lewis

1858 John Brinton took into partnership John Lewis who was a nephew of his brother-in-law Sir Francis Crossley of Halifax. William Adam came from Templetons to install new Chenille power looms.

1867 More capital was invested in the town site with the building of a five-storey wool warehouse, the Piano Building, and a large weaving and spinning shed. Spinning was transferred from Hill Pool and a new boilerhouse and chimney were added.

GOLD MEDAL, PARIS, 1867.

PRIZE MEDAL, PRIZE MEDAL, JURORS' MEDAL,

LONDON, 1851. DUBLIN, 1865. LONDON, 1862.

BRINTON & LEWIS,

Manufacturers of

BRUSSELS, WILTON, INDIAN - AXMINSTER

CARPETS & RUGS,

WORSTED SPINNERS, &c.

WORKS, KIDDERMINSTER.

LONDON WAREHOUSE, 14, BERNERS STREET, OXFORD STREET, W.

John Brinton & Company

{Map B.23, C.24, C.26}

1870 John Lewis resigned with ill health and John Brinton became the sole owner.

1876 The main office block was opened. By now the company was the biggest in town with spinning and 156 Brussels power looms, 50 Tapestry power looms and they still retained some hand looms for weaving Venetian.

John Brinton & Co. Ltd.

In 1881 the company became a limited liability company. One year later they bought the adjacent Waterside Mill Company *{Map C.25}*.

1887 Two of Brintons directors, J.Bennie and H.Chaytor, formed an independent company funded by Brintons called **J.Bennie & Co.** They were housed in the buildings of The Waterside Mill Company. The whole of the Tapestry operation and some Brussels looms was transferred. The enterprise only lasted five years and Brintons again took over the Mills and the equipment.

1890 After six years of development Brintons patented the Gripper Axminster Loom.

BRINTONS LIMITED,

MANUFACTURERS OF
AXMINSTER, BRUSSELS, and WILTON CARPETING,
SEAMLESS AXMINSTER CARPETS, and of
SEAMLESS HAND-MADE AXMINSTER CARPETS & RUGS,
WOOLLEN SPINNERS.

Brintons Limited *{Map B.23, C.24, C.25, C.26}*

1891 John Brinton was chairman and in 1898 Reginald Seymour Brinton, John's third son, became a director. The company continued to invest and build.

In 1906 they set up **The Brinton Carpet Company of Canada**, Peterborough, Ontario. The enterprise was managed by Percy Preen, who was married to one of John Brinton's daughters. The venture was short-lived and wound up in 1910.

About this time the industry was in decline and the company was nearly bankrupt. Their position was strengthened when George Richard (Dick) Woodward joined the board as Managing Director. Later Cecil Brinton became a director.

1914 John Brinton died aged eighty-four. He is buried in St.Mary's Churchyard.

1914-18 The First World War. The companies engineering workshops made shells and aeroplane parts and the looms wove blankets and webbing. After the war more land was developed between the river and Corporation Street.

The directors were now Reginald and Cecil Brinton, Dick Woodward and Percy Preen. In a controversy over the families share-holding Percy Preen tried to take the company over and in 1921 the Old Bailey heard the case of Brinton v Preen. Brintons won the day and Percy Preen left the company and joined Carpet Trades.

1923 John F.C.Brinton, Reginald's only son, joined the company after a period with Bigelow-Sandford in America. He introduced modern management techniques.

1926 The Main Office block was extended and Waterside Mill was gutted by fire.

1929 Brintons bought Spennels and built a Sports and Social Club. Weaving now comprised 122 Gripper Axminster, 110 Wilton and 84 Chenille looms with a full Worsted and Woollen spinning operation.

Between 1938 and 1952 the company had a weaving factory in Bridgewater. In later years they also occupied premises in Green Street *{Map C.36}*.

1939-45 The Second World War. Brintons were a "Nucleus" company. Engineering capabilities were extensively used and many looms wove blankets and webbing.

1945 18 acres of land were purchased at Oldington for a new sports ground. Cecil Brinton was now Chairman and his son Tatton and Dick Woodward's son Derek were appointed to the board.

1948 The company bought Slingfield Spinning Mills from Carpet Trades. Between 1955 and 1968 Brintons were part-owners of the Kosset tufting company in Brighouse, Yorkshire.

BRINTONS LIMITED
KIDDERMINSTER

1960 **Brintons Pty. Ltd.**, Geelong, Australia was formed to manufacture Axminster and Wilton carpet. Initially, 43 Kidderminster workers and their families emigrated.
1963 Castle Mills was acquired from Carpet Trades, new spinning equipment was bought for Slingfield and in 1966 No.5 Factory was started on the Stourport Road.
1964 Tatton Brinton was knighted and became the Member of Parliament.
1968 No.6 Factory opened, also on the Stourport Road. The Telford Factory was acquired for the Spinning operation which had outgrown Slingfield Mills.
1971 & 1973 Sales companies were set up in America and Germany.
1973 Brintons acquired the adjacent buildings to their No.6 site. In the mid-1980s the Telford spinning plant was extended and by 1988 Slingfield Mill was empty. Just afterward the No.6 Factory was considerably extended.

In 1991 **Brintons Industria de Alcatifas Limitada**, Portugal opened for Axminster weaving and in 1994 the company bought **Christchurch Yarns** in New Zealand. Between 1995 and 2000 Brintons gradually transferred the looms and equipment from their No.1 town centre factory in readiness for the new town centre development. During the same period they extended the Portuguese factory, built a factory in India **Brintons Carpets Asia Private Ltd.** and bought US Axminster Inc. Greenville, Mississippi to form **Brintons U.S.Axminster Inc.**

In this country it reorganised Telford and No.6 Factory, extended No.5 and bought The Firs building for its extensive engineering facility.

At the Millennium Brintons continue to occupy their Exchange Street Offices as Headquarters for their Kidderminster, Telford and overseas companies and the main town-centre factory is empty awaiting the developers.

Brintons carpets

EXCHANGE STREET, STOUR VALE
John & William Stooke
John Stooke was a clerk at Thomas Humphries' factory in Vicar Street and his brother, William Stooke, was a hand loom weaver. Around 1863 they started a small factory in Exchange Street. Two years later they became tenants of the Stour Vale Mill Company with 12 looms. In 1870 William retired and John Stooke ran the factory until it ceased trading in 1876.

WORCESTER STREET
George Holloway
1818 George Holloway was born in Vicar Street. He started work as a draw-boy.
1835 Butcher, Worth & Holmes appointed him foreman and when the company ceased he became landlord of The Nags Head in Bewdley Street and later The Falcon in Mill Street. He was a character of the town and known as "Honest" George. Later he set up a carpet factory in Worcester Street {Map B.29} making Carpets and Rugs.

WORCESTER CROSS WORKS, OXFORD STREET *{Map C.31}*
WORCESTER CROSS FACTORY & OFFICES, WORCESTER ST. *{Map C.30}*

James Holmes

1831 James Holmes was a Scot who went into partnership with George Butcher and William Henry Worth in Callows Lane. In 1844 the partnership dissolved and James Holmes started his own factory in Mill Street. In 1849 he invested in Tapestry.

1852 James Holmes built Worcester Cross Works, Oxford Street, and installed the power version of the Tapestry Brussels process. He later added Brussels Wilton. After some years without profit he sold the business to John Crossley of Halifax.

John Crossley and Sons *{Map C.31}*

1857 Crossleys took over and James Holmes remained as their Works Manager.

1869 H.R.Willis, Potter and Company bought the business.

H.R.Willis & Company

Around 1863 Henry Richard Willis founded a company in Church Street making Chenille Rugs.

1868 He expanded with the purchase of another Chenille company.

HENRY WILLIS,
Merchant & Commission Agent,
OFFICE: 23, OXFORD ROAD,
KIDDERMINSTER.

LINEN YARNS, WORSTED YARNS, DRYSALTERY GOODS, &c.

Agent for the MUTUAL LIFE ASSURANCE COMPANY, 39, King Street, Cheapside, London, E.C.

H.R.Willis, Potter and Company

1869 Henry Willis joined Edmund Potter. They purchased Worcester Cross Works, Oxford Street. Chenille hand and Brussels power looms were included in the sale.

1878 Edmund Potter left the partnership to form his own company.

H.R.Willis and Company *{Map C.31, C.30}*

1879 Henry Richard Willis expanded with the building of Worcester Cross Factory and Offices, Worcester Street. These buildings were directly opposite his Oxford Street Works. In 1883 the company became unprofitable and to raise capital sold Worcester Cross Factory and Offices to Woodward, Grosvenor and Company.

1896 Willis was declared bankrupt and the Union provided finance to keep going.

Worcester Cross Carpet Company

Willis was the general manager but within one year the company had closed. Worcester Cross Works remained empty until bought by the Cooke Brothers.

Cooke Brothers *{Map C.31}*
1903 Brothers William and Joseph Cooke began the manufacture of Chenille carpet
and rugs at Worcester Cross Works, Oxford Street. Later they added Axminster.
Cooke Brothers (Kidderminster) Ltd.
1907 The company became a limited company and traded well for a number of years.
For a while Empire Carpets leased part of the factory.
1938 The company ceased trading and the factory and Chenille plant was sold.
Also included in the sale were two, one-yard wide (4/4), Anglo-Turkey knotting looms.
Worcester Cross Works were occupied by Lockheed during the Second World War.
The buildings never returned to carpet manufacture. They were demolished in the
1970s and in the 1980s the site became a Safeway Supermarket

CHURCH STREET, WORCESTER CROSS
Woodward & Morton
John Woodward came to Kidderminster from Evesham. Around 1809 he joined
James Morton in the manufacture of Bombazine at a factory in Vicar Street.
1829 John Woodward resigned and the company became James Morton & Sons.
John Woodward and Company.
1829 John Woodward set up his own carpet company in Church Street.
Woodward and Widnell
Around 1825 John's son Benjamin Higgins Woodward was in partnership with
Henry Widnell in Church Street; they had 60 looms. In 1836 the company failed.
Woodward Brothers
Benjamin and another brother Henry formed a company in Church Street.
1838 The partnership failed and the brothers formed their own companies.

BENJAMIN WOODWARD & Co.,
MANUFACTURERS BY POWER OF
Brussels & Velvet Carpeting
AND RUGS.
Works and Offices:
Mill Street, Kidderminster.

B.H.Woodward and Company
1838 Benjamin Woodward's Church
Street factory controlled over 100 looms.
1860 Benjamin died and his sons took
over. They expanded into Mill Street
and in 1865 installed power looms.
Twenty years later the company was
sold.

Henry Woodward and Company
In the late 1790s Henry Woodward's factory was also in Church Street.
(A design paper, dated 1798, exists in Woodward, Grosvenor's Archives).
By 1850 Henry's sons, Henry Toye and George Gower, were with the company.
Henry Woodward & Sons
1855 They leased a section of Stour Vale Mill and installed power looms.
1864 Henry Woodward died and the sons' partnership was dissolved.
George Gower Woodward joined Palmer & Radford at the Waterside Mill, Back
Market Street. Henry Toye Woodward formed Woodward, Grosvenor & Company.

Palmer & Radford in 1864 became **Woodward, Palmer & Radford.**

Gower Woodward and Company *{Map C.25}*

By 1866 Samuel Palmer had retired and Thomas Radford left the company to join Morton & Sons. The company was eventually renamed **The Waterside Mill Company**. In 1882 it failed and Waterside Mill was purchased by John Brinton.

Benjamin and William Grosvenor

1790 Benjamin Grosvenor came to Kidderminster from Shropshire to make ropes and loom harness cordage in Fish Street, later Orchard Street. Benjamin was joined by his son William and they started the production of Bombazine dress material, furniture upholstery silk and Brussels carpet.

1864 William died. He had an 18-years-old son called George William Grosvenor.

Joseph Kiteley

Around 1817 Joseph Kiteley was a draw-boy and he later became a weaver.

Humphries and Kiteley

1835 Joseph Kiteley became a partner in business with John Humphries.

Fawcett and Kiteley

1837 The partnership broke up and Kiteley joined his brother-in-law William Fawcett at a factory in Mill Street. They had 46 hand looms and 105 employees.

1842 Fawcett and Kiteley broke up and formed their own companies.

Joseph Kiteley

Joseph Kiteley ran his own company until 1856 when he sold up to become General Manager of The Stour Vale Mill Company.

STOUR VALE MILLS, GREEN STREET

The Stour Vale Mill Company *{Map C.32}*

1855 Lord Ward of Witley Court provided the finance for William Grosvenor and Joseph Kiteley to build the Stour Vale Mills on open land near Worcester Cross.

Woodward, Grosvenor and Company *{Map C.30, C32}*

1864 Henry Toye Woodward purchased the Henry Woodward Company and went into partnership with George William Grosvenor to form Woodward, Grosvenor. Since George William Grosvenor was a minor his mother had to sign the partnership deeds. Henry Toye Woodward became Chairman and Managing Director. They remained tenants of the Stour Vale Mill Company.

1873 The company also had small premises in Waterloo Street.

1883 The company bought a Royal Axminster weaving plant and with a need to expand purchased the Worcester Cross Factory in Worcester Street from H.R.Willis. The offices and showroom were transferred to the Worcester Cross Factory.

Henry Toye Woodward died. In the following years, as others left to build their own factories, Woodward, Grosvenor gradually became sole occupants of Stour Vale Mills.

Woodward, Grosvenor and Company Ltd. *{Map C.30, C.32}*

1890 Woodward, Grosvenor became a limited liability company with George William Grosvenor as Chairman and Managing Director.

LONDON WAREHOUSE:-
PANYER HOUSE.
TELEPHONES { Nº 2 KIDDERMINSTER. (2 LINES)   1-4, PATERNOSTER ROW. E.C.4.   TELEGRAMS: { GROSVENOR, KIDDERMINSTER.
{ Nº 3989 CITY, LONDON.   { EXSIRATOS, CENT. LONDON.

WOODWARD, GROSVENOR & Cº. LIMITED.

MANUFACTURERS OF

WILTON, BRUSSELS & ROYAL AXMINSTER CARPETS.

EXHIBITION AWARDS,
LONDON, 1851. 1862 & 1871.
PARIS, 1867 & 1878.   **KIDDERMINSTER.**
DUBLIN, 1872.
SYDNEY, 1879.

1892 Woodward, Grosvenor paid off Lord Ward and became the owners of Stour Vale Mills. They wove Brussels and Wilton at Stour Vale and Axminster at Worcester Cross. Around this time a dyehouse and drying room was added. The letter heading above shows telephone No.2 (2 lines).

1905 George William's son John Ernest Grosvenor joined the company.

1909 Maitland Kempson also joined as joint Managing Director and Sales Director.

1914-18 In the war years the production of carpets was significantly reduced due to the lack of skilled labour and raw materials. The company also wove army blankets.

1923 The Grosvenor-Picking Wilton loom was patented and manufactured.

1923 George William died and John Ernest Grosvenor became chairman.

1938 Maitland Kempson died and his son Charles B. was appointed to the board.

1939-45 During the Second World War the company came under the same restrictions as the rest of the carpet industry. Some carpet was woven with their ration of raw materials, looms were converted to weave canvas and some of the sheds converted to making light engineering war components. Others were Ministry of Supply stores.

1945 John Ernest Grosvenor was nearing retirement and planned to become a Church of England minister. He had no sons to come into the business and considered selling the company. In 1946 the company was sold and became part of a consortium with Grays of Ayr. The company still traded under its own brand name.

Grays Carpets

1967 Rationalisation meant that all products were marketed as Grays Carpets.

1970 Grays were taken over by the **Guthrie Corporation** group and the company became part of **British Carpets Ltd.**

1971 The Axminster plant closed and Worcester Cross Factory was sold to the Borough Council. Stour Vale remained but significantly reduced in capacity.

Woodward, Grosvenor & Co. Ltd. *{Map C.32}*

1982 A group of managers bought the company and returned it to its former name.

1993 The company was further restructured with some changes in directorship. During the 1990s the dyehouse closed. The company also leased buildings at Crossley Park where they ran Platt Spool Axminster looms originally owned by Coloroll.

At the Millennium Stour Vale Mill is the centre of operations with Wilton and Axminster production.

CHURCH STREET, DRAYTON, GREEN STREET

Richard Watson & Son

Around 1800 cotton spinner John Watson's son, Richard, started his own carpet company in Church Street. Richard had two sons called John and Richard Jr.
1831 Richard Sr. died and the company was taken over by the eldest son John. The company owned 34 Brussels hand looms.

John Watson, Son and Badland

1835 Charles Davies Badland joined the business and the company expanded.
By 1838 they had 90 Brussels hand looms and a workforce of about 200.

John Watson & Son

1860 Charles Davies Badland left the partnership and John Watson retired to concentrate on his Dry Salter business. John had a brother Richard Jr.

Richard Watson

In the 1840s Richard Watson set up a Worsted Spinning Company at Drayton near Chaddesley Corbett. The Broom family were involved.

Watson & Naylor

1853 Richard Watson was joined in partnership by Joseph Naylor who came to the area from Halifax where he was a Spinning Mill manager. The business expanded.
1855 Watson & Naylor were tenants of the Lord Ward Shed at Stour Vale Mills. They had two units for their spinning operation.
1857 The company built Pike Mills {Map C.33}. Pike Mills was a large five-storey brick mill building with additional sheds built on meadowland opposite Stour Vale. New Worsted spinning equipment was installed, they later added Woollen spinning.
1869 Watson & Naylor invested in Kidderminster carpet power looms. In the early 1870s both owners brought two sons into the company, they were John Harold and Richard Talbot Watson and Thomas Fox and Arthur Naylor.
1873 Richard Watson Sr. retired. His sons took over; but there was family friction.
1878 Part of Pike Mills was leased to **G.W.Oldland and Company**. They later became associated with **The Princess Carpet Company Ltd.** and both traded at Pike Mills until 1894. George Weight Oldland also had associations with others in the town including **Oldland, Naylor & Lloyd** in Mill Street {Map A.8, A.9}.
About the same time **A.Standage and Company** leased part of the Mill.
By 1883 the friction, in business, between the Naylor and Watson families had increased to the point where they decided to split the Pike Mills operation.

Watson Brothers {Map C.33, C.36}

1883 Watson Brothers concentrated on the Worsted Spinning operation including Drayton Mills which had remained part of the company.
1932 Watson Brothers ceased trading and Pike Mills was sold.

Pike Mills.

Pike Mills was subsequently occupied by other companies including Brintons and the Boucher Engineering Company. It was demolished in 1968.
At the Millennium the area forms the car park between Safeway and Aldi.

T.& A.Naylor *{Map C.33}*

1883 Thomas Fox and Arthur Naylor retained the carpet weaving and Woollen spinning operation. Thomas Fox became the Chairman. A little later they further expanded the weaving into the Chenille and rug markets.

In 1886 Pike Mills was gutted in a major town fire. In the following years the company specialised in Kidderminster carpet, they had over 30 power looms.

1906 Lance Naylor joined the company as did Claud Naylor in 1911.

TELEGRAPHIC ADDRESS
NAYLOR KIDDERMINSTER

TELEPHONE Nᵒˢ 2261 & 2262

LONDON ADDRESS
11 ROSE STREET E.C.4

T.& A. NAYLOR LTD

CARPET & RUG MANUFACTURERS
YARN SPINNERS AND DYERS

KIDDERMINSTER

T.& A.Naylor Ltd. *{Map C.33, C.43}*

1909 The company became a limited private company.

Around 1916 the family purchased Lowland Meadows at the other end of Green Street near the Worcester Road intersection and built Lowland Works *{Map C.43}*. Part of the Chenille and rug making department were transferred from Pike Mills, but some weaving remained at Pike Mills including the Kidderminster looms. During the First World War Naylors wove blankets and other woollen fabrics.

1917 Chairman Thomas Fox Naylor died and was succeeded by Arthur Naylor.

1922 Arthur died and Claud Naylor became Chairman.

1924 Lowland Works further developed with a new office block, showrooms and a two-storey warehouse fronting Green Street. A new dyehouse was built and three years later a large Gripper Axminster plant was added.

1932 When Watson Brothers sold Pike Mills, Naylors had to transfer or scrap the remaining equipment. So the last Kidderminster looms in town were scrapped.

1933 Naylor's Foley Spinning Mill was built on the Stourport Road *{Map D.53}*.

1935 The roof of the warehouse fronting Green Street was raised fifteen feet. A year later a bridge link across Green Street was added. This linked the main factory to premises across the road purchased earlier.

Naylors became one of the larger town companies and a major employer with over 700 employees. They remained woollen spinners, dyers and manufactures of Gripper and Chenille Axminster woven carpet and rugs up until the Second World War.

1939 The wartime effort concentrated on the Chenille looms weaving 350,000 blankets and the Gripper looms weaving 280,000 square yards of heavy duty canvas. However, when raw materials ran out in October 1941 the company closed. Some of the weaving sheds were seconded as an Admiralty store.

The restart after the war took a long time. Spinning commenced at Foley Mills at the end of 1944 but it was not until 1946 that the looms of Lowlands Works wove again. During the postwar boom the company, like all other companies, prospered. 1965 Claud Naylor retired and his son David H.Naylor became Chairman. New Spool-Gripper Axminster looms were installed to replace the obsolete Chenille plant.

Naylors also set up a small pilot plant for Tufting in Lisle Avenue {Map D.54}. This was followed by the installation of a full Tufting Section at the Lowland Works. In the 1970s the whole industry suffered from over production. This was particularly true for the Tufted carpet sector. The company began to lose money on its Tufting operation although the Axminster production continued to be profitable. By 1975 the company was in serious financial difficulties and in May of the following year the receivers were called in to run

Naylor Carpet

the company. In July 1976 the company ceased trading with a loss of 600 jobs. Lowland Works became the Lowland Trading Estate. Between 1976 and 1980 David Bamford, formerly Morris Carpets, leased the Gripper-Spool plant and operated under the company name **Cakebole Carpets.** Rowe Carpets retail shop and Carpets of Kidderminster were also tenants.

GREEN STREET, FOLEY PARK
Samuel Fawcett
Samuel Fawcett was a hand loom weaver at Lea's factory in Mill Street.
1843 He started his own company in Mill Street.
1855 The company became one of the first tenants at Stour Vale Mill with Brussels power looms. The business was profitable and his son Henry Fawcett took over.
Winnall and Fawcett {Map C.34}
1872 Henry Fawcett went into partnership with Henry Walter Corbyn Winnall. They built a new mill and factory next door to Stour Vale Mill on Back Brook. At the front, on Green Street, were a multi-storey block for offices, stores and winding room and to the rear a large weaving shed with a dyehouse and drying room.
Henry Fawcett and Company
Henry Winnall left the partnership and Henry Fawcett took control and brought his brother, Francis Best Fawcett, into the business.
In 1882 they patented the principle for manufacturing the "Chlidema Square". (Chlidema is a word derived from the Greek "chlide" meaning luxurious).
William Fawcett
Samuel Fawcett's brother, William, worked with **Wagstaff and Bayliss** before going into partnership with Joseph Kiteley.
Fawcett and Kiteley
Between 1837 and 1842 Joseph Kiteley and William Fawcett were in partnership.
William Fawcett and Company
1842 William Fawcett had a factory in Mill Street but he could not raise the financial backing to convert to power loom and by 1856 he was bankrupt.

THE CHLIDEMA CARPET Co. LTD

MANUFACTURERS OF

BRUSSELS, WILTON & AXMINSTER CARPETS

Telegrams:
CHLIDEMA CO. KIDDERMINSTER.
A.B.C. CODE. 5TH EDITION.

INCORPORATING THE OLD-ESTABLISHED BUSINESS OF
G.M. WHITTALL & CO. LTD.

Kidderminster

LONDON:
31. PATERNOSTER SQUARE AND
12 ROSE ST., NEWGATE ST., E.C.
TELEPHONE No. 3351 CENTRAL.

The Chlidema Carpet Company Ltd. Green Street *{Map C.34}*

1887 A new company was formed with Henry Fawcett as Managing Director. Over the following years the company's indebtedness to the bank meant that James Trenfield Johnson, the company accountant, gained control using his good standing with Lloyds Bank. By the time Henry Fawcett died, in 1891, J.T.Johnson was in control. At the turn of the century Chlidema were prosperous with over 100 employees producing bordered Brussels and Wilton Chlidema squares.

1906 Chlidema purchased the plant from G.M.Whittall of Park Mills.

1927 Extensions were added to maximise the buildings on the site.

1929 J.T.Johnson died and his sons, Cyril and Eric Johnson took charge.

1935 The company invested in Gripper Axminster.

1967 Chlidema bought the Empire Carpet Company.

The Empire Carpet Company *{Map D.51}*

1907 Thomas Griffin and Henry Johnson started in a part of the Worcester Cross Works leased from Cooke Brothers. They installed 16 Dobcross Brussels looms.

   Thomas Griffin owned land in Foley Park and around 1912 he built the Foley Park Factory in Beauchamp Avenue. The looms and equipment were transferred. After the Second World War they added a Gripper Axminster plant.

1956 The first Tufter in Kidderminster was installed. Empire did not invest further capital into tufting and the original tufter was eventually sold to Georgian Carpets. In the postwar boom years Empire employed over 100 in their Wilton and Gripper Axminster departments. These were profitable years. But, in 1967, the company became insolvent and the receivers were called in. In the following year the buildings and equipment was sold to The Chlidema Carpet Company.

The Chlidema Carpet Company, Chlidema Mill and Foley Park Factory

Eric and Cyril Johnson both retired and the business passed to Eric's two sons.

1970 The Chlidema Mill site was sold and the production concentrated at Foley Park using the Chlidema Company name. The troubled times of the late 1970s resulted in the operation going into receivership during May 1979.

FOLEY PARK FACTORY *{Map D.51}*

The Chlidema Carpet Co. Ltd.

In 1979 Lenagrange, a Harris Queensway company, bought the business but within a year the company had ceased trading.

Gateway Carpets

In the summer of 1980 Adrian and Oliver Johnson started the company with Axminster and Wilton looms purchased from Chlidema's liquidation sale.

Gateway Carpets Limited

1983 Gateway became a limited company and were successful for the next ten years. However, they did not survive the recession of the early 1990s and the company went into liquidation.

Gateway Carpet Manufacturing Company Ltd.

Between 1993 and 1995 a new company, owned by three businessmen, ran Gateway.

Traditional Weavers

1995 Cavalier Carpets of Blackburn bought the assets of Gateway.
At the Millennium they have a small Axminster and Wilton plant with 50 employees.

GREEN STREET

Carpet Products Ltd., Abercynon, South Wales

In 1946 the Boucher Engineering Company set up a carpet factory in South Wales to manufacture Wilton carpet. In 1972 Bouchers transferred to Chlidema Mill, Green Street, bringing together their engineering business and the Carpet Company.

C.P.Carpets, Chlidema Mills, Green Street *{Map C.34}*

1972 The company's production concentrated on the contract market with Wilton body and broadloom products.

C.P.Carpets (Kidderminster) Ltd.

1976 In a restructuring the company became the trading name for **Deepile Limited**.

In the mid-1980s they added Axminster narrow and broadloom and in the 1990s Wilton broadloom.
At the Millennium, with around 90 employees, after a number of changes in ownership the company continues to specialise in the bespoke contract market.

Frank Stone

1830 Thomas Stone came to Kidderminster from Wilton to set up in business with his uncle William Stone. They initially had 6 Wilton hand looms.

1853 Thomas died leaving the company to his son James Edward who was eighteen years old. James Edward Stone gained experience by working in other companies in the town including Henry Brinton & Sons. Later he was Works Superintendent at Woodward, Palmer and Radford, Waterside Mills, Back Market Street.

1870 He became a yarn agent and chemical merchant selling in this country and America.

1884 James Edward's son, Frank, entered the business which was then located in Corporation Street opposite Waterside Mill {Map C.27} and also part of Brintons. Around the turn of the century they reintroduced some old looms for the manufacture of hand-knotted rugs.

Frank Stone (Kidderminster) Ltd. {Map C.35}

1914 The business was transferred to the corner of Green Street and Dixon Street where they wove canvas during the First World War. After the war they introduced Brussels and plain Wilton.

Two years later they started making carpet fringes and a product known as Boucle (French for curly) which was a hard wearing carpet of hair and wool.

1928 Frank Stone died leaving his son, also called Frank, in control.

1960 The company decided to concentrate on fringes and canvas. From this time onwards the carpet production ceased and the looms were dismantled.

1975 The business was sold to **Youghal Carpets (Holdings)**.

1984 The company again changed hands with a management buy-out. The new owners continued trading as Frank Stone Ltd. and they improved the production with the installation of 14 new high-speed cloth weaving looms.

1995 The Company again changed hands becoming part of The Craft Collection Group, Britain's largest craft mail order company.

At the Millennium the products included canvas for rugs, and knotted rug fringes.

William Green

In the early 1830s William Green was a draw-boy. In 1858 he leased a unit of the Lord Ward Shed at Stour Vale Mill and commenced the manufacture of Tapestry Brussels. He also had premises at Green Valley Mills.

1869 He built the New Road Mill {Map C.38} further down the new road from Stour Vale on Back Brook. There he installed a large Tapestry plant with 42 looms.

William Green & Sons

William's sons, James Ernest, George Richard and William Clement Green joined the company. In 1886 William Green died and his sons took over the business.

William Green & Sons Ltd.

1890 The brothers expanded with the introduction of Brussels, Wilton and the latest Spool Axminster. However, things did not work out and they sold up.

1899 Victoria Carpets of Kirkcaldy bought the equipment and leased the buildings.

Isaak Hampton & Company

1869 Isaak Hampton took over William Green's Green Valley Mill factory and the Tapestry looms when New Road Mills was built. The company failed in 1878.

Castle Works, New Road and Pump Street {Map C.44}

Stanley and Laughton Goodwin's Castle Road Motor Company occupied the factory until around 1922 when Victoria Carpets took over the buildings.

The Victoria Carpet Company, Kirkcaldy

1895 The company was formed with three partners, George Anton, Alexander Hamilton and John Johnson. Their first factory was in Kirkcaldy, Fifeshire, and lay

at the corner of two roads, Victoria Road and Dunnikier Road. There they produced Tapestry rugs and squares.

Victoria took its company name from Victoria Road although their office address was Dunnikier Road. The area had a thriving linoleum industry and this created competition for the skilled workforce. The three partners were ambitious and determined to expand and develop so, in 1899, they decided to move the whole operation to Kidderminster, including some equipment and any of the workforce who were prepared to travel south.

THE VICTORIA CARPET CO. LTD.
GREEN STREET
KIDDERMINSTER

TELEPHONE:
KIDDERMINSTER 2278
2279
2270

DIRECTORS
C. S. ANTON
J. G. ANTON
G. S. F. ANTON
P. J. ANTON
J. H. H. ANTON

TELEGRAMS
VICTORIA, KIDDERMINSTER

The Victoria Carpet Company, Kidderminster {Map C.38}

William Green's New Road Mill in Green Street was empty and leased as their new headquarters. The Mill contained power looms for Brussels, Wilton, "Nyanza" Axminster and a full plant for Tapestry including over 20 printing drums. The relocation took two years to complete and involved the charter of two complete trains full of looms and equipment together with the families and their furniture. The story is told of some loyal workers who walked from Kirkcaldy to Kidderminster to keep their jobs. Initially Victoria concentrated on the printed Tapestry carpets, but, by 1911, they were investing in the growing Chenille Axminster market.

1918 John Johnson retired and the two sons of George Anton, Charles and James, came into the business. In 1920 they built extensions to the Green Street factory towards Back Brook and to the side, they also purchased over 50 Dobcross Chenille looms. The company continued to produce some Tapestry until 1946.

A programme of further investment followed with new Gripper Jacquard plant and a Plain Wilton range specialising in car carpeting for Standard Motors and Rover. This was mainly housed in the nearby Castle Works {Map C.44}.

A 14 bay warehouse was added in 1927 and in the same year Alexander Hamilton died, his interests in the company being purchased by the Anton family.

In 1936 the main office complex on the corner of Green and Dixon Street was built.

179

During the Second World War Victoria were one of the town's "Nucleus" companies. The older employees assembled Ford V8 engines under licence for the British Bren-Gun carriers. They also reconditioned machine tools and made parts for gun mountings. Some looms were converted to weave knapsack webbing.

However, the cotton mills of Lancashire were also producing to excess so the direction was given to concentrate on the manufacture of armaments. Two-hundred women employees travelled to Oldbury for many weeks to help out at an armament factory. The aircraft builders Short Brothers had their factory at Rochester destroyed and so they transferred 100 employees in their design team to Victoria's offices. The Stirling Bomber was said to have been designed during that occupation.

In 1946 the Tapestry plant was scrapped and the sheds turned over to weaving, while in 1953 the Australian subsidiary factory opened in Dendenong, Victoria. Initially weaving Gripper Axminster they added Tufting in 1968.

In this country Victoria were one of the Tufting pioneers when, in 1956, a small evaluation plant was installed in the Green Street factory.

GREEN STREET, WORCESTER ROAD
Victoria Carpets Ltd. *{Map C.38, C.44, E.63}*
1963 Victoria became a public limited company. There were over 500 employees. In the same year they built a new factory on the Worcester Road *{Map E.63}* for

their Tufted operation. In the following years the company developed and consolidated their position in the Tufting market. However, they also retained a buoyant woven section at the Green Street factories. In the early 1990s they added the Castlemaine Spinning Company, Australia.

Towards the Millennium, the company planned to extend the buildings at the Worcester Road site to contain all their production machinery. The Green Street factories were sold for development. During 1999 the majority of this work was completed including the transfer of the dyehouse and main offices.

At the Millennium the Green Street premises were in the process of being finally cleared and vacated.

WORCESTER ROAD
William Hill (Kidderminster) Ltd. *{Map E.64}*
William Hill was a Wilton loom tuner. Prior to the Second World War he ran a small company in Worcester with two Wilton plain looms.
1946 William Hill built a factory on the Worcester Road. He initially concentrated on Wilton but in later years added Spool Axminster. In the 1960s the company had 80 employees.
1978 The Company went out of business and the looms were sold.

HOOBROOK

Hoobrook Mill *{Map E.61}* **and Spennels Mill** *{Further up stream}*

Hoobrook gets its name from the stream that flows through the village before joining the River Stour. The Hoo was also known as the "Throw" and on this stream two mills became part of the industry. Both mills were located upstream on the Spennels side of the railway viaduct. Hoobrook Mill was originally a corn and paper mill.

John Broom & Son

In the 1820s John Broom occupied the mills for Worsted Spinning.

James and George Humphries took over and continued Worsted Spinning.

After the 1851 Great Exhibition the Bigelow Power Loom was set up in Hoobrook Mill for demonstration.

Around 1869 **Crabtree Bros.** continued the Worsted Spinning operation and, in 1872, they added a small Tapestry Brussels plant. They later added Chenille but in 1877 Crabtree Brothers ceased carpet production.

The original mill buildings have been demolished.

CRABTREE BROTHERS,

MANUFACTURERS, BY POWER, OF

Tapestry Carpets, Axminster & other Rugs,

WORSTED SPINNERS, & COMMISSION AGENTS.

WORKS—HOO BROOK & SPENNELLS MILLS.
OFFICES—17, MILL STREET,
K I D D E R M I N S T E R.

LONDON WAREHOUSE—12, OAT LANE, NOBLE STREET, E.C.

COMBERTON HILL, ANCHORFIELDS, HOOBROOK

Garford, Lilley and Brother (Kidderminster) Ltd., Comberton Hill

1931 The company sold webbing and tapes, A.G.(George) Brockway was a partner.

A.G.Brockway Ltd. *{Map E.61}*

1934 George Brockway started his own carpet company at Hoobrook where he had a small Wilton plant. Just prior to the Second World War the works were sold to Morris & Company who were expanding at the time.

1948 Brockways resumed production in Hoobrook Carpet Mill which was built on the other side of the viaduct *{Map E.62}*.

In the 1950s the company was developed further with new buildings, Gripper Axminster looms and Face-to-Face Wilton.

Brockway Carpets Ltd. *{Map E.62.}*

1964 George Brockway retired and Roy Annable and Skene Walley became the new owners. The company expanded its broadloom Gripper Axminster plant. In the mid 1970s the Wilton plant closed and they invested in Tufting equipment.

1974 A new office block and showroom was opened.

1978 When Morris-Gloucester failed Brockways took over part of their factory.

In the mid-1990s the Axminster plant was scrapped as they extended their Tufting operation. In 1998 a new despatch office was added to the warehouse *{Map E.61a}*.

At the Millennium Brockways employ a workforce of 180 in the Tufting operation.

Morris and Company

1902 Alfred Morris started his textile-waste business in Anchorfields.

1932 John and Norman Dutfield and Mrs E.Whatmore became the new owners and they expanded into carpets. Additional premises were acquired for narrow Wilton.

1939 The Bamford family entered the business, they eventually became the owners. Just before the Second World War Morris took over the Hoobrook factory from A.G.Brockway. During the war the factory, now called Viaduct Works, was the home of a light engineering concern called Clifford Aero who were engaged in war work.

1946 Morris Carpets restarted the looms and in the years following extended production into Gripper Axminster. They now had a workforce of around 200.

Morris and Company (Kidderminster) Ltd. *{Map E.61}*

1965 Morris became a public limited company and employed over 300.

1968 The Irish Company **Youghal Carpets (Holdings)** of County Cork bought Morris and one year later the Gloucester Carpet Company.

Morris-Gloucester Carpets

1975 The companies were integrated together. Youghal Carpets got into financial difficulties and in 1978 they closed the Hoobrook operation with a loss of 250 jobs.

FRANCHISE STREET

Dutfield & Quayle Ltd.

1928 W.Harry Dutfield and Stephen.K.Quayle started making reversible Chenille rugs in a small shed on the old waste tip in Franchise Street.

1931 The Franchise Street Factory was built with offices at the front. They continued to concentrate on Chenille but added Gripper Axminster. By 1935 they had over 100 employees. In the following year Dutfield and Quayle were approached by members of Axminster Town Council who wanted to revive the weaving industry in the Devon town. Stephen Quayle decided to stay in Kidderminster.

Axminster Carpets Ltd.
1937 Harry Dutfield moved to Axminster to form the new company.

QUAYLE & TRANTER LTD

Carpet Manufacturers

Quayle & Tranter Ltd.
1937 Stephen Quayle continued in partnership with his
brother John C.Quayle and accountant W.Neville Tranter.

FRANCHISE STREET
KIDDERMINSTER
TELEPHONE   KIDDERMINSTER 3643
TELEGRAMS QUALITY, KIDDERMINSTER

During the war the company produced blankets, webbing and some gun parts. In the years following the company successfully produced a series of Celtic designs. In the 1960s they introduced a range of Scandinavian designs which sold around the world. Quayle & Tranter also set up **Broadloom Carpets Ltd.** in Blackburn in association with D.G.Gaskell and Company. Later the Quayle and Tranter partnership ended. Neville Tranter took over the assets of the Blackburn company and Stephen Quayle remained in Kidderminster with the weaving operation.

Quayle Carpets Ltd.
1965 Quayles invested in Tufting in part of
the old Richard Thomas & Baldwin factory in
Wilden Lane. The late 1970s proved to be a

difficult period for the company and in 1979 Quayle Carpets went into receivership. New owners sold the Franchise Street factory and concentrated the business in Wilden Lane.

WILDEN FACTORY UNITS
Quayle Carpets (1980) Ltd.
1979 A new company trading under its previous name produced Tufted broadloom and Gripper Axminster. Six years later the company was in receivership.
1985 Lionel Rowe's company bought the Wilden works and the equipment.
Carpets of Kidderminster Ltd.
Around 1980 Carpets of Kidderminster was started by Lionel Rowe, his son Roger and two other businessmen at Lowland Trading Estate, Green Street *{Map C.43}*.
Initially, they ran the Gripper-Spool looms originally owned by Naylors.
1985 The Rowe company bought the Wilden factory of the failed Quayle Carpets (1980) Ltd. They also bought the subsidiary company **Saxon Carpets** which produced and sold in the tufted market. In the mid-1990s the production was considerably expanded with the purchase of Axminster looms and designs from the American owners of the reformed Kosset Company in Bradford.
  Towards the Millennium, now with 150 employees, they finalised plans to vacate the Green Street premises and further develop the buildings and production at Wilden.
The Wilden Carpet Company Ltd.
1965 Small company producing Wilton until around 1980 when the buildings were taken over by **Classic Carpets (Stourport).**

FRANCHISE STREET FACTORY
Thomson Carpets Ltd.
1978 Eric Thomson leased a unit at Lowland Trading Estate (formerly Naylors) for a small tufting operation. In 1986 he relocated to a unit at the Franchise Street factory where he added Axminster. The company ceased trading in 1987.
Heathfield Carpets Ltd.
1986 Manufactured contract carpet in part of Franchise Street factory until 1988.
Master Weavers Ltd.
1987 A company set up in part of the Franchise Street factory. Starting with Wilton the company expanded into Gripper and later Spool Axminster.
  At the Millennium Master Weavers continue their woven production.

OTHER LOCATIONS AROUND KIDDERMINSTER
Between 1950 and 1967 **Hardwick & Austin Ltd.** of Fair Street were a small company weaving Spool Axminster. In the mid-1960s they had 20 employees.
  Lisle Avenue has been the home of many companies including Naylors. For a time Brintons leased a building for part of their Engineering Department. In the 1960s **Winwood Textiles** manufactured Wilton and in 1978 **A. & J.Classics (Carpets)** produced narrow Gripper Axminster for the contract market. At the Millennium **Valetta Carpets**, started in 1997, wove narrow Spool Axminster.
  David Bayliss started **David Bayliss (Carpets) Ltd.** in Sandy Lane, Stourport, in 1972. There he manufactured Jacquard Wilton, Gripper and Spool Axminster for the contract market. In 1985 the company was reformed as **David Bayliss (1985) Ltd.** in part of the former Carpet Manufacturing Company factory in Green Street. At the Millennium, now called **Contract Carpet Weavers**, the company weaves Spool Axminster exclusively for the contract market. In the same buildings **Aftcraft** wove Axminster between 1984 and 1987.
  P.J.H.Carpets was the trading name of the company started in Green Street in 1955. In the mid-1960s they moved to a new factory on the Oldington Trading Estate. With a workforce at around 70 the company concentrated on Wilton and Gripper Axminster. The problems of the 1970s proved insurmountable and the

company closed in 1979. Across the main Stourport Road at the Firs Industrial Estate **Enterprise Weaving** started up in 1997. At the Millennium their developing business included a seven-frame Wilton.
  Hartlebury Trading Estate also housed the carpet industry with **Dalton Carpets** who, in 1980, made Gripper Axminster for contract. In 1985 they were linked with **Quest Carpets**. About the same time **Custom Carpet Manufacturers** produced narrow Wilton and Gripper, also for the contract market.

STOURPORT-ON-SEVERN

Stourport town and the Staffordshire and Worcestershire canal were very important to the growth of Kidderminster and the carpet industry.

The early 1800s were troubled times for the manufacturers in Kidderminster and a few decided to set up outside the town's boundaries. The Stour at Lower Mitton, near where the river joins the Severn, was an ideal location and so a small carpet industry started in this area of Stourport.

LOWER MITTON

Robert Shirley had premises in Lower Mitton in the mid-1820s.

Tyler & Humphries *{Map F.71}*

1828 Tyler & Humphries established the first carpet factory on the river Stour at Farm Bed near the Lower Mitton bridge. It was called the Farm Bed Carpet Factory. Note: 1828 was the year of the Weavers Strike in Kidderminster.

Harris & Cumming, George Harris *{Map F.71}*

1836 George Harris was the owner of the Farm Bed factory in partnership with John Cumming. They were Worsted spinners, they also built a dyehouse *{Map F.71a}*.

By 1849 they had 16 hand looms weaving Brussels.

1850 Cumming retired and George Harris continued until his retirement in 1854.

Charles Harrison *{Map F.71}*

Charles Harrison came to Stourport from Liverpool. He worked for George Harris and in 1854 took over the factory. Power looms were replacing the old hand looms and so within three years he had invested in 17 Brussels Bigelow-Collier looms.

Charles Harrison & Sons.

The business expanded and outgrew the Lower Mitton factory. Around 1890 Harrison's three sons became partners and in 1896 Harrison and his sons moved the operation to Long Meadow Mills in Kidderminster. The company went on to become part of Herbert Smith's Carpet Trades Ltd.

Samuel Broom or Broome

In the 1840s Samuel Broom was part of the industry in Lower Mitton. He was reported to have been involved with the dyehouse *{Map F.71a}* and the building of the Mitton Works as a Spinning Mill *{Map F.73}*, probably the site of Anglo House. John Brinton was also involved in association with Samuel Broom.

William Underhill and Issak Window

Both had small rug weaving ventures in the late 1800s.

Butcher, Worth & Holmes

1831 George Butcher, William Henry Worth and James Holmes were in partnership in Callows Lane, Kidderminster. In 1844 the partnership broke up and William Henry Worth together with his sons, William and Joseph, continued the carpet business at a small factory in Callows Lane, Kidderminster.

Worth Brothers

1850 Worth Brothers became the registered name when William Henry retired and another brother Thomas Bond, aged 17 years, joined the company.

1853 The business relocated to a new factory in Stourport. With a steam engine and line shafting the building housed the new Bigelow-Collier Brussels power looms. The location is uncertain, possibly one of Broom's sites {Map F.71a or F.73}. However, the factory soon became too small for the rapidly growing company.

Worth & Head

1858 Thomas Bond Worth became the sole family member working in the company when his two brothers retired. John Head was taken into the partnership. Head left in 1864 to form his own company with Russell Broome in Mill Street, Kidderminster.

T.Bond Worth {Map F.74}

1866 Thomas Bond Worth became the owner of the company.

1868 The Severn Valley Mills were built. Following the lead given at Stour Vale in Kidderminster other companies leased sections of the factory, these included

Fawcett & Spurway, James Bough and Thomas Garlick

1883 Lower Dudbridge Mills in Stroud was acquired for rug manufacture.

T.Bond Worth & Sons Ltd.

1896 The company became a limited company and just after this Thomas Bond Worth died and his two sons, Roland and Edward became joint Managing Directors. They now owned 75 Brussels and Wilton looms.

T.Bond Worth & Sons LIMITED. MANUFACTURERS OF HIGH CLASS CARPETS, BRUSSELS, WILTON, ROYAL AXMINSTER, SEAMLESS CHENILLE SQUARES, RUGS & MATS. ADDRESS ALL COMMUNICATIONS TO Severn Valley Mills, Stourport on Severn, Worcestershire.

1899 A new extension shed was built for the latest Royal Spool Axminster looms.

1900 In Stroud, Ham Mills became available and was purchased. Both Stroud Mills were soon equipped with new power Chenille Axminster looms. Around this time the company operated some 120 looms and had over 500 employees.

1920 Yet another Stroud mill, Eagle Spinning Mill at Bowbridge, was bought.

1926 In Stourport a large new shed was added for Axminster and Wilton broad looms. In the same year the company's Works Manager, Arthur Davis, invented and patented the Spool Axminster "split shot" process for the weft insertion. This later became the standard for all looms and it significantly increased production.

1927 New offices and showrooms were completed.

1939-45 During the Second World War the Stourport factory worked with Albright & Wilson of Oldbury filling bombs and hand grenades. Other space at Stourport and the Stroud factories was used for government storage.

1943 Roland died and Edward retired leaving Edward B.Worth Jr. and Colonel Phillip W.Robinson as joint Managing Directors. Robinson was related being the son of Thomas Bond Worth's second daughter. Both had joined the board in 1928. After the war the company quickly returned to full carpet production.

1954 The Eagle Spinning Mills at Stroud were destroyed by fire. Around this time the company ceased the manufacture of Chenille. Ham Mills became a Spinning Mill.

1955 Bond Worth became a partner in Kosset Carpets at Brighouse, Yorkshire.

1958 The Australian Factory at Mornington in Victoria State was opened.

1960 Colonel Robinson died and Edward B.Worth became Chairman with Dr J. T. Murray as Managing Director. Dr Murray had joined the company in 1952.

1961 **Bond Worth (Exports) Ltd.** was set up to deal with the growing export market.

1963 The company bought **Jelleyman & Sons Ltd.**, Townshend Mills, Puxton. The Kidderminster factory had an existing Axminster plant and in the early 1970s Bond Worth installed six new Crabtree 15 foot wide Gripper-Spool Axminster looms.

1964 Bond Worth bought their own Tufting company **Thomas Taylor & Bros.** of Wigan and withdrew from the Kosset Carpets consortium.

1964 **Bond Worth Vergani SRL.** The company went into partnership with the Italian Wilton specialists Vittorio Vergani of Cantu, north of Milan in Italy.

1969 They extended their stake in Tufting with the acquisition of **Rivington Carpets**.

Bond Worth Holdings Ltd.

1973 The company changed its name to Bond Worth Holdings Ltd. and they increased their sales efforts especially in the export field. At the time the workforce in Stourport was over 1000 employees. However, the worldwide recession of the mid-70s affected the company adversely and in 1977 the receivers were called in. The receivers ran the company for a further 18 months under a number of company names.

Carpets of Worth Ltd.

In 1979 the Stourport, Kidderminster and Stroud factories were purchased by a consortium of Middle Eastern businessmen and the name was changed. The company continued to market Spool Axminster and their own development Bondax, a patterned non-woven bonded product that took over 15 years to perfect. In 1983 **The Bondax Company** was set up to market the product. In 1994 Worths bought the marketing rights of the Northern Ireland Axminster company **Clandeboye Carpets**.

Like most other companies during the 1990s Carpets of Worth started a programme of restructuring and consolidation which resulted in the transfer of equipment between the Stourport and Kidderminster sites and locations abroad.

At the Millennium Carpets of Worth main offices remained at Severn Valley Mills but equipment was being transferred from the site.

LOWER MITTON, STOURPORT

Fawcett & Spurway, Fawcett & Watson, Fawcett Brothers

1868 Robert Fawcett and William Spurway, a Kidderminster company with offices in Church Street, were tenants at Severn Valley Mill. Around 1875 Spurway retired and Robert Fawcett was joined by George Watson. They had a factory at the Island Mills, Lower Mitton *{Map F.72}*. When George Watson retired, in 1880, William Lea Fawcett, Robert's brother, became a partner. The company ceased trading in 1882.

Richard Smith & Sons

1882 Richard Smith, at the time a large Kidderminster company, bought Island Mills and installed Chenille Axminster looms.

Anderson, Lawson and Company *{Map F.72}*

Around 1894 James William Anderson and John Lawson came to Island Mills from Glasgow. Richard Smith was now part of The Carpet Manufacturing Company and he provided some finance for the venture. The company was also known as **The Textile Manufacturing Company** making Chenille curtain material.

In the late 1890s Chenille carpets, rugs and later "Alcosto" squares were added to the production. During the 1920s the Lawson family left the business and in 1931 the company became fully integrated with The Carpet Manufacturing Company. In 1934 Island Mills was sold and the equipment transferred to Kidderminster.

The Sultana Carpet Company, Sandy Lane, Stourport

1997 The Sultana Carpet Company was formed by three Kidderminster businessmen. Full story on page 133.

At the Millennium the developing company had six looms in operation

BEWDLEY

Bewdley had a thriving cloth industry in the houses around town but there appears to have been only one carpet factory on the River Severn.

Sturge & Lloyd started in 1828, the year of the Weavers Strike. Henry Sturge and Theodore Lloyd built the new carpet factory in the Butt Town Meadow on the Wribbenhall side of the river near the bridge. The four-storey brick mill-style factory was complete with dyehouse, warehouse and hand loom-shops. Around 1832 Theodore Lloyd left the partnership but Henry Sturge continued until 1838.

In 1840 **Reginald New** of Wribbenhall possibly occupied the factory until 1844 when one of Kidderminster's largest employers **Pardoe, Hooman & Pardoe** took control. In the early 1850s Charles Collins and George Thomas Rose, trading as **Collins & Rose**, were the owners.

In 1863 **G.M.Gilbert** took over and ran the carpet company until 1884. It is doubtful if the factory was ever converted to power loom weaving. The mill was ultimately used for other things and became locally known as "The Chocolate Factory". It was destroyed by fire in 1968.

BRIDGNORTH

Bridgnorth, also on the River Severn, was a cloth-weaving town with the hand looms scattered around the houses. Early records confirm that a Society of Weavers controlled the production. However, the carpet factories needed the river location. Early plans indicate that there were three areas where the factories were located. One in Hospital Street which was known as Pale Meadow Mills, in more recent years it was the home of Decca. The second was in Friars Lane. Friars Works was the largest location and became the factory of the Southwell family and later The Carpet Manufacturing Company, both major employers in the town. The third was a much smaller factory on the riverbank opposite the Friars Works.

George and William MacMichael and Company

Around 1800 Joseph MacMichael is thought to have been the first carpet weaver in Listley Street, Bridgnorth. Over the following years John and William MacMichael, Thomas Gitton and Alexander McMath all became part of the company which failed in 1818 The company was restarted by George and William MacMichael in Hospital Street, the factory was known as Pale Meadow Mills.

MacMichael & Grierson

In the 1830s Thomas Grierson came into the company. In the 1840s they were associated with Thomas Whitmore in a spinning operation at Pendlestone Mills. However, by 1863 the company had closed.

In 1851 **Law & Grierson** were Worsted spinners at Spital Works.

In the mid-1800s a number of carpet companies are listed. **Ball & Baker**, Richard Ball and John Baker had a small hand-weaving factory near the river in Mill Street. **Thomas Elcock** had looms in Friars Street and **Benjamin Saloway** together with a Mr Yates set up a small carpet and rug factory in Friars Street. Yates left the partnership and Saloway continued with hand-knotted carpet until 1858. **John Tyler** had premises in Cartway until he merged with Southwells. The Southwell family were the largest and most influential carpet manufacturers in Bridgnorth.

Southwell Family

1809 Joseph Southwell started weaving Kidderminster carpet at premises in Friars Lane near the River Severn. The site was originally a Franciscan Monastery. Other members of the Southwell family worked in the industry.

1820 Joseph Southwell built the first factory called Friars Works, hand looms were leased to weavers in the town.

Southwell and Company

1828 The Company was formed with Joseph and William Southwell as joint Managing Directors. They manufactured Kidderminster, Brussels and Venetian. Note: This was the year of the Weavers Strike in Kidderminster.

1855 The Friars Works was extended and 22 Brussels power looms installed. The factory was a complete unit with weaving sheds, dyehouse and drying rooms.

H. & M.Southwell

1860 The company was restructured and Henry Foxall and Thomas Martin Southwell became Joint Managing Directors. One year later Henry Foxall retired.

1879 The company obtained the licence and installed Royal Spool Axminster looms.

1888 Thomas Martin's three sons, Horace Baden, Edmund Martin and William Lascelles, became partners in the company.

H. & M.Southwell Ltd.

1890 Southwell became a limited company and added further extensions for Spool Axminster.

**H. & M. Southwell, Ltd.,
Bridgnorth.**

Telegrams—Southwell, Bridgnorth.   Telephone No. 12 Bridgnorth.

They now owned 75 Brussels looms and 20 Royal Axminster looms.

1893 A hand knotting section was set up for specials. It only lasted for eight years. Also in 1893 a major fire destroyed part of the factory including their design store.

It may be of interest to our customers to know that the names given to the following qualities :—

BRUGES, SEVERN, FRIARS, SILURIAN, SALOPIAN, STANWAY, MORFE, PRIORY & ABDON,

are of both local and historical interest.

1920s The Company extended its premises purchasing part of Rope Walk Farm.

1923 The North Works was opened. Five years later it was extended and in 1932 new broad Spool Axminster Looms were installed.

1938 William Lascelles Southwell retired he was the last member of the family to be associated with the company. D.A.Spicer and F.W.Head became Joint Managing Directors. Fred Head patented a needle insertion development on Spool looms.

1939-45 During the war Southwells produced blankets and ammunition.

1944 The company was sold to The Carpet Manufacturing Company.

The Carpet Manufacturing Company Ltd.

1944 CMC bought Southwells and added Chenille Axminster to the production.

1963 In conjunction with Storey Brothers of Lancaster, CMC formed **Debron Carpets Ltd.** for the development of a non-woven bonded product called Debron.

The hard-wearing product was suitable for the contract tile market.

Carpets International Ltd.

1969 The Carpet Manufacturing Company became Carpets International Ltd.

1971 Carpets International formed a Southern Division which included the Bridgnorth factory. A programme of rationalisation was introduced.

1975 The Spool Axminster broadlooms were gradually transferred from Bridgnorth to the appropriately named "Bridgnorth Shed" at the Mill Street factory in Kidderminster. The Debron production equipment travelled north to the Group's Tile Division at Shelf Mills in Yorkshire.

In 1977 The Friars Carpet Works closed and became available for development.

OUT OF TOWN

Globe Carpets was formed by Arthur Pagett, who had previously been a Wilton loom tuner with Chlidema and Carpet Trades. In 1967 he put together a small company at Globe Works, Lye, near Stourbridge. In 1986 he moved his production to Park Lane, Cradley Heath. Globe produced a full range of narrow Wilton, Spool and Gripper Axminster for the Contract market and employed around 25 people. In mid 1999 the company reduced capacity and ultimately stopped trading.

GLOBE CARPETS

A.J.P. CONTRACTS LIMITED
Contract Carpet Manufacturers

Park Lane, Cradley, Halesowen
West Midlands, B63 2RA

Telephone: 01384 633772
Fax: 01384 411476

In 1971 **Axwoven Carpets** started on the Hawne Trading estate in Halesowen where they wove Gripper Axminster for the retail trade.

Carpet Weavers started in Lye in 1948. Twenty years later they moved to a purpose built factory in Shelah Road, Halesowen. They also had a showroom in Lion Street. The company specialised in Gripper Axminster and Wilton body carpet. In 1980 the company closed and the plant was sold at auction.

Alveley Carpets started as **Chanter Carpets** at the factory in Alveley. Gripper Axminster production started in 1971 but later they went into Tufted carpet at a factory in Newtown in Wales. The company went into receivership in 1978 and was bought by **Cakebole Carpets** who ran the factory until 1981 when a consortium of Middle Eastern businessmen took over. They later ceased trading.

Some you win, some you lose

In the early years a number of carpet manufacturers who became better known in other areas either lived in or spent time working in the factories in Kidderminster. For example, in 1795, William Peabody Cooke left Kidderminster to make rugs in Heckmondwike. He expanded the business into Brussels carpet and, together with his sons, formed the famous Cooke, Sons & Company.

Richard Whytock, inventor of the Tapestry process in 1832, started his own company in Lasswade near Edinburgh. His first partner was Henry Henderson and when Whytock died without heirs Henderson replaced him with Kidderminster's Henry Widnell. In 1851 the company expanded into a factory at Bonnyrigg In later years the company was known throughout the world as Henry Widnell & Stewart.

In 1879 Henry James Homfray started a five years indentured apprenticeship with John Brinton. In 1889 he left the town for Sowerby Bridge in Yorkshire to start up on his own. Homfray & Company was to become one of the country's giants encompassing such names as The Birstall Carpet Company and Riding Hall Carpets.

These are just three examples of what was a significant movement of personnel between the Scottish and Yorkshire industries and Kidderminster. There were more including many shop-floor workers.

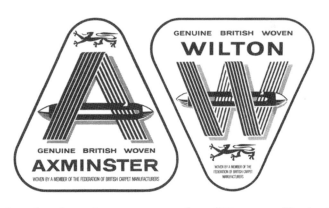

for looks, for wear, the Woven Pair!

Weaving & Tufting

Warp. Parallel yarn threads running lengthways (towards the weaver) often referred to as the chain, stuffer or pile warp ends. They are generally fed from a beam or a creel.

Weft. Threads running across the carpet. These are inserted by a shuttle or a "needle".

Weave. The interlacing of the warp and weft yarns forms the weave.

Backing. The carpet backing keeps the pile tufts in position and gives the structure of the carpet its stability. The loom weaves the backing but the tufter needs a pre-woven primary and a secondary backing to achieve the same stability.

Pile. Pile ends are the coloured yarns which form the visible pattern surface.

Finishing. The process of making the off-loom product fit for sale. The "picking" process sews in any missing tufts. The back of the carpet then receives a coating of latex or size to lock in the tufts and add bulk to the carpet. In a final process, called "shearing", the pile surface is levelled removing any weaving marks and loose tufts.

Pitch (gauge in tufting). The pitch is the number of warp ends per inch. The loom or tufter is set for the pitch and cannot be easily altered. The normal standard for Axminster is 7 pitch whereas Wilton is often 8 pitch. Tufters have many standards.

Rows per inch. This refers to the number of ends in the weft direction and can be altered at the loom. It is the one variable that can be used to alter the quality.

Quality. Generally determined by the number of pile ends in one square inch. A popular rule of thumb is that the more tufts per square inch the better the quality.

Note : Other weaving terms are explained within the Chapters where they are more relevant.

Carpet Materials

Natural fibres. Yarn ends made by nature. Wool, cotton, jute, flax, linen, silk, etc.

Spinning. The conversion of these loose fibres into yarn threads.

Woollen spun yarns are bulky and used for the majority of carpet pile yarns.

Worsted yarns are leaner and used for the finer pitched high quality products.

Synthetic fibres. Made by man imitating the natural fibres. Nylon, Acrylan, etc. Pile materials use blends with wool; 80/20 Wool Nylon became the woven carpet standard for wearability. Synthetic fibres, though generally stronger, are more prone to soiling. The high speed tufting operation makes extensive use of man-made fibres. Polypropylene has become a substitute for backing warp and weft materials.

Cloth and Carpet

Hand Knotted (Turkey Work) Carpet - Early times until the 1900s.
The carpet is formed by knotting the precut tufts of pile yarn individually into the warps on a vertical frame. A weft shot is introduced to complete the weave.
More details in Chapter 1 - page 2 and Chapter 4 - page 88.

Bombazine Cloth - 1700s and 1800s (hand loom only).
A light weight twilled or corded woven dress material made from silk and worsted yarns. Generally woven in black for mourning but sometimes in other clerical colours.
More details in Chapter 1 - page 6.

Kidderminster Stuff - Early times until the 1700s (hand loom only).
Multi-purpose heavy-weight cloth woven with coarser yarns.
More details in Chapter 1 - page 8.

Kidderminster Carpet (Scotch or Ingrain) - 1735 to 1932 (hand and power loom).
A coarse flat weave, reversible, patterned carpet woven as a double or triple thickness.
More details in Chapter 2 - page 9.

Mounture - Cloth and early carpet looms up to 1830s (hand loom only).
A device above the loom for the selection of the pile ends to appear on the patterned surface. It was later superseded by the Jacquard.
More details in Chapter 2 - page 11.

Jacquard - Developed in 1801, first used on the town's carpet looms in 1825.
A mechanism above the loom which selects a set or "frame" of warp pile yarns of differing colours to form the surface pattern.
More details in Chapter 2 - page 12.

Brussels Wilton - From 1749 to the present day (hand and power loom).
A woven carpet where the coloured pile yarns run continuously through the carpet as warp ends. There are normally up to five colours, these are known as "frames".
The weaving process uses the Jacquard (earlier Mounture) to select the pattern pile yarns and individually bring them above the surface of the backing to form a raised pile over flat wires on end. The depth of the flat wire is the depth of the pile.
The wire is withdrawn to the side leaving a looped pile surface. In some cases a normal round wire is used to give a flat looped or corded pile surface.
More details in Chapter 2 - page 11.

Stouts or "common goods" - 1800s (hand loom).
A Brussels carpet where the number of yarn ends, backing and pile, were reduced to produce a cheaper quality carpet.

Wilton Velvet - From 1750s to the present day (hand and power loom).
The weave is exactly as described for Brussels but in this case the pile wire has a knife blade in the end which cuts the pile on withdrawal forming a velvet surface.

Wilton and Brussels Plain - Still in production (power loom).
Woven on the standard loom in a single colour. The single frame does not require the Jacquard or the tray creel therefore pile ends are generally fed from a beam.

Face-to-face Wilton - In Kidderminster 1940s onward (power loom).
A traditional Wilton Velvet weave where two carpets are woven at the same time facing each other. The pile yarns pass from the top carpet to the bottom carpet to form the raised pile. In this weave the pile wire is not needed. A travelling knife slits the woven "sandwich" into two carpets.

Tapestry Carpet - 1832 to 1946 (hand and power loom).
Tapestry was the cheapest form of patterned carpet. The pile yarns were printed in sections around a drum before steaming and beaming for the loom. Tapestry or "Tap-looms" were traditional Wilton or Brussels looms adapted for the process. Tapestry Velvet refers to the cut pile, Tapestry Brussels refers to the loop pile.
More details in Chapter 2 - page 34, Photographs in Chapter 3 - page 65.

Axminster - General description.
A carpet where successive weft-wise rows of pile are inserted during the weaving process to a predetermined arrangement of colours to form a cut-pile patterned velvet surface. With Axminster the pile ends are individually placed into the weave.

Spool Axminster - 1878 to the present day (power loom only).
The pile yarns for each weft-wise row are wound onto separate spools according to the design. There can be any practical number of colours in the design - normally less than 20. The spools are held in a large endless chain in pattern order. The spools are removed from the chain and taken to the weaving position. The pile ends are woven in, the tufts are cut and the spool returned to the chain which then indexes to the next spool and so on. A weft shot is inserted to complete the weave.
More details and photographs in Chapter 3 - page 61.

Gripper Axminster - 1890 to the present day (power loom only).
The pile tufts are inserted at the point of weaving by a row of grippers which hold the individual tufts across the loom. The colour is selected by the Jacquard. Normally up to eight colours are supplied from a large creel of bobbins. With electronic Jacquards more than eight colours can be included.
More details and photographs in Chapter 3 - page 69.

Gripper-Spool Axminster - 1950s to present day (power loom only).
A traditional Gripper Loom with the spool feed replacing the Jacquard. The advantage lies in the unlimited number of colours of the Spool system.

Chenille Axminster - 1839 to the mid 1900s (hand and power loom).
The process has two separate weaving operations. The first involves the weaving of the Chenille fabric on the weft loom. The fabric is steamed and then cut into strips which have the pile tufts, or "fur", held in pattern order. The second operation weaves the actual carpet on a setting loom using the fur as a weft to form the pile.
More details in Chapter 2 - Page 35, Photographs in Chapter 3 - page 66.

Venetian Carpet - 1800s (probably hand loom only).
A striped carpet made for corridors and stairs in a number of colours with a woollen visible warp and a binding weft of hemp or cotton.

Tufted Carpet - in Kidderminster from 1956 onward (tufting machine or "tufter"). The pile yarn ends are fed from a creel or beam to a row of reciprocating needles which penetrate the primary backing, a looper below catches the pile yarn as the needle withdraws and so forms a loop. The carpet can be cut pile, loop pile or a mixture of cut and loop. There are attachments to introduce simple patterns and textured surfaces. More recent developments have improved the pattern potential. A secondary backing is added as a subsequent process.
More details in Chapter 5 - page 113.

Carpet Widths

For many years the carpet industry expressed the width of the woven carpet in quarters of a yard. Many looms today weave at the "body" width of 27 inches.
More details in Chapter 1 - page 7.

27 inches = 3/4 (yard)   36 inches = 1 yard = 4/4   9 feet = 3 yards = 12/4
12 feet = 4 yards = 16/4   15 feet = 5 yards = 20/4

In the shops the carpet was sold as 27 inch, 9 feet, 12 feet and 15 feet.
When metrication came in the metre became another standard, looms and tufters are now available up to five metres wide.

The Raw Material Suppliers

'When I grow up my thick white fleece will make extra special carpets'

BRITISH WOOL
naturally

Book Presentation

In addition to those from the industry named on page 136 there a number of other people to whom I am particularly indebted.

My son, Andrew, is my computer consultant. He was responsible for page layouts and his expertise in combining the sketches and photographs with the text produced some interesting options.

Roger Sullivan's artistic talents have added considerably to the overall appearance of the book. His oil painting of Slingfield Mill forms the outer cover and he produced some remarkable sketches of the industry and the town. These are featured on pages 12, 20, 21, 22, 37 and 54.

A special thank you to Mrs Mavis Morrissy and Michael Stone who were my proof readers. Believe me, they earned their corn!

I am also grateful to my colleagues within the Carpet Museum Trust who encouraged me and gave their opinions, good and otherwise, but always constructive!

Photographs

The photographs are an essential part of the book, my thanks to the following -
The Charter Trustees of Kidderminster and the Carpet Trades Collection.
The extensive archive collections of Brintons and Tomkinsons.
The Naylors Collection donated by Mrs Barbara Naylor.
Individual donations from Goff Jones; Dave Duffield, Woodward, Grosvenor; John Fudge, Greatwich; Chris Brighton, CMC and Sultana; Ruth Walker, Carpet Trades and Charles Talbot, the wartime photograph. The remaining were taken by myself or are from the extensive collection retained by The Carpet Museum Trust.

Further Reading - *I found the following books particularly helpful.*

The Story of British Carpets	Bertram Jacobs
Carpet Weavers and Carpet Masters	L.D.Smith
The Carpet Weavers of Kidderminster	Arthur Marsh
Ridiculous Refinement	Nigel Gilbert
Carpeting the Millions	J.Neville Bartlett
The History of British Carpets	Tattersall & Reed
Broadlooms and Businessmen	Ewing and Norton
Tufting: An Introduction	Derek Ward.
Carpets	George Robinson
Weaving in Bridgnorth	Frederick W.Head
Kidderminster Since 1800	Ken Tomkinson & George Hall
Carpets	R.S.Brinton
Carpets and Rugs	Otis A.Kenyon {The Hoover Co.]
Dean Clough and the Crossley inheritance	Eric Webster
The Illustrated History of the Kidderminster & Stourport Electric Tramway Company	Melvyn Thompson & David Voice

Hoobrook Spinning Mill in 1915, viewed from the Spennels side.
The Bigelow Power Loom was installed here in 1852.

Inside Cover Pictures

The factories, past and present, photographed at the Millennium.

Brinton's Waterside Mill,
Corporation Street.

Victoria's New Road Mill,
Green Street.

Brinton's Castle Road Building.

Morton's Factory, New Road.
Formerly The Carpet Manufacturing Co.

Tomkinson's "Carpet Manufactory".
Mount Pleasant.

Worth's Severn Valley Mills.
Stourport.

Worcester Cross Factory,
Worcester Street.
Formerly Woodward, Grosvenor.

Woodward, Grosvenor's Stour Vale Mills.
Green Street.